A WELSH GRAMMAR

STEPHEN J. WILLIAMS

CAERDYDD

CARDIFF
UNIVERSITY OF WALES PRESS
1980

© University of Wales, 1980
Reprinted, 1981, 1986, 1991, 1993

British Library Cataloguing in Publication Data

A catalogue record for this book
is available from the British Library

ISBN 0-7083-0737-X

Printed in Wales by:
Dinefwr Press, Llandybïe, Dyfed

FOREWORD

The book on Modern Welsh Grammar entitled *Elfennau Gramadeg Cymraeg* (University of Wales Press, 1959) was intended for readers studying Welsh through the medium of the language itself. It appears that there is a demand for a similar work written in English, and it was at the request of The Board of Celtic Studies and the University Press Board that the present edition was prepared. It is hoped that it will meet the needs of readers desiring to become acquainted with standard literary Welsh whether they have a knowledge of colloquial Welsh or not.

The standard of literary Welsh has been greatly influenced in the present century by the researches of scholars in the various fields of Welsh studies. For example, the reform of the orthography was gradually adopted by Welsh writers in general; the re-classification of Accidence was accepted without demur; a fresh study of Syntax has been welcomed, and re-appraisal of the context and history of our literature has been most beneficial.

The salient features of the language form the basis of all formal teaching and studying of the subject. The classification of Accidence and Syntax is essential, and that is why this handbook is so much concerned with these matters. The interspersion of frequent syntactical notes in the treatment of Accidence is intended to make it more meaningful. The sections on Syntax, as such, are therefore devoted to the Sentence, in addition to the syntactical significance of the consonantal mutations summarized in APPENDIX A. The many references to colloquial and dialect words and expressions are intended sometimes for comparison of spoken and written forms, and sometimes to draw attention to debased colloquial usages. The use of a recent Welsh-English Dictionary with this handbook is recommended.

The references under ABBREVIATIONS give some indication of my indebtedness to some writers, but there are many more from whose work in books, articles, etc. I have greatly profited.

My sincere thanks are due to the University of Wales Press for publishing the book, to the printers for their care and especially to Mr. Alun Treharne and Mr. John Rhys for their interest and help.

S.J.W.

October, 1979.

CONTENTS

	Page
Foreword	v
Abbreviations	ix
The Alphabet	1
Diphthongs	4
Accentuation	5
The Article	6
Nouns	9
Adjectives	26
Numerals	40
Pronouns	45
The Verb	72
The Regular Verbs	80
Contracted Forms	88
Irregular Verbs	92
Other Irregular Verbs	105
The Verb-Noun	109
Verbal Adjectives	120
Compounds	122
Prepositions	127
Adverbs	143
Pre-Verbal Particles	146
Conjunctions	151
Interjections	162
The Sentence	163
Appendix A	174
Appendix B	177
Index	181

ABBREVIATIONS

A.G.   *Gwaith Ann Griffiths,* gol. O. M. Edwards, Cyfres y Fil, Conwy, 1905.

Alun   *Ceinion Alun* (John Blackwell), gol. G. Edwards (Gutyn Padarn), Rhuthun, 1851.

AN   Yr argraffiad newydd o'r Beibl, Llundain, 1955 (gol. Henry Lewis).

BBCS   Bulletin of the Board of Celtic Studies.

BBN   *Bob Bore o Newydd, Llyfr Gweddi y Gwasanaeth Darlledu,* Llundain, 1938.

B.Cw.   Ellis Wynne, *Gweledigaetheu y Bardd Cwsc,* gol. J. Morris-Jones, Bangor, 1898.

BE   *Blodeuglwm o Englynion,* gol. W. J. Gruffydd, Abertawe, 1920.

BU   *Barddoniaeth yr Uchelwyr,* gol. D. J. Bowen, Caerdydd, 1957.

CAN   *Y Caniedydd,* Abertawe, 1960. (Reference to hymns).

CFG   Melville Richards, *Cystrawen y Frawddeg Gymraeg,* Caerdydd, 1938.

CN   Y cyfieithiad newydd o'r Testament Newydd, (Adran Ddiwinyddol Urdd Graddedigion Prifysgol Cymru), Rhydychen, Caerdydd, Wrecsam, 1921—.

D.C.   David Charles. 1762—1834.

Dewi Medi   (David Lewis). 1844—1917.

DG   *Gwaith Dafydd ap Gwilym,* gol. Thomas Parry, Caerdydd, 1952.

DGG   *Dafydd ap Gwilym a'i Gyfoeswyr,* gol. Ifor Williams a Thomas Roberts, Caerdydd, arg. 1935.

DIG   *Datblygiad yr Iaith Gymraeg,* Henry Lewis, Caerdydd, 1931.

D.J.   D. Jones, Tre-borth. 1805—68.

D.N.   *The Poetical Works of Dafydd Nanmor,* ed. T. Roberts and Ifor Williams, Cardiff, 1923.

Ehedydd Iâl   (William Jones). 1815—99.

Eifion Wyn   (Eliseus Williams) i. *Telynegion Maes a Môr,* Caerdydd, 1908. ii. *Caniadau'r Allt,* Llundain, 1927.

ETM	*Emynau a Thonau y Methodistiaid,* Caernarfon a Bangor, 1929.
E.R.	Edward Richard. 1714—77.
EWG	*An Elementary Welsh Grammar.* J. Morris-Jones, Oxford, 1921.
FG	*Y Flodeugerdd Gymraeg,* gol. W. J. Gruffydd, Caerdydd, 1931.
FN	*Y Flodeugerdd Newydd,* gol. W. J. Gruffydd, Caerdydd, 1909.
GC	*Gramadeg Cymraeg,* J. J. Evans, Aberystwyth, 1946.
GCC	D. Simon Evans, *Gramadeg Cymraeg Canol,* Caerdydd, 1951.
GG	*Gemau'r Gogynfeirdd,* gol. Arthur Hughes ac Ifor Williams, Pwllheli, 1910.
G.M.D.	Gruffudd ab Maredudd ap Dafydd. XIV ganrif.
G.O.	*Barddoniaeth Goronwy Owen,* gol. I. Ffoulkes, 8fed arg., Liverpool, 1924.
GTA	*Gwaith Tudur Aled,* gol. T. Gwynn Jones, Caerdydd, 1926.
Gwyrosydd	(Daniel James). 1847—1920.
HB	*Hen Benillion,* casgl. T. H. Parry-Williams, Llandysul, 1940
Hedd Wyn	(Ellis Humphrey Evans), *Cerddi'r Bugail,* gol. J. J. Williams, Caerdydd, 1918.
I.D.	*Gwaith Ieuan Deulwyn,* gol. Ifor Williams, Bangor, 1909.
I.G.	Ieuan Gwynedd (Evan Jones). 1820—52.
IGE	*Iolo Goch ac Eraill,* gol. Henry Lewis, Thomas Roberts, Ifor Williams, Caerdydd, 1937 (arg. newydd).
I.G.G.	Ieuan Glan Geirionydd (Evan Evans), *Detholion o waith Ieuan Glan Geirionydd,* gol. Saunders Lewis, Caerdydd, 1931.
J.J.W.	J. J. Williams, *Y Lloer a Cherddi Eraill,* Aberystwyth, 1936.
J.M.-J.	John Morris-Jones, *Caniadau,* Rhydychen, 1907.
J.P.R.	J. Price Roberts. 1853—1905.
J.R.	John Roberts. 1804—84.

K.R.   Kate Roberts, *Traed Mewn Cyffion*, Aberystwyth, 1936.

L.G.C.   Lewis Glyn Cothi, XV ganrif. i. *Llên Cymru*, casgl. T.
                Gwynn Jones, Caernarfon, 1922; ii. FN.

LlGG   Llyfr Gweddi Gyffredin.

LlTA   'Llyfr y Tri Aderyn'; dyfynnir o *Gweithiau Morgan
                Llwyd*, gol. T. E. Ellis, Bangor, 1899.

Morswyn   (S. J. Griffiths). 1850—93.

Pedr Fardd   (Peter Jones). 1775—1845.

RBS   Ellis Wynne, *Rheol Buchedd Sanctaidd*, adarg. Caerdydd,
                1928.

R.E.   Roger Edwards. 1811—86.

R.G.D.   *Robert ap Gwilym Ddu, Detholion o'i Weithiau*, gol.
                Stephen J. Williams, Caerdydd, 1948.

R.T.J.   R. T. Jenkins, *Yr Apêl at Hanes*, Wrecsam, 1930.

R.W.P.   R. Williams Parry, *Yr Haf a Cherddi Eraill*, Y Bala,
                1924.

T.A.   *Gwaith Tudur Aled*, gol. T. Gwynn Jones, Caerdydd,
                1926.

TC   T. J. Morgan, *Y Treigladau a'u Cystrawen*, Caerdydd,
                1952.

T.G.J.   T. Gwynn Jones, i. *Manion*, Wrecsam, 1932.
                ii. *Caniadau*, Caerdydd, 1934.

T.H.P.-W.   T. H. Parry-Williams. i. *Ysgrifau*, Llundain, 1928.
                ii. *Cerddi*, Aberystwyth, 1931.

T.J.   Thomas Jones, Dinbych. 1756—1820.

T.R.   Thomas Rees, Abertawe. 1815—85.

T.W.   Thomas Williams, Bethesda'r Fro. *Gwaith Prydyddol*,
                gol. T. Rees, Abertawe, 1882.

W.J.G.   W. J. Gruffydd. i. *Caneuon a Cherddi*, Bangor, 1906.
                ii. *Ynys yr Hud*, Wrecsam, 1927.

W.LL.   *Barddoniaeth Wiliam Llŷn*, gol. J. C. Morrice, Bangor,
                1908.

PHONOLOGY

§ 1. (a) **The Alphabet.** The Welsh alphabet consists of twenty simple letters and eight digraphs. These are signs denoting sounds or phonemes, and each sign has a traditional name (shown below in Welsh spelling):

sign	name	sign	name	sign	name
a	â	ng	èng	r	èr
b	bî	h	âets	rh	rhi, rho
c	èc	i	î	s	ès
ch	èch	l	èl	t	tî
d	dî	ll	èll	th	èth
dd	èdd	m	èm	u	û
e	ê	n	èn	w	ŵ
f	èf	o	ô	y	y
ff	èff	p	pî		
g	èg	ph	ffî		

Vowels: **a, e, i, o, u, w, y,** but **i** and **w** may be consonantal in diphthongs (see § 4). Vowels are either long or short; but a vowel that is long in a final syllable becomes medium in a non-final syllable before a single consonant, e.g., *cân,* (long *â*), *canu* (medium *a*).

(b) **Vowel-sounds:**

LONG

a, as in *tad,* is like *a* in E. *father.*

e, as in *gwên,* is like Northern E. *a* in *make.*

i, as in *gwin,* i slike E. *ee* in *meet.*

o, as in *bod,* is like Northern E. *o* in *so.*

u, as in *pur,* resembles Fr. *u,* but is less rounded.

w, as in *sŵn,* is like *oo* in E. *moon.*

y has two sounds: (1) *clear,* as in *byd,* has the same sound as *u* in North Wales; in South Wales it is sounded like *i.*

(2) obscure, as in *y* (the definite article), is like *e* in E. *her* and *u* in E. *hurdle.* It is medium in length in non-final syllable, e.g., *byddaf, cryfaf.*

SHORT

a, as in *mam,* is like Northern E. *a* in *cab.*

e, as in *pen,* is like E. *e* in *let.*

i, as in *dim,* is like E. *i* in *pit.*

o, as in *hon,* is like E. *o* in *cod.*

u, as in *ust,* is somewhat less rounded than long *u* in North Wales, and is the same as short *i* in South Wales.

w, as in *cwm,* is like E. *oo* in *hood.*

y, (1) clear, as in *bryn*, is like short *u* in North Wales and like short *i* in South Wales.

(2) obscure, as in some unstressed words (*y, yr, yn, fy, dy, myn, ys, syr*), is like E. *u* in *sun*. The sound occurs in closed non-final syllables (i.e. with two or more consonants following the vowel) as in *dynion, cysgodd, syrthio*.

(c) Consonant-sounds:

The following are sounded as in E.: **b, d, h, l, m, n, p, t. c** is sounded like E. *k* (never as *s*) and **g** like E. hard *g* (never as *j*). **ch** is sounded like Scotch *ch* in *loch*. **f** has the sound of E. *v* or *f* in E. *of*. **ff** and **ph** are both sounded like E. *f* or *ph*, the Welsh *ph* being often a mutation of *p*, as in *a phan* from *a* + *pan*. **ng** usually has the same sound as E. *ng* in *long*, but in a few words **ng** is sounded *ng* + *g* like E. *finger*, e.g. *Bangor* and *dangos* (except in North Wales where the latter has now no hard *g* sound). **ll** is a voiceless *l* produced with the tongue in the *l* position by emitting the breath sharply on one side of the mouth. **rh** and **r** are both trilled like strong Scotch *r*. The former is an *r* sound followed by a strong emission of breath which makes it voiceless, while **r** is voiced. In the consonant change known as the Soft Mutation *rh* is regarded as the radical and *r* the mutated form. **s** has the sound of *ss* in E. *miss*, and never the sound of E. *z*. *si-* followed by a vowel is sounded like E. *sh*, e.g. *siop*, E. *shop*. **th** is sounded like E. *th* in *thin, heath*. **dd** has the sound of E. *th* in *this*. In words borrowed from English *j* is used in writing and speaking, e.g. *jam*. As noted above **i** and **w** are often consonants and correspond to E. *y* and *w* respectively. They occur thus mainly in rising diphthongs, but also in the combination *gw* in such words as *gwlad, gwraidd, gwlyb*.

The sounds of the E. symbols *k, v* and *x* are represented by *c, f* and *cs* respectively in Welsh.

§ 2. Length of vowels:

(a) When two consonants follow the vowel in a monosyllable the vowel is usually short: *sant, perth, corff, cwrt, pyrth, hynt*. By the same token the following words have a short vowel in South Wales: *gwallt, gwellt, (g)allt, mellt, hollt, swllt, Pasg, tasg, gwisg, cosb, tyst, cwsg, llesg, hesg, tost, cist, hesb, cost,* etc. In North Wales the vowel in each of these is sounded long, i.e. a vowel preceding *-llt, -sb, -sg, -st*. In a few verbal forms the vowel is long before *-nt*, and in writing the circumflex accent (ˆ) is used to mark the length: *cânt, ânt, gwnânt, dônt, trônt*, etc. In such cases the long vowel is the result of contracting two short vowels: *cânt < ca-ant, bûm < bu-um*.

(b) In monosyllables ending in **p, t, c, m, ng**, the vowel is short: *swp, het, lwc, llam, llong*. In the exceptions the long vowel should be marked with a circumflex: some verbal forms, *ŷm, bûm, bôm*, and some borrowings such as *siâp, tâp, sêt, ffrâm, côt, grôt* (but *cot, grot* in South Wales). The vowel is long in monosyllables ending in **b, d, g, f, dd, ff, th, ch, s.** There is no need to mark the vowel-length in such words: *mab, gwlad, cig, dof, af, rhodd, rhaff, hoff, peth, coch, pas, cas, nos, nes* ('nearer'). Exceptions: the vowel is short in *os, nes* ('until'), *och, fflach, hwb, nid, nad, heb* (but long in S. Wales). For clarity the long vowel in a few cases should be circumflexed, e.g. *nâd* ('cry'), *ôd* ('snow'), *ŷd* ('corn').

(c) In every unaccented syllable the vowel is short, e.g. in final syllables, *canu, gweithdy, meini, cytgan, pentan;* and in syllables preceding the stress in polysyllabic words, *cariadon* (car-iád-on), *cofiadur* (cof-iád-ur), *mabolaeth* (mab-ól-aeth).

Prolitics such as *y, yr, yn, fy, dy* are normally unstressed and have short vowels (§ 1), but *fy, dy* may be stressed for emphasis, the vowel thus being lengthened. In other monosyllables ending in a vowel such a vowel is always long: *pla, lle, bo, da, ti, llu, llw, try.* The circumflex is not needed in such words except to distinguish between *dŷ*, a mutated form of *tŷ* 'house' and *dy* 'thy'.

(d) A vowel preceding -ll in monosyllables varies in length according to local custom. It is generally short in North Wales and long in South Wales, but in neither region is there consistency of usage. No attempt is therefore made to denote quantity in writing. Vowel-length varies before -l, -n, -r (not in respect of region) according to derivation of the word. In writing one should become accustomed to using the circumflex where needed, as in *môr, ôl, dêl, gên, câr, cân, tân, sŵn, côr.* As a rule *i* and *u* are long before these consonants, and vowel-length need not be marked, e.g. *hir, min, ffin, hil, mul, llun, cur.* The few exceptions have a short vowel: *prin, swil, bil, pin, pen;* but it is long in *pin* 'pine'. In *cnul* 'knell' *u* is short, except in some dialects. Although *y* in *dyn* is long, it is written traditionally without circumflex, but when *tyn* 'tight' undergoes mutation the double *n* of the mutated form *dynn* shows that the *y* is short. Similar doubling serves the same purpose in *ynn* 'ash-trees', *yrr* (from *gyr*) 'drives', *syrr* (from *sorri*) 'sulks'. Some speakers pronounce *pryn* 'buys' and *cryn* 'quakes' with a long, and others with a short vowel. *Cŷff* 'trunk' is often mispronounced *cyff*.

If by adding to a syllable containing a long vowel two or more consonants come together the vowel becomes short: *môr, morglawdd; pûr, purdeb; cûl, culni; môr, morio* (§ 4). If a single consonant follows, the vowel is medium: *cân, canodd.*

§ 3. The two sounds of the symbol **y** are noted above (§ 1 (b)). They occur as vowels, (1) clear, e.g. in *dyn* (long), *llym* (short); (2) obscure, e.g. in *tyfu* (medium), *cysgu* (short). They also form the vocalic elements in diphthongs, both clear and obscure, as shown below. It is shown below in Appendix B (ii) that obscure *y* is a 'mutation' of clear *y* or of *w* in the majority of cases.

§4. Diphthongs. A dipthong is the combination of two´vowels, the one sonantal and the other consonantal. When the sonantal (or pure vowel) element comes first the combination is a *falling diphthong*. When the consonantal element comes first it is a *rising diphthong*.

(a) *Falling Diphthongs:* **ai, ei, oi, ŵy, ey, ae, oe, au, eu, ou, aw, ew, iw, yw, ow, uw.** Examples: t*ai*, c*ei*r, rh*oi*, ll*wy*, t*eyr*n, m*ae*, c*oes*, d*au*, h*eu*log, cyffr*ou*s, ll*aw*, t*ew*, ll*iw*, u*w*ch, rh*ow*ch, afr*wy*dd. The sound of *y* is either clear or obscure according to the position of the diphthong in the word. It is clear in monosyllables and final syllables (but *yw* is often sounded as if it were *iw*), e.g. ll*yw*, unrh*yw*; it it is obscure in the penultimate, e.g. cl*yw*sant, cl*yw*ed, b*yw*yd, ll*yw*ydd, c*yw*ydd. Following the rule the sound in North Wales is obscure in such words as b*yw*iol, rh*yw*iog, c*yw*ion; but in South Wales the sound in these is usually clear. The sound tends to be clear too in such compounds as rh*yw*beth, rh*yw*rai, rh*yw*un, rh*yw*fodd, but the obscure is followed by the clear in b*yw*yd, as in m*y*nydd.

(b) *Rising Diphthongs:* **ia ie io iw iy wa we wi wo wy.** The first element in these is either **i** or **w** and is consonantal. At the beginning of a word this consonantal **w-** is always the mutated form of *gw-*. Examples: *i*ach, cof*i*er, cof*i*o, *iw*rch, s*iw*r, *iy*rchod, en*w*ad, *we*di (from earlier g*we*dy), g*we*n, (merch) *we*n, g*wi*n, (dy) *wi*n, gal*w*odd, g*wy*n, (yn) *wy*n, g*wy*nnaf (obscure *y*).

§5. In writing the sound of *wy* cannot always be denoted. The following are examples of the various sounds:

(a) The falling diphthong:

1. monosyllables where the circumflex is not needed: m*wy*, h*wy*, *wy* (*ŵy*) 'egg', ll*wy*, b*wy*d, rh*wy*d, rh*wy*f, *wy*t, s*wy*dd, ch*wy*dd, c*wy*mp, rh*wy*sg, s*wy*n, d*wy*s, *wy*th, ll*wy*r, t*wy*m.

2. words where the circumflex is needed to distinguish between them and other words: g*ŵy*l, *ŵy*n ('lambs'), g*ŵy*r, ('knows', 'bending'), *ŵy*r ('grandchild'), (dy) g*ŵy*n, (ei) ch*ŵy*n, (y) g*ŵy*s ('the furrow'), (a) ch*ŵy*s ('and a furrow'), g*ŵy*dd ('goose', 'presence'), *Ŵy*sg ('Usk'), c*ŵy*r ('wax').

3. words of more than one syllable normally written with no circumflex (although it could be used to denote the correct pronunciation): c*wy*no, ll*wy*do, *wy*bren (*ŵy*bren), *wy*lo (*ŵy*lo), *wy*neb, (*ŵy*neb), cyd*ŵy*bod, g*ŵy*bod (particularly in reciting and singing poetry), ar*wy*dd, mor*wy*n,

gwanwyn (gwanŵyn), cannwyll, cadwyn, aswy, Conwy, galwyn, gwyliau, gwenwyn (gwenŵyn), synnwyr, egwyddor, nodwydd, annwyd, ysgwydd.

(b) The rising diphthong: 1. monosyllables with no accent marks: (short *y*) *gwyn, gwynt, gwyrth, chwyrn;* (long *y*) *chwys* ('perspiration').

2. monosyllables with *y* circumflexed: *gwŷr* ('men'), *gwŷdd* ('trees'), *gwŷn* ('pain, passion'), *gwŷs* ('summons'), *gwŷs* ('it is known').

3. in final syllables without circumflex: *tywydd, celwydd, arwyr* ('heroes'), *enwyn* ('buttermilk'), *palmwydd, pinwydd, myrtwydd, olewydd.*

4. with obscure *y* in any syllable except finally: *gwynnaf, gwyntoedd, tywyllwch.* N.B. The diphthong in which an obscure *y* occurs must be a rising diphthong, i.e. one in which *w* is a consonant and *y* a vowel.

§6. Accentuation. (a) The general rule is that in polysyllables the accent falls on the penult: *gwelaf (gwélaf), héfyd, cymháru, cymariáethol.*

(b) A prefix in a word of more than two syllables bears a secondary accent, e.g. in *annibynnol* the prefix *an-* bears a secondary, while the main accent falls on *-byn-* in the penult. Each of the following words then bears a secondary and a main accent: *amherffaith, angharedig, digyffelyb, direswm, cydgyfarfod, cydredeg, adolygu, rhagfynegi, rhagacen, gwrthwynebu.* (More examples can be seen under § 187). Many other 'loose compounds' are similarly accented, e.g. *tirfeddiannwr, croesholi;* § 186(i)(c).

(c) Many words are accented on the final syllable instead of on the penult: 1. words in which the last syllable is a contraction of two syllables, e.g. *Cymraeg (<Cym-ra-eg), crynhoi (<cryn-ho-i), parhad (<par-ha-ad), glanhau (<glan-ha-u), canfûm (<can-fu-um), cytûn (<cyd-du-un), amheus (<am-he-us).*

2. a few words with *ys-* in the first syllable, e.g. *ystryd, ystên, ystôl, ystwc, ysgrech.* Initial *y* is very often dropped from such words *(stryd, stên,* etc.). This applies also to *yrhawg* and *rhawg.*

3. A few words with *ym-* in the first syllable: *ymwêl, ymweld, ymhel, ymdroi (<ym-dro-i), ymroi.* Some are regularly accented sometimes, with a difference of meaning according to the position of the accent, as in *ymlâdd* ('to tire oneself'), *ýmladd* ('to fight'); *ýmddwyn* ('to behave'), *ymddŵyn* ('to bear (child)'). There is no difference of meaning between *ýmdrin* and *ymdrîn* ('to deal'), nor between *ýmolch* and *ymólch* ('wash thyself').

4. Several adverbial or prepositional compounds, e.g. *heblaw, drachefn, uwchlaw, islaw, gerllaw, gerbron, goruwch, erioed, ymysg, ymhlith, ynglŷn, ymlaen, ymhell, cyhyd, gwahân, paham.*

5. A few other compounds such as *prynhawn, penrhaith* ('lord'), *Caer-dydd, Llandâf, Aberdâr. Pen-rhos* varies with *Pénrhos* according to local pronunciation.

6. A few words borrowed from E.: *apêl, balŵn, perswâd, cysêt, diclein, carafán.*

7. Some words borrowed from E. are accented on the ante-penultimate: *testament, paragraff, polisi, ambiwlans, melodi* (but *melodaidd* is accented regularly).

ACCIDENCE

(With Syntactical Notes)

THE ARTICLE

§7. The definite article in Welsh has three forms: *yr, y, 'r.* Welsh has no indefinite article.

(i) The full form is *yr.* This occurs (a) before a vowel, *yr afon, yr enw;* (b) before a diphthong, except one beginning with a consonantal *w, yr aur, yr eira, yr oen, yr Wyddfa, yr ŵy, yr ŵyneb, yr iaith;* (c) between a word ending in a consonant and a word beginning in a vowel or diphthong (as above), *blaen yr afon, pen yr Wyddfa, masgl yr wy, troed yr iâr;* (d) before *h, yr haf, yr haul, yr hwn.*

(ii) *'r* occurs after a vowel or diphthong, *o'r tŷ, i'r afon, lliw'r afal, gyda'r iâr, dringo'r wal,* 'Canu'r dydd a chanu'r nos'.

(iii) *y* occurs between two consonants or between a consonant and consonantal *w, ymyl y cae, Tal-y-bont, pen y rhiw, Pen-y-waun, wrth y wal, yn y wlad, at y wraig.*

Until fairly recently *y* or *yr* (instead of *'r*) would often be written after words ending in a vowel (especially nouns, verbs and adjectives):

'Fy enaid, bendithia *yr* Arglwydd' (Salm ciii. 1); 'A phan wybu *yr* Iesu' (Mk. viii. 17; 1955 edn. 'A phan wybu'*r* Iesu').

This is still done if the sense demands a slight pause after the vowel:

'Ni ddaeth neb yma *y* noson honno'.

Note. In some of the phrases given as examples under (i)(c) and (iii) above the second noun in each instance is in the genitive case and depends on the first noun, e.g. *ymyl y cae* means 'the edge of the field' or 'the field's edge', *pen y rhiw* means 'the top of the hill', *blaen yr afon* means 'the source of the river'. As each of these genitives is preceded by the article it is definite. If the genitive is not preceded by the article it is indefinite, e.g. *pen ceffyl* 'the head of a horse'. Although a personal name is definite it is not preceded by the article, e.g. *Llyfr*

Dafydd 'David's book'. *Yr Iesu* is an exception and occurs more frequently than *Iesu*. The article is also used before a personal name that is followed by a demonstrative adjective or by a definite adjectival pronoun etc., e.g. *y Dafydd hwn* 'this David', *tad yr Iago hwnnw* 'the father of that James', *y Fair arall* 'the other Mary'.

§ 8. The Soft Mutation, or Lenition, after the Article. (See page 174)

The nine consonants that undergo soft mutation, or lenition, are:

Radical Consonants: **p t c b d   g m ll rh**

Soft Mutation: **b d g f dd   - f l r**

(i) When a feminine singular noun follows the article the initial consonant of the noun is mutated: pont, y *b*ont; torth, y *d*orth; cyllell, y *g*yllell; buwch, y *f*uwch; dafad, y *dd*afad; gardd, yr *a*rdd; gŵyl, yr *ŵ*yl; gwên, y *w*ên; mam, y *f*am; tref, y *d*ref, i'r *d*ref.

Note that **ll** and **rh** do *not* mutate after the article in feminine singular nouns: y *ll*ong; a'r *ll*aw; y *ll*euad; y *rh*aff; y *rh*eol.

Many names of places, mountains, localities, etc. consist of feminine singular nouns preceded by the article, which causes mutation: *Y Waun; Y Gelli; Yr Wyddfa; Y Gaer; Y Foel; Y Felinheli*. The article in such names is often dropped, but remains understood, and the mutation remains: *Felindre; Garn Goch; Waun-fawr; Faerdre; Gelliwastad; Efail-fach; Gilfach-goch; Borth; Gors-las*. Sometimes the mutation is irregular because no article is understood before the noun: *Gorseinon; Garndolbenmaen; Waunarlwydd; Gelli'r Ynn*.

The word *pobl* 'people' is a feminine singular noun, though collective in meaning. The mutation in *y bobl* is regular, but the same change in the plural is irregular, *y bobloedd*, because plural nouns do not undergo mutation after the article.

(ii) Lenition occurs at the beginning of an adjective between the article and a fem. s. noun: y *f*wyn fam; y *dd*u nos; y *w*en ferch; yr *a*rw groes. **ll** and **rh** also mutate in an adjective in such a position: y *l*wyd wawr; y *r*ydd wlad. When the noun, being understood, is omitted the mutation remains: y *l*wyd 'the grey (one)'; y *f*echan 'the little (girl)'; y *d*los 'the beautiful (lady)'; y *l*onnaf 'the happiest' (woman). Following are the names given to certain features in Welsh metres: Y Gynghanedd *G*roes; y Gynghanedd *D*raws; y Gynghanedd *L*usg. These are often abbreviated to: Y *G*roes; y *D*raws; y *L*usg.

(iii) The numerals *dau* and *dwy* mutate after the article: y *dd*au ddyn; y *dd*wy wraig; 'mae pobl wedi mynd i fyw i'r *dd*au dŷ ar bymtheg' ('People have gone to live in the seventeen houses').

This change (>*dd*) occurs in *deu-* and *dwy-* in compounds, e.g. y *dd*euddyn; y *dd*wyfron; y *dd*eutu; but *y dwylo* and *y deuddeg* retain the radical.

(iv) The prime numbers, with the exception of *dau* and *dwy*, retain the radical after the article: y *t*air gwraig; y *p*edair gwlad; y *p*um heol; y *d*eg adnod; y *p*ymtheg merch hyn ('these 15 girls'); y *c*anpunt.

The ordinal numerals are mutated when they are fem., i.e. when they qualify a fem. s. noun either expressed or understood: y *d*rydedd bennod; y *b*edwaredd flwyddyn; y *b*umed adnod; y *dd*egfed salm; y *g*anfed ferch; y *d*rydedd ar ddeg o'r llongau ('the thirteenth of the ships'); § 208 (iv).

§9. (i) When adjectival demonstrative pronouns, such as *hwn, hon, hyn, hynny*, are placed after nouns the article must precede the nouns: *y tŷ hwn* 'this house'; *y ferch honno* 'that girl'; *i'r lleoedd hynny* 'to those places'; *y pethau hyn; yr aur hwn.*

This rule applies if the pronoun *rhai* takes the place of a noun before *hyn(ny): y rhai hyn; y rhai hynny.* These expressions are usually contracted to *y rhain; y rheiny, y rheini,* but in writing the article should not be omitted (See §90).

(ii) The article is used in a few Welsh expressions without a corresponding use in English: *yn y gwaith* 'at work'; *yn yr ysgol* 'in, at school'; *yn yr eglwys* 'in church'; *mynd i'r farchnad* 'going to market'; *mynd yn (ar) y trên* 'going by train'; *yn yr ysbyty* 'in hospital'; *yn y gwely* 'in bed'.

(iii) The article is used also in expressions denoting price standard, measurement etc. where English has the indefinite article: *swllt y llath* 'a shilling a yard'; *deg ceiniog y pâr* 'ten pence a pair'; *ceiniog yr un* 'a penny each' 'a penny (for) one'; *deg punt yr wythnos* 'ten pounds a week'; *deugain milltir yr awr* 'forty miles an hour'; *punt y dydd* 'a pound a day'.

(iv) The article should not be placed before the Welsh names of a river: *Clwyd, Gŵy, Hafren, Ŵysg, Tafwys* (Thames), *Nîl* (Nile); *Donaw* (Danube). The rule is kept in place-names: Aber*teifi;* Aber*tawe;* Glyn *Nedd;* Dyffryn *Clwyd;* Cwm*tawe;* Glyn *Dyfrdwy.* The river-name is mutated where necessary: Pontar*gothi* (Cothi); Pontar*ddulais* (Dulais).

The irregularity is allowed in *Y Fenai* and *Yr Iorddonen,* but these names also occur without the article: *Menai* and *Iorddonen* (Jordan).

NOUNS

§ 10. Nouns are either *common* or *proper*, e.g. common nouns: *tŷ, dyn, môr, cariad, cyfoeth;* proper nouns: *Gwen, Ifan, Bangor, Tywi.*

Nouns can also be classified as abstract and concrete. A concrete noun relates to a substance or object, e.g. *carreg, cnawd, dŵr, tân, lliw.* An abstract noun relates to a concept or idea, e.g. *hiraeth, cariad, gwynder, dewrder, drygioni, pleser, delfryd, dawn.*

Number. Most common nouns have a singular and a plural number. Some nouns have no plural and others have no singular. Some nouns, though singular in form, denote a number or collection of individual objects or substances. These are called *collective* nouns; but collective nouns in most cases have further plural forms, e.g. *haid* 'swarm', *heidiau;* *tyrfa* 'crowd', *tyrfaoedd.*

The plural can be formed from the singular in seven ways:

  (i) By vowel change.
  (ii) By adding a plural termination.
  (iii) By adding a termination together with a vowel change.
  (iv) By losing a singular ending.
  (v) By losing an ending together with a vowel change.
  (vi) By changing a singular for a plural ending.
  (vii) By changing a singular for a plural ending together with vowel change.

FORMING THE PLURAL

§ 11. Vowel change:

a becomes **ai**

		pl.			pl.
brân	'crow'	brain	arddodiad	'preposition'	arddodiaid
sant	'saint'	saint	gleisiad	'young	gleisiaid
llygad	'eye'	llygaid		salmon'	
dafad	'sheep'	defaid*	deiliad	'tenant'	deiliaid

a becomes **ei**

		pl.			pl.
iâr	'hen'	ieir	march	'steed'	meirch
car	'car'	ceir	bardd	'bard'	beirdd
sarff	'serpent'	seirff	carw	'stag'	ceirw
gafr	'goat'	geifr	tarw	'bull'	teirw

a becomes **y** (clear)

		pl.			pl.
bustach	'steer'	bustych	aradr	'plough'	erydr*
alarch	'swan'	elyrch*	paladr	'ray'	pelydr*

*a in the penult becomes e

ae becomes **ai**

		pl.			*pl.*
draen	'thorn'	drain	maen	'stone'	main
					(old pl.)

(N.B. Irregular change: gwaell 'skewer', '(knitting) needle'; *pl.* gweyll, gweill).

e becomes **y** (clear)

		pl.			*pl.*
castell	'castle'	cestyll	bachgen	'boy'	bechgyn
astell	'shelf'	estyll	llawes	'sleeve'	llewys
asgell	'wing'	esgyll	cyllell	'knife'	cyllyll
padell	'pan'	pedyll	angel	'angel'	engyl
aberth	'sacrifice'	ebyrth	maharen	'ram'	meheryn
Gwyddel	'Irishman'	Gwyddyl	llannerch	'glade'	llennyrch

o becomes **y** (clear)

		pl.			*pl.*
ffordd	'way'	ffyrdd	corff	'body'	cyrff
post	'post'	pyst	ffon	'stick'	ffyn
Cymro	'Welshman'	Cymry	porth	'gate, porch'	pyrth
corn	'horn'	cyrn	porthmon	'drover'	porthmyn

w becomes **y** (clear)

		pl.			*old pl.*
asgwrn	'bone'	esgyrn	arddwrn	'wrist'	erddyrn,
					pl.
					arddyrnau

oe becomes **wy**

		pl.			*pl.*
oen	'lamb'	ŵyn	croen	'skin'	crwyn

Changes in other vowels and diphthongs:

		pl.			*pl.*
haearn	'iron'	heyrn	gŵr	'man'	gwŷr
caseg	'mare'	cesig	maneg	'glove'	menig
cragen	'shell'	cregyn	gweithiwr	'worker'	gweithwyr

§12. Adding a termination:

-au: arf 'weapon', arfau; afal 'apple', afalau; llong 'ship', llongau; cae 'field', caeau; coes 'leg', coesau; poen 'pain', poenau.

-iau: esgid 'boot', esgidiau; het 'hat', hetiau; glin 'knee', gliniau; grudd 'cheek', gruddiau; llanc '(a) youth', llanciau; gofid 'sorrow', gofidiau.

-ion: ysgol 'school', ysgolion; esgob 'bishop', esgobion; ŵyr 'grandchild', wyrion; atgof 'memory', atgofion; rhodd 'gift', rhoddion.

-on: cysur 'comfort', cysuron; gofal 'care', gofalon; cennad 'messenger', cenhadon ('missionaries'); nwy 'gas', nwyon; gweddw 'widow', gweddwon; Iddew 'Jew', Iddewon.

-i: proffwyd 'prophet', proffwydi; ffenestr 'window', ffenestri; perth 'hedge,' perthi; llwyn 'bush, grove', llwyni; llestr 'vessel', llestri; llen 'curtain', llenni.

-ydd: afon 'river', afonydd; bwyd 'food', bwydydd; heol 'road', heolydd; bro 'vale, region', broydd; fferm 'farm', ffermydd; ffos 'ditch', ffosydd; diod 'drink', diodydd.

Either -i or **-ydd** may be added to a few nouns: tref 'town', trefi/trefydd; plwyf 'parish', plwyfi/plwyfydd; eglwys 'church', eglwysi/eglwysydd.

-edd: ewin '(finger) nail', ewinedd; teyrn 'monarch', teyrnedd; bys 'finger', bysedd; dant 'tooth', dannedd.

-oedd: môr 'sea', moroedd; dinas 'city', dinasoedd; ardal 'district, region', ardaloedd; gwisg 'dress', gwisgoedd; brenin 'king', brenhinoedd; oes 'age', oesoedd.

-ed: merch 'girl', merched; pryf 'worm, insect', pryfed.

-aint: gof 'smith', gofaint; (with no singular) ysgyfaint 'lungs'.

-od: cath 'cat', cathod; llwynog 'fox', llwynogod; geneth 'girl', genethod; colomen 'pigeon, dove', colomennod; baban 'baby', babanod; corrach 'dwarf', corachod; gwiber 'viper', gwiberod; cor 'spider, dwarf', corrod.

-iaid: pechadur 'sinner', pechaduriaid; creadur 'creature', creaduriaid; Methodist, Methodistiaid; person 'parson', personiaid; gwennol 'swallow', gwenoliaid. Also, mostly in plural, names of nations, peoples, families, etc.: Groegiaid 'Greeks'; Rhufeiniaid 'Romans'; Normaniaid 'Normans'; y Llwydiaid 'the Lloyds'; y Morganiaid 'the Morgan family'.

Note I. The accent falls normally on the penult in polysyllables‧ (§6, i).

By adding a syllable the accent moves, and this may cause a spelling change. **-nn** and **-rr** in an accented syllable become **-n** and **-r** when it becomes unaccented, and an original **h** is restored, e.g. *corrach, corachod; carrai* 'thong', *careiau; annedd* 'abode', *anheddau; cennad* 'messenger', *cenhadon* 'missionaries'; *cenedl* 'nation', *cenhedloedd; cannwyll* 'candle', *canhwyllau; cynnen* 'contention',

cynhennau; cynnyrch 'product', *cynhyrchion.* Note that there is no **h** in
cynneddf 'faculty', *pl. cyneddfau.* **h** disappears with the loss of accent,
e.g. in *cynghanedd* 'harmony', (metrical term), *cynganeddion,* and the s.
cangen 'branch', pl. *canghennau.* It moves with the accent in *dihareb*
'proverb', *diarhebion.* The s. form *brenin* is now so written, but was
formerly written *brenhin;* the **h** is kept under the accent in the pl.
brenhinoedd (cf. brenhines 'queen').

In many monosyllables **-n** *and* **-r** *stand for* **-nn** *and* **-rr,** and if a syllable
is added the double consonant should be shown, e.g. *ton* 'wave'
tonnau; llan 'church', *llannau; man* 'place', *mannau; gwar* 'nape of
neck', *gwarrau; cwr* 'border', *cyrrau.*

II. In a few words **-nt** and **-nc** mutate to **-nn** and **-ng** on adding a
termination, but this is not a general rule: *cant* 'hundred', *cannoedd;*
punt (£), *punnoedd, punnau; tant,* 'harpstring', *tannau; meddiant*
'possession', *meddiannau; amrant* 'eyelid', *amrannau (amrantau); dant*
'tooth', *dannedd; crafanc* 'claw', *crafangau; cainc* 'branch', *cangau
(ceinciau); braint* 'privilege', *breintiau (breiniau,* cf. the adj. *breiniol).*

§13. Adding a termination together with a vowel change:

	a becomes **ei**				**a** becomes **e**	
		pl.				*pl.*
sant	'saint'	seintiau	nant		'brook'	nentydd
mab	'son'	meibion	gardd		'garden'	gerddi
gwas	'servant'	gweision	gwlad		'country'	gwledydd
cymar	'mate'	cymheir-iaid	câr		'kinsman'	ceraint

	e becomes **ei**				**ae** becomes **ei**	
		pl.				*pl.*
capten	'captain'	capteiniaid	maen		'stone'	meini
gefell	'twin'	gefeilliaid	saer		'carpenter'	seiri
pencerdd	'chief of song'	penceirdd-iaid	maer		'mayor'	meiri

	ae becomes **ey**				**aw** becomes **ew**	
		pl.				*pl.*
maes	'field'	meysydd	cawr		'giant'	cewri
caer	'fort'	ceyrydd				

	ai becomes **ei**				**au** becomes **eu**	
		pl.				*pl.*
iaith	'language'	ieithoedd	haul		'sun'	heuliau
nain	'grandmother'	neiniau	traul		'expense'	treuliau
ffair	'fair'	ffeiriau	aroglau		'smell'	arogleuon
rhaid	'need'	rheidiau	gwaun		'meadow'	gweunydd
nai	'nephew'	neiaint				

aw becomes **o**

		pl.
awr	'hour'	oriau
brawd	'brother'	brodyr
bawd	'thumb'	bodiau
traethawd	'essay'	traethodau

w becomes **y** (obscure)

		pl.
ffrwd	'stream'	ffrydiau
cwm	'glen'	cymoedd
hwrdd	'ram'	hyrddod
cwestiwn	'question'	cwestiynau

clear **y** becomes obscure **y**

		pl.
llyn	'lake'	llynnoedd, llynnau
bryn	'hill'	bryniau
gwynt	'wind'	gwyntoedd

		pl.
pryf	'worm'	pryfed
ych	'ox'	ychen

uw becomes **u**

		pl.
buwch	'cow'	buchod

au becomes **aw** or **af**

		pl.
cenau	'whelp'	cenawon, cenafon
edau	'thread'	edafedd

ei becomes **a**

		pl.
lleidr	'thief'	lladron
neidr	'snake'	nadredd, nadroedd

ai becomes **a**

		pl.
gwraig	'wife'	gwragedd
rhiain	'maiden'	rhianedd
celain	'corpse'	celanedd
cainc	'branch'	cangau
adain	'wing'	adanedd

(old forms of modern *aden, adenydd*)

ai becomes **ae**

		pl.
Sais	'Englishman'	Saeson

The vowel changes noted in the above paragraphs, (§§ 12, 13) are classified below in Appendix B.

§ 14. Dropping a singular ending:

		pl.
plufyn	'feather'	pluf
pluen	'feather'	plu
mwyaren	'blackberry'	mwyar
gwelltyn	'straw'	gwellt

		pl.
rhosyn	'rose'	rhos
mochyn	'pig'	moch
ffäen	'bean'	ffa
pysgodyn	'fish'	pysgod

§ 15. Dropping a singular ending together with vowel change:

a becomes **ai**

		pl.
dalen	'leaf' (of book)	dail (*also* dalennau)
gwialen	'twig'	gwiail
hwyaden	'duck'	hwyaid
asen	'rib'	ais (*also* asennau)

a becomes **ei** or clear **y**

		pl.
tywarchen	'turf'	tyweirch, tywyrch

	ei becomes **ai**			**o** becomes clear **y**	
		pl.			*pl.*
deilen	'leaf'	dail	collen	'hazel'	cyll
meipen	'turnip'	maip	onnen	'ash-tree'	ynn
eisen	'rib'	ais	cortyn	'cord'	cyrt
			corcyn	'cork'	cyrc

	o becomes **aw**			**eu** becomes **au**	
		pl.			*pl.*
conyn	'stalk'	cawn	blodeuyn	'flower'	blodau
cosyn	'(a) cheese'	caws	cneuen	'nut'	cnau
		(also s.)	lleuen	'louse'	llau

	obscure **y** becomes clear **y**			**e** becomes **a**	
		pl.			*pl.*
gwenynen	'bee'	gwenyn	plentyn	'child'	plant
celynnen	'holly'	celyn	aderyn	'bird'	adar
rhedynen	'fern'	rhedyn	dilledyn	'garment'	dillad
cnewyllyn	'kernel'	cnewyll	rhecsyn	'rag'	rhacs

	ew becomes **au**			obscure **y** becomes **w**	
		pl.			*pl.*
llysewyn	'herb'	llysau, llysiau	cacynen	'hornet'	cacwn
giewyn, gewyn	'sinew'	gïau			

§16. Substituting a plural ending for a singular ending:

		pl.			*pl.*
rholyn	'roll'	rholion, rholiau	crwydryn	'wanderer'	crwydraid
			cardotyn	'beggar'	cardotwyr
unigolyn	'individual'	unigolion	cwningen	'rabbit'	cwningod
diferyn	'drop'	diferion			

§17. Substituting a plural ending for a singular together with vowel change:

		pl.			
miaren	'bramble'	mieri	teclyn	'tool'	taclau
cerdyn	'card'	cardiau	cerpyn	'rag'	carpiau

§18. Forming the plural irregularly:

(i) Anomalous in form or change, e.g.

		pl.
blwyddyn 'year'		blynyddoedd, blynedd *(after numeral)*
ci 'dog'		cŵn
credadun 'believer'		credinwyr

cydymaith 'companion'   cymdeithion
chwaer 'sister'   chwiorydd
dydd 'day'   *(formerly)* diau, *as still in* tridiau
                               'three days'

dyniawed 'yearling'   dyniewaid
haearn 'iron'   heyrn
llaw 'hand'   dwylo (dwylaw)
llo 'calf'   lloi (lloeau)
morŵyn 'maid'   morynion, morŵynion
pared 'partition'   parwydydd
pennog *(formerly* penwag)   penwaig
  'herring'
troed 'foot'   traed
tŷ 'house'   tai (teiau)

Compounds ending in **-dy** (**-ty**):

beudy 'cowshed'   beudyau, beudai (beudái)
elusendy 'almshouse'   elusendai
gweithdy 'workshop'   gweithdai (gweithdái)
gwallgofdy 'madhouse'   gwallgofdai
gwesty 'hotel'   gwestyau, gwestai*
hundy 'dormitory'   hundyau
llety 'lodging'   lletyau
ysbyty 'hospital'   ysbytyau, ysbytai

The ordinary plural of *rhaeadr* 'waterfall' today is *rhaeadrau,* but we also have:

rhaeadr   rhëydr, rhÿeidr

(ii) Forming the plural from a derivative:

Cristion 'Christian'   Cristionogion, Cristnogion
glaw 'rain'   glawogydd
llif 'flood'   llifogydd
addurn 'adornment'   addurniadau
crwydr 'wandering'   crwydradau
dychryn 'terror'   dychryniadau
rheg 'curse'   rhegfeydd
dechrau 'beginning'   dechreuadau
diwedd 'end'   diweddiadau
gwich 'squeak'   gwichiadau
serch 'love, affection'   serchiadau
cas 'enemy'   caseion
gwaith 'work(s)'   gweithfeydd *(also* gweithiau)
     (e.g. gwaith glo 'coal mine'; gwaith haearn 'iron-works')
gras 'grace'   grasusau

Gwestai is also a s. noun, 'guest'

Note that an unaccented syllable is dropped from the plural:

llysywen 'eel'	llyswennod
cystadleuaeth 'competition'	cystadlaethau (cystadleuaethau)
perchennog 'owner'	perchnogion (perchenogion)

§ 19. Double Plural. Many nouns have double plural forms.

(i) The commonest are those which add the diminutive endings -**ach** and -**os** to the plural (sometimes with a vowel change), e.g.

Singular	Plural	Diminutive Double Pl.
ci	cŵn	cynos
crydd 'shoemaker'	cryddion	cryddionach
draen(en) 'thorn'	drain	dreiniach
dilledyn	dillad	dilladach, dillados
gwraig	gwragedd	gwrageddos
merch	merched	merchetos, merchetach
bachgen	bechgyn	bechgynnos, bechgynnach
plentyn	plant	plantos, plantach
pryf	pryfed	pryfetach
tŷ	tai	teios

(-**ach** is sometimes added to dialect forms, such as,

crwt(yn) 'lad'	cryts	crytsach
crotyn 'lad'	crots	crotsach)

Sometimes the ending is added to the singular, e.g.

carreg	cerrig	caregos
gwerin 'folk'	(gwerinoedd)	gwerinos
dernyn 'piece'	dernynnau	dernynnach
gêr (dial.) 'gear'		geriach (dial.)
dŵr 'water'		dwrach (dial.)

-**os** usually expresses endearment, and -**ach** contempt.

(ii) Other double plurals are formed by adding a plural ending to a form already plural, e.g.,

Singular	Plural	Double Plural
celain 'corpse'	celanedd	celaneddau
cloch 'bell'	clych (poetical)	clychau
angel	engyl	engylion, angylion
neges 'errand'	negesau	negeseuau, negeseuon
paladr 'ray'	pelydr	pelydrau
peth 'thing'	pethau	petheuau

mach 'surety'	meichiau	meichiafon
sant	saint	seintiau
tŷ	tai	teiau
llo	lloi	lloeau

§20. Nouns with more than one plural:

Singular	*Plural*
eglwys 'church'	eglwysi, eglwysydd
tref 'town'	trefi, trefydd
plwyf 'parish'	plwyfi, plwyfydd
pêl 'ball'	pelau, peli
pibell 'pipe'	pibelli, pibellau
canhwyllbren 'candlestick'	canwyllbrenni, canwyllbrennau
pelen 'ball'	pelenni, pelennau
cell 'cell'	celli, cellau
celli 'grove'	cellïau, cellïoedd
oes 'age'	oesoedd, oesau
llythyr, 'letter'	llythyrau, llythyron
glan 'bank'	glannau, glennydd
caer 'fort'	caerau, ceyrydd
ffrwyth 'fruit'	ffrwythau, ffrwythydd
gwal (wal) 'wall'	gwaliau (waliau), gwelydd
gwinllan 'vineyard'	gwinllannau, gwinllannoedd
cefnder '(first) cousin'	cefnderoedd, cefndyr
cyfrder '(second) cousin'	cyfrderoedd, cyfrdyr
llyn 'lake'	llynnoedd (llynnau)
amser 'time'	amseroedd, amserau
ach 'lineage'	achau, (achoedd)
porfa 'pasture'	porfeydd, porfaoedd
preswylfa 'dwelling place'	preswylfeydd, preswylfâu
cath 'cat'	cathod (cathau)
Groegwr 'Greek'	Groegwyr, Groegiaid
Gwyddel 'Irishman'	Gwyddyl (Gwyddelod)
Ffrancwr 'Frenchman'	Ffrancwyr (Ffrancod)
padell 'pan'	padelli, padellau, pedyll
awdur (awdwr) 'author'	awduron, awduriaid (awdwyr)˙
cariad 'lover'	cariadon, cariadau
llech 'slate'	llechi, llechau
chwarel 'quarry'	chwareli, chwarelau, chwarelydd
alarch 'swan'	elyrch, eleirch (alarchod)
mynach 'monk'	mynaich, mynachod

§21. Plural variation according to meaning. Where a singular noun has two meanings the difference is sometimes shown in the plural by differing forms, e.g.

Singular	Plural	Plural
cyngor	cynghorau 'councils'	cynghorion 'counsels'
canon	canonau 'rules'	canoniaid '(church) canons'
bron	bronnau 'breasts'	bronnydd 'hill-sides'
llwyth	llwythi 'loads'	llwythau 'tribes'
pwys	pwysau 'weight(s)'	pwysi 'pound-weights'
punt	punnau (punnoedd) 'pounds', £	punnoedd 'amounts of £1s (notes or coins)
pryd	prydiau 'times'	prydau 'meals'
person	personau 'persons'	personiaid 'parsons'
ysbryd	ysbrydoedd 'spirits'	ysbrydion 'ghosts'
helm	helmydd 'stacks, ricks'	helmau 'helmets', '(of ships) helms'
asen	asennau 'ribs'	asennod 'she-asses'
munud	munudau 'minutes'	munudiau 'gestures'
llif	llifogydd 'floods'	llifiau 'saws'
llwyn, lwyn	llwynau, lwynau 'loins'	llwyni (llwynau) 'groves, bushes'
brawd	brodyr 'brothers'	brodiau 'judgements'
mil	miloedd 'thousands'	milod 'animals'

§22. Nouns with two forms of the singular.

Singular	Plural
cleddyf, cleddau 'sword'	cleddyfau
dant, daint 'tooth'	dannedd
dwfr, dŵr 'water'	dyfroedd
cofl, côl 'bosom, lap'	coflau
edau, edefyn 'thread'	edafedd
arf, erfyn 'weapon'	arfau
mil, milyn 'animal'	milod
ysgallen, ysgellyn 'thistle'	ysgall
cawnen, conyn 'stalk, rush'	cawn
hoel, hoelen 'nail'	hoelion
imp, impyn 'sprout'	impion
hwyad, hwyaden 'duck'	hwyaid

§23. Nouns with no singular.

plwyfolion 'parishioners'; trigolion 'inhabitants'; gwehilion 'dregs'; ysgarthion 'refuse'; ysgubion 'sweepings'; pigion 'selections';

ceinion 'beauties'; dychweledigion 'converts'; gwybodusion 'knowledgeable (persons)'; gwartheg 'cows'; aeron 'fruits'; creifion 'parings'; glafoerion 'drivel'; ymysgaroedd 'bowels'; llodrau 'trousers'; teithi 'characteristics'; rhieni 'parents' *(an artificial s. form* rhiant *is being increasingly used).*

§24. Nouns with no plural.

(i) Many abstract nouns, e.g. newyn 'famine'; syched 'thirst'; ffydd 'faith'; gwres 'heat'; caredigrwydd 'kindness'; sirioldeb 'cheerfulness'; tegwch 'beauty'; tywydd 'weather'.

(ii) Nouns denoting substance or material, e.g. cnawd 'flesh'; gwaed 'blood'; llwch 'dust'; eira 'snow'; baw 'dirt'; llaeth 'milk'; llefrith 'milk'; caws 'cheese'; uwd 'porridge'; te 'tea'; glo 'coal'; cynnud 'fuel'; tail 'dung'; iâ 'ice'; mêl 'honey'; medd 'mead'; siwgr 'sugar'.

(iii) Some diminutive nouns in *-ig, -an, -cyn, -cen,* e.g. afonig 'brook'; oenig 'lambkin'; dynan 'a little person'; ffwlcyn (m.), ffolcen (f.), 'fool'. (Many others with these endings have plural forms, e.g. llecyn 'place', llecynnau; tennyn 'tether', tenynnau).

(iv) Proper nouns, e.g. Dafydd, Cymru, Yr Wyddfa, Clwyd, (Y) Pasg, (Y) Nadolig, Ionawr. (But we have the plural forms *Suliau* 'Sundays', *Gwenerau* 'Fridays', *Sadyrnau* 'Saturdays'; and one can say *dyddiau Llun* 'Mondays', *boreau Mawrth* 'Tuesday mornings', *nosau Iau* 'Thursday nights', *dyddiau Calan* 'New Year days', etc.)

§25. The Dual Number.
In the very early period of the language there was a dual number in addition to the singular and plural. A few traces of it remain in compounds with *deu-* and *dwy-* and in the exceptional soft mutation occurring in some cases:

(i) The numerals *dau, deu-, dwy, dwy-* undergo mutation after the article; § 8 (iii).

(ii) Lenition follows *dau, dwy,* and *deu-, dwy-* (in compounds), e.g. *dau beth* 'two things', *dwy geiniog* 'two pence', *deufis* 'two months', *deuddeg* 'twelve', *dwyfron* 'breast, bosom', *dwyfil* 'two thousand'. (Exceptions *deupen, deutu, deuparth, deucant).*

(iii) Lenition follows the article in a few nouns which are 'dual' although not preceded by a numeral: *yr efeilliaid* 'the twins' (s. *gefell)* and names of mountains with dual connotation, e.g. *Yr Eifl* (from *gafl* 'fork'); *Y Gyrn* (from *corn,* pl. *cyrn* 'horn').

GENDER OF NOUNS

§26.
Nouns in Welsh in general are either masculine or feminine in gender. The gender of many nouns (mostly denoting persons) varies:

(i) according to the sex of the individual meant, e.g. *priod* 'spouse', *perthynas* 'relation', *gefell* 'twin', *tyst* 'witness', *ŵyr* 'grandchild', *cariad* 'loved one', *ymwelydd* 'visitor', *ysgrifennydd* 'secretary'. Formerly *dyn* belonged to this class and could mean either 'man' or 'woman', so that *y dyn* 'the man' and *y ddyn* 'the woman' were possible expressions. In some dialects a fem. form *dynes* has come into general use, but it has not been completely adopted into the literary standard. (In the same way many other fairly new fem. forms are commonly used, e.g. *ysgrifenyddes, wyres, cymhares* 'mate', *arweinyddes* 'conductress'. When *peth* is applied to a person it can be fem., *y beth fach* 'the (dear) little thing'.

(ii) according to dialect or local custom. This class includes many nouns in common usage, e.g. *angladd* 'funeral', *breuddwyd** 'dream', *troed**'foot', *munud** 'minute', *rhyfel** 'war', *cinio** 'dinner', *cyflog* 'pay', *clorian* '(weighing) scales'.

(iii) according to meaning, e.g.,

Masculine	Feminine
math: y math *hwn* 'this kind'	y fath 'the kind'; y fath beth 'such a thing'
golwg: yn y golwg 'in sight'	yr oedd golwg *wael* arno 'he was ill in appearance'
	mae gennyf olwg *fawr* arni 'I regard her highly'
man 'place': yn y man 'presently, on the spot'	yn y fan 'immediately'
coes 'leg': y coes *hwn* 'this stem, handle'	y goes *hon* 'this leg'
to 'roof': y to 'the roof, the generation'	y do (sy'n codi) 'the (rising) generation'

For a discussion of the anomalies in the use of *math* see TC pp. 82-86.

There are also pairs of words of similar forms but different in origin, meaning and gender:

gwaith 'work', masc.;	gwaith 'occasion', fem. (unwaith 'once')
brawd 'brother', masc.;	brawd 'judgement' (y frawd) fem.
llif 'flood', masc.;	llif 'saw', fem.
mil 'animal', masc.;	mil 'thousand', fem.
llith 'mash, bait', masc.	llith 'lesson', fem.
gwasg 'waist' masc. or fem.	gwasg '(printing) press', fem.

(both of probably same origin)

*mostly masc. in N. Wales and fem. in S. Wales.

(iv) according to choice or taste of user, e.g., arfer 'custom', arwydd 'sign', awyrgylch 'atmosphere', cyngerdd 'concert', cri 'cry', dawn '(innate) gift', delfryd 'ideal', ergyd 'blow', nifer 'number', penbleth 'quandary', ystyr 'meaning'.

(v) because of uncertainty as regards gender in fairly recent borrowings, e.g. blows 'blouse', bws 'bus', coler 'collar', crafat 'cravat', piano, stamp, record, tei 'tie', trên 'train'. (The gender of many others is well established, e.g. *fem.* set, gêm 'game', trei 'try', gôl 'goal', wiced 'wicket', sgriw 'screw', sgert, sgyrt 'skirt', cic, 'kick'; *masc.* pensiwn 'pension', credyd 'credit', iws *(beside* llog) 'interest, use', rhent 'rent', telegram', notis 'notice', polisi 'policy'.

§ 27. The gender of nouns denoting animate objects generally agrees with the sex of the object, e.g.

masc.: bachgen 'boy', gwas 'manservant', ci 'dog', tarw 'bull'
fem.: merch 'girl', morwyn 'maid', gast 'bitch', buwch 'cow'

There are also some epicene nouns, i.e. nouns which have their own gender irrespective of the sex of the objects they denote.

Examples of (a) masculine epicenes: plentyn 'child', baban, maban 'babe', bardd 'bard', perchen 'owner', deiliad 'tenant', alarch 'swan', curyll 'hawk', oen 'lamb'.

(b) feminine eipcenes: cath, celain, cennad 'messenger', gwiwer 'squirrel', cog *and* cwcw 'cuckoo', colomen 'pigeon', eos 'nightingale'.

The adjectives *gwryw* 'male' and *benyw* 'female' may be added to an epicene, but by doing so the *gender* is not changed, e.g. in *eryr benyw* the non-mutation of *benyw* shows that *eryr* is masculine although the expression means 'female eagle'. Similarly, in *cath wryw* the mutated adjective shows that *cath* is still feminine although *cath wryw* means 'male cat'. *Llo benyw* follows the rule, but *llo fenyw,* heard in some parts of Wales, seems to be an exception.

§ 28. Some masc. nouns are made fem. by: (1) adding **-es**, e.g.,

Masculine	*Feminine*
arglwydd 'lord'	arglwyddes
brenin 'king'	brenhines
meistr 'master'	meistres
llanc 'youth'	llances
sant	santes
maer	maeres
aer 'heir'	aeres
llew 'lion'	llewes
mul 'ass'	mules
organydd 'organist'	organyddes

The ending is added to a stem which differs from the masc. in the following: athro 'teacher', athrawes; Cymro 'Welshman', Cymraes; Sais 'Englishman', Saesnes; cenau 'whelp', cenawes; lleidr 'thief', lladrones.

(ii) changing **-yn** to **-en** e.g.

hogyn 'boy'	hogen
crwtyn 'boy'	croten
coegyn 'fop'	coegen
ffwlcyn 'fool'	ffolcen
merlyn 'pony'	merlen
asyn 'ass'	asen
clobyn 'huge (fellow)'	cloben

(iii) changing **-wr** to **-es,** e.g.

cenhadwr 'missionary'	cenhades
Almaenwr 'German'	Almaenes
Ffrancwr 'Frenchman'	Ffrances
Albanwr 'Scot'	Albanes

(iv) changing **-(i)wr** to **-wraig,** e.g.

gweithiwr 'workman'	gweithwraig (gweithreg)
pysgotwr 'fisherman'	pysgotwraig
adroddwr 'reciter'	adroddwraig (adroddreg)
cantwr 'singer'	cantwraig (cantreg)

§ 29. Names of family relations and of a few animals have different words or anomalous forms for masc. and fem., e.g.

tad	mam
brawd	chwaer
ewythr 'uncle'	modryb
gŵr 'husband'	gwraig
tad-cu 'grandfather'	mam-gu
taid 'grandfather'	nain
nai 'nephew'	nith
cefnder '1st cousin'	cyfnither
*chwegrwn 'father-in-law'	*chwegr
tad-yng-nghyfraith 'father-in-law'	mam-yng-nghyfraith
*daw 'son-in-law'	*gwaudd
mab-yng-nghyfraith 'son-in-law'	merch-yng-nghyfraith

*(Chwegrwn, chwegr, daw and gwaudd are now known mostly through their use in the Bible.)

masc.	fem.
ceffyl, march 'horse, stallion'	caseg
ceiliog 'cock'	iâr
hwrdd, maharen 'ram'	dafad, mamog 'ewe'
bustach, eidion, ych 'steer, ox'	anner, treisiad 'heifer'
hesbwrn 'yearling ram'	hesbin 'yearling ewe'

For lack of a masc. form corresponding to a fem. noun the nouns *bwch* 'buck' or *ceiliog* 'cock' are used with the fem. to form a masc., e.g. gafr 'goat', bwch gafr; bronfraith 'thrush', ceiliog bronfraith; mwyalch(en) 'blackbird', ceiliog mwyalch.

§30. Nouns denoting inanimate objects or abstractions can not be classified by gender according to definite rules, but the following distribution may serve as a guide:

(i) Masculine: (1) *dydd, diwrnod,* and names of days; *Dydd Sul, Dydd Llun, Y Calan, Calan-mai, Clamai, Y Pasg, Y Sulgwyn, Y Nadolig,* etc. Exceptions: names of feast days (including *gŵyl*) are feminine: *Gŵyl Ifan, Gŵyl Fair, Gŵyl Fihangel,* etc., but both *Gŵyl Ddewi* and *Gŵyl Dewi* occur.

(2) *mis,* and the names of months; *(Mis) Ionawr, Ionor, (Mis) Awst,* etc.

(3) *tymor,* and the names of seasons; *gwanwyn, haf, hydref, gaeaf.*

(4) *gwynt* 'wind', and the names of the points of the compass; *gogledd, dwyrain, de (deau), gorllewin, de-ddwyrain,* etc.

(5) Nouns denoting substance or material: *arian, aur, derw, efydd, calch, dŵr (dwfr), glaw, eira, rhew, iâ, brethyn, gwlân, pren, pridd, mawn, gwydr, lledr, melfed, sidan, bwyd, bara, cig, mêl, te, coffi, ŷd, medd, cwrw, dafn, darn,* etc.

Exceptions: the following are feminine; *torth, teisen, pastai, saig, gwledd, diod, tablen;* names of fruit ending in *-en, gellygen, eirinen.*

(6) Verb-nouns: *canu, gweithio,* etc. (Exceptions: *gafael* and *cyfeddach,* especially when used as nouns, are feminine.)

(ii) Feminine: (1) *gwlad,* and names denoting a country or region, e.g. *Cymru, Lloegr, Ffrainc, Yr Almaen, Israel, Yr Aifft, ardal, bro, ffin, teyrnas, tywysogaeth, talaith, pau, cymdogaeth.*

Exceptions: the following are masculine; *tir, rhandir, cyfandir, parth, rhanbarth, cylch. Goror* may be masc. or fem.

(2) *tref, llan, dinas, caer,* and names of towns and parishes; *Bangor,*

Caerdydd, Llanfair-ar-y-bryn, Llandeilo Fawr, and all place-names beginning in *Tre(f)-, Llan-, Caer-, Ynys-, Ystrad-.*

(3) *afon, nant,* and names of rivers and streams: *Dyfrdwy, Taf, Tawe, Conwy, Hafren, Brân, Sawdde,* etc. (But old names with *Nant-* are sometimes masc., e.g. *Nantgarw.*)

(4) Names of mountains except those in which *mynydd* or *bryn* is part of the name: *Y Fan, Yr Wyddfa, Y Garn, Carnedd Ddafydd, Y Foel, Eryri, Y Farteg.* (*Y Mynydd Du, Bryn-teg, Y Moelwyn,* etc. are masc.).

(5) *iaith,* and names of languages: *Y Gymraeg, Y Saesneg, Yr Wyddeleg,* etc. But when the name denotes an example or specimen or particular piece of a language, it is masc., e.g., *Cymraeg da, Saesneg llafar, Gwyddeleg Diweddar.*

(6) *llythyren,* and the names of the letters of the alphabet: *A fawr, dwy n, r ddwbl.*

(7) *coeden, gwydden, colfen,* and names of trees, e.g. *derwen, onnen, afallen, celynnen, miaren.* But in compounds whose second element is *pren (-bren)* the noun is masc.; *ffigysbren, cambren, esgynbren.* According to rule *croesbren* and *crocbren* should be masc., but they are often treated as fem., because *croes* and *crog* are both fem.

(8) Collective nouns denoting groups or communities: *cenedl (y genedl), ciwed (y giwed), ach, llinach, hil, cymanfa, cynhadledd, cymdeithas, cenfaint, diadell, buches, haid, (h)aig, mintai, byddin, catrawd, torf, tyrfa, cyngres, cyfeillach, sasiwn, seiat, gwerin, Gorsedd (y Beirdd, yr Orsedd), y glêr* 'minstrels', *pendefigaeth, cynulleidfa, corfforaeth, cwt* 'queue', *urdd, ysgol, prifysgol, henaduriaeth.*

Masculine exceptions: *llu, teulu, tylwyth, llwyth, côr, cyngor, pwyllgor, gweithgor, bwrdd, undeb, cyfundeb, ciw, cwmni, coleg, enwad, cynulliad.*

§31. Derivative nouns can be classified according to terminations as follows: (i) Masculine nouns (mostly abstract):

-ad: cyflenwad, enwad, troad, cyflead.
-aint: henaint.
—awd, -od: traethawd, unawd, triawd, cryndod, cardod, segurdod.
-deb: undeb, (sometimes fem.), *duwioldeb, uniondeb, cywirdeb.*
-der: poethder, blinder, ysgelerder, hyder, braster, dicter.
-did: glendid, gwendid, aflendid, ieuenctid.
-dra: glanweithdra, mawrdra, ffieidd-dra, cyfleustra.
-dwr: cryfdwr, sychdwr.
-edd: amynedd, cydbwysedd, gwirionedd, atgasedd.
-had: mwynhad, eglurhad, glanhad, parhad, caniatâd, ymwacâd.
-i: tlodi, llwydi, diogi, chwyddi, cwrteisi.
-iad: rhodiad, cariad, gwelediad, cysylltiad.
-iant: mwyniant, nodiant, tarddiant, ffyniant.

-ineb: ffolineb, doethineb, taerineb, claerineb.
-ni: noethni, bryntni, dellni, syrthni, llwydni, glesni.
-ioni: daioni, drygioni, haelioni.
-id: cadernid, rhyddid (formerly *rhydd-did*).
-rwydd: caredigrwydd, helaethrwydd, addasrwydd, ardderchowgrwydd.
-wch: heddwch, tywyllwch, brawdgarwch, hawddgarwch, dedwyddwch.
-yd: iechyd, dedwyddyd, esmwythyd, seguryd.

Exceptions: the following are feminine: *trindod, buchedd, cynghanedd, trugaredd, ordinhad, cenadwri; galwad, ymgeledd, addewid* can be either masc. or fem., and *doethineb* is sometimes fem.: Mt. xiii. 54, 'y doethineb hwn'; Mk. vi. 2, 'a pha ddoethineb yw hon?'

(ii) Feminine nouns (mostly abstract):
-aeth, -iaeth: gwybodaeth, darbodaeth, dirnadaeth, tywysogaeth, esgobaeth, amheuaeth, athrawiaeth, athroniaeth, gwyddoniaeth, barddoniaeth, rhagoriaeth, swyddogaeth, gweinidogaeth, rhagluniaeth.
-as: priodas, galanas, teyrnas, perthynas 'relationship'.
-fa: noddfa, amddiffynfa, graddfa, porfa.

Exceptions: many nouns in *-aeth, -iaeth* are masc. e.g. *hiraeth, gwasanaeth, gwahaniaeth, lluniaeth, darfodedigaeth; amrywiaeth, claddedigaeth* are mostly masculine.

(iii) Feminine nouns having the following suffixes:
-en, -cen: hogen, seren, ffolcen (§ 28(ii)).
(Exception: *maharen,* which is masc.)
-es: santes, llewes (§ 28(i)).
-ell: llinell, cronnell, iyrchell, tarddell, pothell.
(*hanes, castell, cawell* are masc., as *-es, -ell* are not suffixes in these cases.)

(iv) Masculine nouns having the following suffixes:
-yn, -cyn: asyn, dernyn, llencyn, llecyn.
(Exceptions, words in which *-yn* is not a suffix: *blwyddyn, odyn, telyn, twymyn.*)
-wr: gweithiwr, glöwr, morwr, dyrnwr.

(v) The suffixes *-aid* ('-ful') and *-od* ('blow') do not change the gender of the nouns to which they are added:

fem.	*masc.*
dysgl, dysglaid	*tŷ, tyaid*
llwy, llwyaid	*crochan, crochanaid*
basged, basgedaid	*dwrn, dyrnod* 'blow with fist'
ffon, ffonnod 'blow with stick'	*cwpan, cwpanaid* (in some dialects *cwpan, -aid* are fem.)

cern, cernod	cleddyf, cleddyfod
'blow on cheek'	'blow with sword'

nyth, nythaid: feminine in S. Wales; masculine in N. Wales.

(vi) (1) As a rule the gender of a proper compound (§§ 185-6) is that of its chief (i.e. final) element, e.g.

masculine: gwaith; trymwaith, caledwaith.

        tŷ; ffermdy, gweithdy, beudy, ysbyty.

        ci; milgi, corgi, bleiddgi.

feminine: tref; hendref, maerdref, melindref, maestref.

Exceptions: *canrif* and *pendro* 'giddiness' are feminine (though *rhif* and *tro* are masc.)

(2) The gender of an improper compound (§ 186) is that of its first element, e.g.,

masculine; pentan, pencerdd, penrhyn, cartref, brawdmaeth, prynhawngwaith.
feminine: treftad, pontbren, noswaith, chwaerfaeth.

ADJECTIVES

NUMBER

§ 32. Many adjectives have a plural as well as a singular form, and in many cases the singular feminine has a distinctive form.

§ 33. The plural is formed from the singular masculine, viz. in one of the following ways:

(i) By vowel change:

a becomes **ai**		**a** becomes **ei**	
Singular	*Plural*	*Singular*	*Plural*
bychan 'little'	bychain	balch 'proud'	beilch
buan 'quick'	buain	garw 'rough'	geirw
cyfan 'whole'	cyfain	hardd	heirdd
ieuanc, ifanc	ieuainc, ifainc	'beautiful'	
'young'		marw 'dead'	meirw
llydan 'wide'	llydain	ysgafn 'light'	ysgeifn
truan 'wretched'	truain		
byddar 'deaf'	byddair		

a-a become **e-y**		**a-e** become **e-y**	
cadarn 'firm'	cedyrn	caled 'hard'	celyd

The above changes are discussed below in Appendix B (i).

(ii) By adding *-ion, -on:*

blin 'weary'	blinion	hir 'long'	hirion
blith 'milch'	blithion	llwyd 'grey'	llwydion
caled 'hard'	caledion	mawr 'big'	mawrion

cul 'narrow'	culion	mud 'dumb'	mudion
dewr 'brave'	dewrion	sur 'sour'	surion
doeth 'wise'	doethion	tew 'fat'	tewion

The ending is -on (i) after -u, -eu; (ii) after consonant + r; (iii) after -oyw or after consonant + consonantal w:

du 'black'	duon	gloyw 'bright'	gloywon
tenau 'thin'	teneuon	hoyw 'lively'	hoywon
budr 'dirty'	budron	tryloyw 'trans-	
		parent'	tryloywon
		croyw 'clear'	croywon
		gwelw 'pale'	gwclwon
		gweddw	
		'widowed'	gweddwon

(In the triphthong oyw the y and the w are consonantal).

(iii) By vowel together with adding termination:

a becomes ei

balch 'proud'	beilchion
garw 'rough'	geirwon
hardd 'beautiful'	heirddion
marw 'dead'	meirwon
cam 'bent'	ceimion
dall 'blind'	deillion
gwag 'empty'	gweigion
hallt 'salt'	heilltion

clear y becomes obscure y

gwyn 'white'	gwynion
gwyllt 'wild'	gwylltion
gwyrdd 'green'	gwyrddion
hyll 'ugly'	hyllion
melyn 'yellow'	melynion
byr 'short'	byrion
llyfn 'smooth'	llyfnion

ai becomes ei

main 'slender'	meinion
cain 'elegant'	ceinion

w becomes obscure y

crwn 'round'	crynion
dwfn 'deep'	dyfnion
llwm 'poor'	llymion
trwm 'heavy'	trymion
pwdr 'rotten'	pydron

aw becomes o

tlawd 'poor'	tlodion

au becomes eu

brau 'brittle'	breuon
tenau 'thin'	teneuon

§ 34. Many adjectives have no distinctive plural forms, e.g.,

(i) Simple adjectives: aeddfed, aml, araf, bach, briw, byw, call, cas, cau, crog, chwim, chwith, da, dig, dwys, drwg, ffiaidd, gau, glân, gwâr, gwir, hagr, hen, hoff, hawdd, llawen, llon, llesg, llwyr, llosg, mad, mân, mwll, onest, pŵl, pur, rhad, rhwydd, sâl, serth, sobr, sicr, siwr, siŵr, syn, tal, teg, tywyll.

(ii) Adjectives in the equative and comparative degree, *teced*, *cryfach*, etc., § 44.

(iii) Adjectives ending in: -adwy, -aid, -aidd, -gar, -in, -lyd, -llyd, e.g., *gweladwy, euraid, prennaidd, gwlatgar, derwin, myglyd, oerllyd.*

Note that *-ion* can be added to several adjectives ending in *-ig, -ol, -us*, e.g., *caredigion, nefolion, cyfoethogion, anffodusion*. These plurals are used mostly as nouns, or else preceding nouns: *y cyfoethogion, nefolion leoedd*. (Formerly they could be used after nouns, as in *gwŷr boneddigion* for the modern *gwŷr bonheddig*). There are, however, many adjectives having these endings to which *-ion* can not be added to form the plural, e.g., *canolig, pigog, swynol, hapus*.

(iv) Compound adjectives such as *hirben, gwynlliw, prydlon, hyglyw, hyfryd, melynwallt*. If, however, the second element of the compound is an adjective which may take *-ion*, the compound may also do so, e.g., *claerwynion (claer + gwynion)* 'brilliant white', *brithfeilchion* 'speckled-proud', *pengrynion* 'round-headed', *gruddgochion* 'redcheeked'.

§ 35. Some plural forms are used as adjectives and nouns, while others are used as nouns only. Most of these nouns denote kinds or classes of persons (or animals) but a few are abstract.

(i) *Singular adj.*

Singular adj.	Plural adj.	Plural noun
tlawd	tlodion	tlodion
cyfoethog	cyfoethogion	cyfoethogion
doeth	doethion	doethion
dall	deillion	deillion
gwan	gweinion, gweiniaid	gweinion, gweiniaid
blwydd	(blwyddi), blwydd-iaid	blwyddiaid 'yearlings'
truan *(noun also)*	truain	trueiniaid, truain
caeth	caethion	caethion
ffyddlon		ffyddloniaid
prydferth		prydferthion
marwol		marwolion
rheidus		rheidusion
enwog		enwogion
gorau *(superlative)*		goreuon
hynaf *(superlative)*		hynafiaid 'ancestors'
cyfnesaf *(superlative)*		cyfneseifiaid 'nearest kin'
eithaf *(superlative)*		eithafoedd, eithafion
pellaf *(superlative)*		pellafoedd
anwar		anwariaid
cyfoed		cyfoedion
cain		ceinion

(ii) *Singular adj.*	*Plural adj.*	*Plural abstract noun*
uchel	uchelion*	uchelion

dirgel	dirgelion*	dirgelion
cyfrin	cyfrinion*	cyfrinion
eithaf		eithafion

*These plural adjectives precede nouns which they qualify, e.g. *dirgelion bethau.*

CONCORD

§ 36. The general rule is that an adjective agrees with its noun in number, but the singular form of an adjective is often used with a plural noun.

§ 37. When the plural of the adjective is formed by vowel change only it is that plural form that is generally used with a plural noun, e.g., *pethau bychain, dynion ifainc (ieuainc), caneuon ysgeifn, calonnau celyd.* The singular form is also used, e.g. *llwybrau garw; plant mud a byddar;* 'dwfn *gerbydau hardd'* (R.W.P. 30); 'Och *galed newyddion'* (G.O. 125).

§ 38. When the plural adjective is formed by adding *-ion, -on* (with or without vowel change) either the singular or the plural may be used with a plural noun, e.g., (i) dyfroedd dyfnion, bryniau mawrion, eglwysi rhyddion, llestri llawnion, llwybrau ceimion, llyfrau gleision, adar duon, nentydd gloywon, cerrig pydron 'soapstone', tai llwydion.

(ii) gwŷr mawr, geiriau cryf, dynion gwan, gwartheg tenau, dannedd pwdr, heolydd cul.

(iii) Although *pobl* 'people' is a singular noun, it is collective in meaning, and for that reason the adjective qualifying it is often plural in form: *pobl dlawd* or *pobl dlodion; y bobl ieuainc; pobl wynion.* (Cf. the irregular mutation in *y bobloedd,* § 8(i)).

GENDER

§ 39. In many adjectives **w** or **y** become **o** or **e** respectively in the corresponding feminine forms:

Masc.	*Fem.*	*Masc.*	*Fem.*
blwng	blong*	brych	brech (*as noun,* 'pox, vaccination')
brwnt	bront	bychan	bechan
crwm	crom	byr	ber
crwn	cron		
cwta	cota	cryf	cref
dwfn	dofn	cryg	creg
llwfr	llofr	ffyrf	fferf
llwm	llom	gwlyb	gwleb

mwll	moll*	gwyn	gwen
tlws	tlos	gwyrdd	gwerdd
trwm	trom	hysb	hesb
trwsgl	trosgl	hyll	hell
twn	ton 'broken'	gwymp	gwemp
swrth	sorth	llym	llem
pendwll	pendoll	sych	sech
pengrwn	pengron	syth	seth*
		syml	seml
		melyn	melen
		claerwyn	claerwen

In *brith* 'speckled', fem. *braith*, **i** becomes **ai**.

*These feminine forms, though found in literature, are now regarded as obsolete.

§ 40. The masculine forms are often used instead of the above listed feminine forms with feminine nouns, e.g. *Y Gelfyddyd Gwta* (the title of a book by T. Gwynn Jones) in contrast with *buwch* goch *gota* 'ladybird'; *daear wlyb* 'wet soil' is the common expression, but *daear wleb* occurs in poetry (BE 60); and the forms *llofr, sorth, ton, creg, hell* are confined to poetry.

There is a tendency to use the masc. form in sentences like the following: *Y mae* + *(s. fem. noun)* + *yn* + *(masc. adj.)*, e.g., *Y mae'r nant yn sych* 'the brook is dry'; *'Yr oedd y ferch yn gryf* 'the girl was strong'.

§ 41. The following adjectives have no distinctive fem. form: *brwd, crin, drwg, dwbl, dygn, glwth, gwych, gwyllt, hy, prŷn (pryn), rhydd, rhwth, sydyn, disymwth, syn, dwl, twp, tywyll* (except that *nos dywell* and *ynys dywell* occur in poetry).

Also the following adjectives (not containing **w** or **y**) may be either masc. or fem.: *llon, rhonc, hen, teg, clên, ffel, lleddf, llesg, gweddw, pêr, pert, serth, sobr.*

§ 42. Mutation in the feminine adjective. Soft mutation occurs in the initial consonant of an adjective following a fem. s. noun: *merch fawr, gwlad fach, porfa las, gŵydd dew, cân dlos, geneth fechan, het goch, daear lom.*

The rule is followed in such combinations as *ynys ddu, pais ddu, wythnos ddymunol, Cymraes dda, ffos ddofn,* but *d* replaces *dd* sometimes after *-s,* e.g. *nos da, ewyllys da, yr wythnos diwethaf.* In some parts of North Wales *bach,* though fem., remains unmutated: *geneth bach, Mari bach,* but in general the rule is observed: *geneth fach, Mari fach.*

After a s. fem. noun *braf* is not mutated, e.g. *noson braf, hogen braf* (cf. 'Mae hi'n *braf* yma', § 213, Note (b)). However, in parts of South

Wales one hears *noson fraf, noswaith fraf, merch fraf.* (This is explained by T. J. Morgan in TC 443).

When an adj. precedes a noun in a compound, the noun is mutated, whether it be masc. or fem.: (loose compound) *gwir ddyn, hen ferch, annwyl wlad;* (mutation or non-mutation in adjectives in degrees other than the positive are dealt with in § 53); (strict compound) *gwenferch, cromlech, hirddydd, hendref, glasfro.*

§ 43. When a genitive noun follows another noun (masc. or fem.) no compound is formed, and the genitive noun is not mutated: *mab bardd* 'a bard's son'; *merch bugail* 'a shepherd's daughter'; *gwallt bachgen* 'a boy's hair'; *gwallt merch* 'a girl's hair'; *calon mam* 'a mother's heart'. But a noun following another noun may qualify it adjectively, and thus a noun + adjective relationship is formed. The qualifying noun accordingly mutates after a s. fem. noun:

masc.: *tŷ pridd* 'a house of earth'; *ceffyl gwedd* 'a team horse';

fem.: *côt law,* 'a rain-coat'; *padell bridd* 'an earthen-ware pan'; *cyllell fara* 'a bread-knife'; *caseg wedd* 'a team-mare'; *y fedel wenith* 'the wheat-reaping (party)'; *gwal gerrig* 'a stone-wall'.

The rule applies when the second noun is replaced by a verb-noun:

masc.: *cae pori* 'grazing-field'; *maes glanio* 'landing-ground'; *tŷ golchi* 'wash(ing)-house'.

fem.: *gwialen bysgota* 'fishing-rod'; *cymanfa ganu* 'singing-festival'; *ystafell gysgu* 'bedroom'; *buddai gorddi* 'butter-making churn'.

In the same way proper names mutate after a s. fem. noun: *teml Dduw* 'God's temple'; *llaw Fair* '(St.) Mary's hand'; *Gŵyl Ddewi* 'St. David's Day (Festival)'; *Gŵyl Fihangel* 'Michaelmas'; *Eglwys Loegr* 'The Church of England'; *Ynysforgan; Llandeilo* ('St. Teilo's').

The following are exceptions to the rule: *Gŵyl Dewi, Dinas Dafydd* (*dinas* being masc. formerly); *Dinas Mawddwy; Tremadog; Llancarfan* (for a former *Nantcarfan,* when *nant* was masc.); *Nantgarw* (§ 30. (ii) (3); § 54.).

COMPARISON

§ 44. There are four degrees of comparison of adjectives in Welsh: positive, equative, comparative and superlative. The endings *-ed, -ach, -af* are added respectively to the positive to form the other degrees. When the positive ends in *-b, -d, -g, -dr, -gr* these are unvoiced (or hardened) to *-p, -t, -c, -tr, -cr* respectively before the endings of the other degrees. There are some vowel changes (mostly clear *y* becoming obscure and *w* becoming obscure *y*) as in § 33 (iii). In speaking, and often in poetry, the final -*f* of the superlative is dropped, e.g. *ucha* for *uchaf.* Also *n* and *r* are written doubled after a short vowel in the penult, e.g. *gwynned, llonnach, byrraf:*

Positive	Equative	Comparative	Superlative
budr 'dirty'*	butred	butrach	butraf
brau 'brittle'	breued	breuach	breuaf
byr 'short'	byrred	byrrach	byrraf
cas 'hateful'	cased	casach	casaf
cryf 'strong'	cryfed	cryfach	cryfaf
dewr 'brave'	dewred	dewrach	dewraf
glân 'clean'	glaned	glanach	glanaf
gwyn 'white'	gwynned	gwynnach	gwynnaf
gwlyb 'wet'	gwlyped	gwlypach	gwlypaf
hagr 'ugly'	hacred	hacrach	hacraf
hyfryd 'pleasant'	hyfryted	hyfrytach	hyfrytaf
llawn 'full'	llawned	llawnach	llawnaf
llon 'cheerful'	llonned	llonnach	llonnaf
pur 'pure'	pured	purach	puraf
tlawd 'poor'	tloted	tlotach	tlotaf
huawdl 'eloquent'	huotled	huotlach	huotlaf
tlws 'pretty'	tlysed	tlysach	tlysaf
trwm 'heavy'	trymed	trymach	trymaf
teg 'fair'	teced	tecach	tecaf
ysgafn 'light'	ysgafned	ysgafnach	ysgfnaf
melys 'sweet'	melysed	melysach	melysaf
caredig 'kind'	carediced	caredicach	caredicaf
grymus 'powerful'	grymused	grymusach	grymusaf

Note. Adjs. with positive ending in -*aidd* have -*ied*, -*iach*, in other degrees, and the few ending in -*aid* change *d* to *t* before -*ied*, -*iach*, -*iaf:*

peraidd 'fragrant'	pereiddied	pereiddiach	pereiddiaf
mwynaidd 'gentle'	mwyneiddied	mwyneiddiach	mwyneiddiaf
telaid 'graceful'	teleitied	teleitiach	teleitiaf
rhaid 'necessary'	rheitied	rheitiach	rheitiaf

§ 45. Distinctive forms for masc. and fem. occur only in the positive, except for a few rare examples in poetry, e.g. *gwennaf* (in the song 'Mentra Gwen': *Wennaf Wen), tlosaf, berraf, tromaf.*

§ 46. Irregular comparison. The following adjs. are compared irregularly:

agos 'near'	nesed	nes	nesaf
bach, bychan 'small'	lleied (bychaned)	llai	lleiaf
{ buan 'swift, early'	cynted	cynt	cyntaf
cynnar (*also compared regularly*)			
da 'good'	cystal (daed)	gwell	gorau

*In S. Wales it has the colloquial meaning of 'remarkable'.

drwg 'bad'	cynddrwg (dryced)	gwaeth	gwaethaf
hawdd 'easy'	hawsed	haws	hawsaf
anodd 'difficult'	anhawsed	anos	anhawsaf
hen 'old'	hyned	hŷn (hynach)	hynaf
hir 'long'	cyhyd	hwy	hwyaf
ieuanc, ifanc 'young'	ieuanged, ifanged	iau, ifangach	ieuaf, ieuangaf
isel 'low'	ised	is	isaf
llydan 'wide'	cyfled, lleted	lletach	lletaf
mawr 'big'	cymaint	mwy	mwyaf
uchel 'high'	uched, cyfuwch (cuwch)	uwch	uchaf

Instead of some of the forms of irregular comparison given above several colloquial forms are heard, e.g. *llydanach* for *lletach; hawsach* for *haws; anhawsach* for *anos;* henach for *hŷn; iseled, iselach, iselaf* for *ised, is, isaf; ucheled, uchelach, uchelaf* for *uched, uwch, uchaf; hirach, hiraf* for *hwy, hwyaf.* These colloquialisms are avoided by good writers.

By prefixing *cyf-* many nouns become equative adjs., e.g. *lliw — cyfliw* 'of the same colour'; *urdd — cyfurdd 'of the same order'; gwerth — cyfwerth* 'of the same value'; *oed — cyfoed* 'of the same age'; *rhyw — cyfryw* 'of the same kind, such'. *Un* is used in the same way: *unlliw* 'of the same colour; *unwedd* 'of the same appearance, like'.

Some equatives have the prefix *cy-* and these may have a further prefix *go-: gogymaint, gogyfuwch, gogyhyd.*

Defective comparison.

	Comparative	Superlative
	trech 'stronger'	trechaf
	amgen(ach) 'different'	—
	—	eithaf 'extreme'

§ 47. A few nouns used as adjectives take degrees of comparison endings:

Noun-adj.	Equative	Comparative	Superlative
pen 'head'	—	—	pennaf 'chief'
blaen 'front'	—	—	blaenaf 'foremost'
rhaid 'necessary'	rheitied	rheitiach	rheitiaf 'most necessary'
diwedd 'end'	—	—	diwethaf 'last'
dewis 'choice'	—	dewisach 'preferable'	—
ôl 'rear'	—	—	olaf 'last'
lles 'benefit'	—	llesach 'more advantageous'	—

elw 'profit'	—	elwach 'more profitable'
rhagor 'more, difference'	—	rhagorach 'superior'
amser 'time'	—	amserach 'more timely'

§ 48. Many adjs. (mostly polysyllabic) are compared periphrastically, i.e. by placing *mor, mwy, mwyaf* before the positive. The soft mutation follows *mor,* except that *ll-* and *rh-* are not mutated. Examples:

Positive	Equative	Comparative	Superlative
brawdol 'brotherly'	mor frawdol	mwy brawdol	mwyaf brawdol
cyndyn 'stubborn'	mor gyndyn	mwy cyndyn	mwyaf cyndyn
diog 'lazy'	mor ddiog	mwy diog	mwyaf diog
llwfr 'cowardly'	mor llwfr	mwy llwfr	mwyaf llwfr
rhesymol 'reasonable'	mor rhesymol	mwy rhesymol	mwyaf rhesymol
gwaradwyddus 'shameful'	mor waradwyddus	mwy gwaradwyddus	mwyaf gwaradwyddus

Adjs. ending in *-aidd, -ig, -og, -us* can be compared regularly, e.g. *mwynaidd, pwysig, ardderchog (ardderchoced,* etc.), *truenus.*

Every adj. can be compared periphrastically except the irregular adjs. listed in §§ 46, 47. But *mor* can be used with any adj., e.g. *mor fawr, mor dda, mor ifanc, mor llydan.* Note that *m-* in *mor* is never mutated: *Mae hi'n ferch mor gall.* The South Wales use of *mor* instead of *cyn* with the equative *(mor laned)* is not in the literary tradition. § 50(i).

§ 49. Compound adjs. are generally compared periphrastically; a few are compared regularly, e.g. *gloywdduaf, claerwynnaf. Gwerthfawr* can be compared thus: *gwerthfawroced, gwerthfawrocach, gwerthfawrocaf;* and both *clodfawr* and *clodforus* have a superlative *clodforusaf* 'most renowned'.

SYNTAX OF ADJECTIVAL FORMS OF COMPARISON

§ 50. Equative Degree. (i) In simple comparison the usual pattern is the following: Copula *(Y mae,* etc.) + noun or pronoun + *cyn* + equative form + *â (ag)* + noun or pronoun: *Y mae'r dillad cyn wynned â'r eira* 'The clothes are as white as snow'. *Yr oedd ei gwallt cyn dded â'r frân* 'her hair was as black as the crow'. *Yr wyf fi yn fwy nag ef* 'I am bigger than he'.

The spirant (or aspirate) mutation (Appendix A (i)) follows *â* 'as': *cymaint â chath* 'as large as a cat'; *mor drwm â phlwm* 'as heavy as lead'; *mor gryf â thi* 'as strong as thou'.

The soft mutation follows *cyn* (like *mor*) in all mutable consonants except *ll-, rh-: cyn drymed* 'as heavy'; *cyn gyflymed* 'as swift'; *cyn bured* 'as pure'; *cyn llawned* 'as full'; *cyn rhated* 'as cheap'.

In periphrastic comparison it is the positive form that follows *mor* (and also *mwy, mwyaf*) (§ 48).

The following adjs. are equative in form and can not be preceded by *cyn: cynddrwg* 'as bad'; *cymaint* 'as much'; *cystal* 'as good'; *cyfled* 'as wide'; *cyfuwch* 'as high'; *cyhyd* 'as long'.

The adj. can be adverbial after verbs: *Canodd ef mor fwyn â'i chwaer* 'He sang as gently as his sister'; *Rhedai cyn gyflymed ag ewig* 'He would run as swiftly as a hind'.

A noun can be replaced by a clause after an adj. + *â*; see § 230.

(ii) An equative form (without *cyn*), or *mor* and the positive, can be placed after a preposition: *er cymaint* 'however much'; *er daed* 'however good'; *rhag teced* 'though so fair'; *gan fwyned* 'so gentle'; *er mor fawr* 'however big'; *rhag mor deg* 'though so fair'; *er mor dda* 'however good'. Sometimes the equative can be regarded as an abstract noun: *rhag garwed y tywydd* 'because of the roughness of the weather'. A pronoun can precede the equative in this use: *rhag ei theced* 'because of her fairness'. Expressions containing the equative can be causal or concessive clauses, e.g. Cariodd ef y plentyn *er trymed oedd* 'He carried the child though he was so heavy'; Ni all hi siarad *gan waeled ydyw* 'She can not speak because she is so ill'; Ni chlywodd ef y sŵn *gan mor drwm y cysgai* 'He did not hear the noise because he slept so heavily'.

(iii) The equative degree is often used to express wonder, but, as with prepositions, *cyn* can not be used with it in such constructions. When it is thus used the equative undergoes soft mutation (unless it is preceded by the conjunction *a* 'and' which takes the spirant mutation): 'Mwyfwy y rhyfeddwn *uched, gryfed* a *hardded, laned* a *hawddgared* oedd pob rhan ohoni' (B.Cw. 45) ('More and more I saw in wonder *how high, how strong* and *beautiful, how fair* and *lovely* every part of it was'.)

(iv) Nowadays the equative is used before an expression or clause denoting consequence:

Yr oedd *cymaint* o lif yn yr afon *fel na allem groesi* 'There was *so much* flood in the river *that we could not cross*').

Yr oedd y bachgen *mor ddrwg fel y gyrrwyd ef adref* 'The boy was *so naughty that he was sent home*'.

(Formerly *ag* was used instead of *fel* in such sentences. § 230).

§ 51. Comparative Degree. (i) When two things etc. are compared the comparative adj. is followed by *na* with the spirant mutation of *p-*, *t-*, *c-*, or by *nag* before a vowel:

Y mae'r pren yn *uwch na*'r to 'The tree is *higher than* the roof'.

Cefais afal *melynach nag a*ur 'I had an apple *more golden than* gold'.

Gwell enw da *na ch*yfoeth *'Better* [is] a good name *than* wealth'.

(ii) The comparative form may be used as a simple adj.:

Ceisio *gloywach* nen 'Seeking a brighter sky'. *Cryfach* dyn 'a *stronger* man'.

(iii) The comparative adj. is sometimes equivalent to a noun:

Ni welsoch erioed ei *gynt* 'You never saw his *swifter* (i.e. anyone swifter than he)'. Mi welais ei *well* 'I have seen his *better'*.

(iv) A comparative may be preceded by a numeral: *mil harddach* 'a thousand (times) more beautiful'; *canmil gwell* 'a hundred thousand (times) better'; *deuwell* 'twice better'.

A noun or adj. denoting size or degree can precede a comparative: *llawer gwannach* 'much weaker'; *ychydig mwy* 'a few (little) more'; *rhywfaint pellach* 'somewhat further'; *llawn cymaint* 'quite as much' (§§ 96, 101, 106).

(v) The following comparatives are often used adverbally: *mwy, mwyach, bellach, gynt;* also the noun *rhagor*, which can have an equative meaning. Ni welwn ef *mwy* 'We shall not see him any more'; Ni ddaw hi heno *mwyach* 'She won't come to-night any longer'; Y mae pawb yma *bellach* 'Everyone is here by now'; Ni all ef weithio *rhagor* 'He can't work any more'; Yr oedd melin yma *gynt* 'There was a mill here formerly'.

(vi) In comparing two objects the superlative (and not the comparative, as English) is used:

Hwn yw'r *gorau* o'r ddau 'This is the *better* of the two'.

Pa un yw'r ochr *orau*? 'Which is the *better* side?'

But if the article is not needed with the adj. the comparative, as well as superlative, can be used:

Pa un o'r ddau sydd *orau gennych*? 'Which of the two do you prefer?' *Y mae'n well* gennyf hwn 'I prefer this one'. Hwn sydd *orau* gennyf 'This is the one I prefer'.

"Rwy'n mynd i weld pa un sydd *well*,
  Ai 'ngwlad fy hun neu'r gwledydd pell". (Folk Song)
'I am going to see which is the *better,* my own land or the far-off lands'.

§ 52. Superlative Degree. (i) The superlative degree may be used to emphasize the quality denoted by the adj. rather than to suggest comparison, e.g. *harddaf gwraig* 'fairest lady'; *ardderchocaf frenin* 'most exalted king'; *eithaf dyn* 'quite a man'. (The soft mutation sometimes follows the superlative here instead of the traditional radical).

(ii) The superlative is used in comparison of two objects when *na(g)* 'than' does not follow (§ 51 (vi)):

Mae'r ddwy yn deg, ond hon yw'r ferch *decaf* 'They are both fair, but this girl is the fairer'.

(iii) To express proportionate equality the superlative is used in Welsh, where the comparative is used in English:

Po uchaf y bo'r tŷ, *gorau oll* fydd yr olygfa 'The *higher* the house is, all the *better* is the view'.

Po *gyntaf* yr êl, *cyntaf* y daw yn ôl 'The *sooner* he goes, the *sooner* will he return'.

Po *brinnaf* y bwyd, *drutaf* yw '*The scarcer* the food, the *dearer* it is'.

Formerly *po* was followed by the radical consonant (see TC 403-4). In such expressions as the following *gorau* precedes *po: gorau po fwyaf* 'the *more*, the *better*'; *gorau po gyntaf* 'the *sooner*, the *better*'.

(iv) In several idiomatic expressions a preposition precedes a superlative:

Rhedwch *am y cyntaf!* 'Run to be first!'; Byddwch *ar eich gorau!* 'Be at your best!'; Yr oedd ef *ar ei waethaf* 'He was at his worst'; *Er gwaethaf* y glaw 'In spite of the rain'; *Ar/er fy ngwaethaf* 'In spite of me'; 'Doctor *er ei waethaf*' (*Le Médecin malgré lui*); Gwna dy waith! *O'r gorau* 'Do your work! Very well'; Mi wnaf y gwaith *o 'r gorau* 'I will do the work well enough'.

Note the following idiom: Mae'n bryd i chwi *roi'r gorau i* weithio 'It is time for you to give up working'.

(v) There is an adverbial use of the superlative: (1) not introduced by *yn* (which takes the soft mutation) if a relative clause follows (§ 79):

Dos adref *gyntaf* y medri! 'Go home as quickly as (the quickest) you can'; Gwnewch *orau* y gellwch! 'Do as best you can'.

(2) with *yn* in a few expressions: *yn gyntaf* 'firstly'; *yn olaf* 'lastly'; *yn bennaf* 'chiefly'.

(3) with or without *yn* when no relative clause follows: Ef a ganodd *orau/yn orau* 'He sang best'; Dyma'r ffordd yr ewch adref *gyntaf* 'This is the way you will go home most quickly'.

Note that the superlative is substantival in such sentences as:

Gwnewch y *gorau* a alloch 'Do the best you can'; Gwna dy *waethaf* 'do your worst'.

It stands for a noun, without the article, in the proverbial saying:

Gwannaf gwaedded. *trechaf* treisied 'Let the weakest cry out, let the strongest oppress'.

§ 53. Adjective preceding Noun. (i) **Positive Degree.** When the noun follows the adj. either a loose or a strict compound is formed, with the noun undergoing soft mutation, e.g. *gwen ferch, gwenferch* (§ 42). In such compounds *ll-* and *rh-* are mutated: *pêr lais* 'sweet voice'; *hen le* 'old place'; *oer rew* 'cold frost'; *hen rwyd* 'old net'; *mwynlais* 'soft voice (soft-voiced)'; *hirlwyn* 'long grove'. Exceptions: *henllan* 'old church', *henllys* 'old court', *perllan* 'orchard', *mawrlles* 'great benefit'. One may regard *truan gŵr* also to be an exception. The adj. *truan* 'poor, wretched' is often used as a noun meaning 'wretch, poor dear', e.g. (masc.) *druan bach!*, (fem.) *druan fach!* (See TC. 126, 449).

(ii) **Equative and Comparative.** These are followed by the radical of the noun: *cystal dyn* 'as good a man'; *teced bro* 'as fair a region'; *cymaint tlodi* 'so much poverty'; *cased peth* 'so hateful a thing'; *dewrach gŵr* 'a braver man'; *gwell lle* 'a better place'; *sicrach gafael* 'a surer hold'; *trech rhedwr* 'a stronger runner'.

(iii) **Superlative Degree.** Nowadays the soft mutation, as well as the traditional radical, may follow the adj.: (1) *cyntaf peth, gorau gŵr, goreugwr, eithaf peth.* (2) *y decaf fro, 'Wennaf Wen', eithaf Gymro, gwaelaf ŵr, prif dref* 'chief town', *prifddinas* 'capital city'. *Prif* always precedes the adj. and takes the soft mutation. (It was borrowed from the Latin superlative *primus).*

(iv) The following positive adjs. are commonly heard before the noun: *annwyl, cam, gau, gwir, hen, unig.*

In some cases there is a difference of meaning according to the position of the adj.: *cam farn* 'wrong judgement'; *pren cam* 'crooked stick'; *hen ddyn* 'old man'; *dyn hen* 'a really old man'. When *hen* comes before the adj. it sometimes expresses the disgust of the speaker rather than the age of the object; *hen dywydd gwael* 'miserable weather'; *yr hen blant yma* 'these brats'. On the other hand the tone of voice can cause *hen* to imply dearness or compassion; *hen blentyn bach* 'a dear/poor little child'. Further, *unig fab* 'only son'; *lle unig* 'a lonely place'; *gwir ateb* 'a real reply'; *ateb gwir* 'a truthful reply'.

Ambell and *cryn* always come before the noun: *ambell ddyn* 'an occasional man'; *ambell dro* 'sometimes'; *cryn amser* 'considerable time'; *cryn drafferth* 'a lot of trouble'. For 'many sins' one may say *aml bechodau* or *pechodau aml.*

When *pur* is an adj. meaning 'pure' it is usually placed after the noun: *awen bur* 'pure/true muse'; *dŵr pur* 'pure water'. When it is an adverb, meaning 'very, fairly', it precedes the adjective: *pur dda* 'very good'; *pur llawn* 'very/quite full'; *purwyn* 'very white'; *purion* (from *pur iawn*) 'fairly good, alright'.

§ 54. An adjective after a proper noun. An adj. after a proper noun often undergoes soft mutation even when the noun is masc.: Arthur *F*awr, Eifion *W*yn, Dewi *W*yn, Hywel *Dd*a, Iolo *G*och, Ieuan *Dd*u, Rhys *G*och, Selyf *Dd*oeth, Seithennin *F*eddw, Gwilym *G*am, Einion *W*an, Wiliam *dd*uwiol, Pulston *r*adlonair, Herod *g*reulon, Llywelyn *B*ren, Dafydd *F*ychan, etc.

In many cases, however, the adj. preserves its radical: Gwilym *T*ew, Ieuan *D*u, Dyfnwal *M*oelmud, Rhodri *M*awr, Ifor *B*ach, Dafydd *B*ychan, Dafydd *Ll*wyd, Gwenno *Ll*wyd, Iesu *d*a, Iesu *m*awr, Duw *d*a, Duw *g*wyn.

§ 55. Noun in apposition. (i) When a proper noun is followed by a noun in apposition, i.e. a noun denoting an office or relationship, the second noun is mutated: Duw *D*ad, Iesu *G*rist, Ioan *F*edyddiwr, Ieuan *F*ardd, Dafydd *F*renin, Branwen *F*erch Lyr, Manawydan *F*ab Llyr, Iago *f*ab Sebedeus (Mt. iv. 21). *Druan* (from *truan*) is mutated after common as well as proper nouns: Owen *d*ruan, fy nhad *d*ruan 'my poor father'.

It is the mutated form *fab* (in Medieval Welsh written *vap*) that has given *ab* (before vowels) and *ap* (before consonants) in personal names, e.g. Gruffudd *ab* Adda, Dafydd *ap* Gwilym 'David son of Gwilym'.

(ii) When nouns denoting kinship (*mab, brawd, tad,* etc.) are used as common nouns, and not as part of recognized personal names, they are not mutated: 'Absolom *m*ab Maachah, *m*erch Talmai *b*renin Gesur' (1 Chr. iii. 2); 'A Phenuel *t*ad Gedor, ac Eser *t*ad Husa' (1 Chr. iv. 4); 'Ioan *b*rawd Iago' (Mk. iii. 17).

(iii) If the name of a historical person follows a common noun which is a title or style, or which denotes office etc., and is preceded by the article, mutation depends on whether this noun is masc. or fem.: *Y Forwyn Fair; Y Wyry Fair; y Brenin Gruffudd; y Tywysog Llywelyn; y bardd Dafydd; Y Prifardd Elfed.*

In modern usage, a fem. personal name has the radical initial after a noun in apposition: *y frenhines Gwenhwyfar; y fonhesig Morfudd; y delynores Mair.* As *Duw* is a masc. noun, *Yr Arglwydd Dduw* has exceptional mutation. In medieval Welsh other masc. nouns were mutated after *arglwydd, brawd* 'friar', *athro,* etc.

(iv) A noun may be in apposition to a pronoun, e.g. 'Wele *fi, b*echadur truan' (T.R. CAN 324); *'tydi, ddyn; Tithau, Dduw'* (Ps. lv, 13, 23).

In older editions of the Bible a noun following a pronoun keeps the radical, but in the 1955 edition such a noun, in apposition, is mutated, e.g. *'chwi feibion'* replaces *'chwi meibion'* (Is. xxvii. 12).

NUMERALS

§ 56. Examples:

Cardinal	Ordinal	Multiplicatives
1. un	cyntaf	unwaith
2. dau *(masc.)*, dwy *(fem.)*	ail	dwywaith
3. tri *(masc.)*, tair *(fem.)*	trydydd *(masc.)*, trydedd *(fem.)*	teirgwaith
4. pedwar *(masc.)*, pedair *(fem.)*	pedwerydd *(masc.)*, pedwaredd *(fem.)*	pedair gwaith
5. pump, pum	pumed	pum gwaith/waith
6. chwech, chwe	chweched	chwe gwaith
7. saith	seithfed	seithwaith, saith gwaith
8. wyth	wythfed	wythwaith, wyth gwaith
9. naw	nawfed	naw gwaith
10. deg (deng, dec-)	degfed	dengwaith, deg gwaith
11. un ar ddeg	unfed ar ddeg	un waith ar ddeg
12. deuddeg	deuddegfed	deuddeng waith, (deuddeg gwaith)
13. tri/tair ar ddeg	trydydd/trydedd ar ddeg	teirgwaith ar ddeg
15. pymtheg (pymtheng)	pymthegfed	pymthengwaith, pymthegfed gwaith
16. un ar bymtheg	unfed ar bymtheg	un waith ar bymtheg
17. dau/dwy ar bymtheg	ail ar bymtheg	dwywaith ar bymtheg
18. deunaw	deunawfed	deunaw gwaith
19. pedwar/pedair ar bymtheg	pedwerydd/pedwaredd ar bymtheg	pedair gwaith ar bymtheg
20. ugain	ugeinfed	ugeinwaith (ugain gwaith)
21. un ar hugain	unfed ar hugain	unwaith ar hugain
22. dau/dwy ar hugain	ail ar hugain	dwywaith ar hugain
30. deg ar hugain	degfed ar hugain	dengwaith ar hugain
32. deuddeg ar hugain	deuddegfed ar hugain	deuddeg gwaith ar hugain
40. deugain	deugeinfed	deugain gwaith
50. deg a deugain, hanner cant	degfed a deugain, hanner canfed	hanner canwaith
60. trigain	trigeinfed	trigain gwaith
80. pedwar ugain	pedwar ugeinfed	pedwar ugeinwaith
100. cant	canfed	canwaith
120. chwech ugain, chweugain	chwech ugeinfed	chwech ugeinwaith
300. tri chant, trichant	tri chanfed	tri chanwaith
1,000. mil	milfed	milwaith
1,000,000. miliwn	miliynfed	miliwn gwaith

For consonant mutations after numerals see § 62.

§ 57. Adjectival numerals. (a) When a cardinal numeral is used as an adj. it is followed by a singular noun, e.g. *dwy awr* 'two hours', *tri bachgen* 'three boys', *ugain ceiniog* 'twenty pence'.

Formerly plural nouns could follow numerals. There are still many examples in the Bible, e.g. *pedair merched* (Acts xxi.9); *seithwyr* (Acts vi.3); *triwyr* (Gen. xviii.2); *deg brodyr* (Gen. xlii.3; 1955 *brawd*). Two old plurals are still used with numerals: *blynedd* 'years' and *diau* 'days'. The latter is seen in *tridiau* 'three days', and *blynedd* is the plural form used after numerals except *un* and *mil: pum mlynedd* 'five years', *chwe blynedd* 'six years', but *un flwyddyn* 'one year', *mil blynyddoedd* or *mil o flynyddoedd* 'thousand years'. The fem. form of the numeral, if used, precedes *blynedd*, e.g. *dwy flynedd, pedair blynedd*.

(b) In composite numbers the noun comes immediately after the first element: *tair merch ar ddeg* 'thirteen girls', *pedwar llyfr ar bymtheg* 'nineteen books', *dau dudalen a deugain* 'forty two pages'. Though 'one year' is *un flwyddyn*, composite numbers containing *un* preserve the old plural: *un mlynedd ar ddeg* 'eleven years', *un mlynedd a deugain*.

The word order is the same in phrases expressing alternatives, e.g. *dwy gyllell neu dair* 'two or three knives' (as well as *dwy neu dair cyllell);* *tair gwaith neu bedair* 'three or four times'; *wyth swllt neu naw* 'eight or nine shillings'. In such expressions *un* is not normally used before the noun: *diwrnod neu ddau* 'a day or two'; *wythnos neu ddwy* 'a week or two'. But for emphasis *un* is included: *un* flwyddyn *neu ddwy* '(only) one year or two'; and also in the multiplicative: *unwaith neu ddwy* 'once or twice'.

A numeral is often compounded with a noun: *dwybunt* '£2'; *deufis* 'two months'; *pythefnos* 'a fortnight (fifteen nights)' or *pythewnos; decpunt* '£10'.

In the literary tradition *pum* and *chwe* are used before a noun: *pum dyn, chwe merch, pum afon, chwe awr;* but if the noun is omitted the full forms, *pump* and *chwech* are used: *Pa sawl afal sydd yna? Pump* 'How many apples are there? Five'; *mae pump yma* 'there are five here'. *Cant* becomes *can* before a noun: *can punt, canpunt, can erw* '100 acres'; *tri chan ceiniog* '300 pence'. The shorter forms of these numerals are used before *blwydd (oed)* 'year (old)': *pum mlwydd (oed)* '5 years (old)'; *chwe blwydd; can mlwydd*. But if *blwydd* is omitted the final consonant is restored: *pump (oed); chwech (oed); cant (oed)*. (In S. Wales dialects the spoken forms are *pump* and *chwech (whech)* with all nouns, except in stable combinations such as *chwe cheiniog* and *chweugain* (standing for *chwe ugain ceiniog* in pre-metric coinage, '120 pence, 10 shillings').

Figures denoting numbers of pages, hymns, vehicles, etc. (i.e. distinctive and not quantitative numbers) are spoken in terms of units, tens, hundreds, etc. This method is now generally used in teaching arithmetic and science subjects in schools, and for this purpose it is found to be very suitable, but learners should also be thoroughly acquainted with the traditional numeration. In stating the age of anybody or anything, by either method, the fem. form, *dwy*, *tair* etc. should be used: *dwy (flwydd) (oed), tair, pedair (blwydd) (oed); pum deg a dwy; saith deg a thair.*

§ 58. In poetical language numerals sometimes follow plural nouns: *dynion dri; angylion gant; tafodau fil; cyfoedion gant; brodyr dri.* The numeral in such expressions undergoes soft mutation.

§ 59. Ordinals. Simple ordinals precede the noun: *ail fab, y drydedd bennod, y seithfed tŷ.* In composite ordinals (as with composite cardinals) the noun follows the first element: *yr unfed tŷ ar ddeg; y drydedd salm ar hugain.* Where large numbers are mentioned such variants as the following are sometimes heard: *y bedwaredd bennod wedi'r ganfed* 'the hundred and fourth chapter'.

Like an adj. *cyntaf* can be placed after the noun it qualifies: *y plentyn cyntaf; y llyfr cyntaf; yr adnod gyntaf; y cartref cyntaf; y bont gyntaf; y pethau cyntaf.* It can also come before the noun: (without the article) *cyntaf peth* '(the) first thing'. Preceded by *yn* it can be adverbial: *yn gyntaf dim* 'first of all'. In a composite ordinal it is *unfed (not* cyntaf) that is used: *yr unfed mis ar ddeg* 'the eleventh month'.

Ordinals are placed after names of kings, popes, etc.: *Siôr y trydydd* 'George the third'; *Rhisiart y cyntaf* 'Richard the first'; *Clement yr ail* 'Clement the second'; *Adda'r ail* 'the second Adam'. Similarly in naming the day of the month: *Awst y cyntaf* 'August 1'; *Medi'r trydydd* 'September 3'; *Rhagfyr y pedwerydd ar hugain* 'December 24'. The masc. noun *dydd* is understood after the ordinal in these examples.

§ 60. Substantival numerals. Numerals are used as substantives thus: numeral + o + plural noun or pronoun, *or* numeral + plural personal form of the preposition *o*, e.g.,

(i) *tri o ddynion* 'three men', *pedwar o blant* 'four children', *chwech o eifr* 'six goats'.

(ii) *deg ohonom* 'ten of us', *saith ohonynt* 'seven of them'.

(iii) *dau o'r dynion* 'two of the men', *un o'r rhain* 'one of these'.

In (i) the noun is indefinite, and as a rule there is no difference of meaning, for example, between *tri o ddynion* and *tri dyn*. This construction is common when the number is large: *mil a phedwar cant o bobl* 'one thousand and four hundred people'. It is invariably used when the numeral is plural: *cannoedd o bobl* 'hundreds of people', *miloedd o bunnau* 'thousands of pounds'. The same construction is used when the speaker is thinking of the component units of the numeral: *mae ganddo bedwar o blant* 'he has four children (thought of singly)'; *A oes gennych bump o geiniogau am ddarn pum ceiniog?* 'Have you five (single) pennies for a five penny piece?'; *Mi dalaf y decpunt yn ddeg o bunnoedd* 'I shall pay the ten pounds in ten single pounds'.

In (ii) and (iii) the noun or pronoun or personal preposition is definite, and the two constructions are not interchangeable; the prep. *o* is essential.

§ 61. Personal pronouns often precede numerals from *un* to *saith*, viz. *ein, 'n, eich, 'ch, ill* (used only with numerls): *ein dau* 'the two of us'; *ni 'n tri* 'the three of us'; *eich pump* 'the five of you'; *ill dau* 'both of them'; *hwy ill tri* 'all three of them'; *aethom yno 'n tri* 'we three went there'.

INITIAL MUTATIONS AFTER NUMERALS

§ 62. Un: with masc. noun, radical; with fem. noun, soft except *ll-* and *rh-*: *un peth, un tad, un bachgen; un ferch, un wraig, un gath, un llaw, un rhwyd.*

Un + adj. + fem. noun, soft in the adj. (and noun, § 42); *un dawel awr* 'one quiet hour'; *un brif dref* 'one chief town': soft of *ll-* and *rh-* in the adj.: *un lon galon* 'one happy heart'; *un ryfeddol gân* 'one wonderful song'.

Un + adj. standing for fem. noun, soft: *un lawen (yw hi)* '(she is) a happy one'; *un gall* 'a wise one (i.e. female)'; *un rydd yw 'r wlad* 'the country is a free one'.

When *un* has the meaning of 'similar', there is soft mutation in both masc. and fem. nouns: *mae'r plentyn yr un ben â'i dad* 'the child has a head like his father's'; but when *un* means 'the one and the same' it is the fem. noun only that is mutated: *yn yr un tŷ* 'in the same house'; *yn yr un dref* 'in the same town'. The mutation in the masc. in *plant yr un dad a'r un fam* 'children of the same father and mother' is exceptional.

After *un* in composite numerals *blynedd* and *blwydd* take the nasal mutation: *un mlynedd ar ddeg* '11 years'; *un mlwydd ar hugain oed* 'twenty one years old'.

Dau, Dwy: Soft mutation of masc. and fem. nouns: *dau fachgen, dwy ferch, deubeth, dwyfron.* Soft mut. also of these numerals after the article *y: y ddau, y ddwy,* § 8 (iii).

In a few words the radical is heard after *dau: dau cant, deucant, dau pen, deupen, dau tu* 'two sides', *deutu* 'about', *deuparth* 'two parts, two thirds'. But the regular mutation is also heard in *dau gant, dau ben, dau beth, deubeth, dau droed/dwy droed.* Nouns with initials *b-, d-, g-* follow the rule: *dau frawd, dau ddant, dau of* (from *gof* 'smith').

Tri, Tair: *Tri* takes the spirant mutation, but no mutation follows *tair: tri chae* 'three fields'; *tri phen, tri thŷ, tri bwrdd; tair gwraig, tair ceiniog, tair pont; y tair merch, y tair bord* (The N. Wales form *bwrdd* 'table' is masc. and the S. Wales form *bord* is fem.). See § 8, iv and note that the spirant mutation occurs in only three consonants: *p, t, c*. (Appendix A (i)).

When an adj. follows *tri* the spirant normally follows, e.g. 'Tri Chryfion Byd' (title of 'Interlude' by Twm o'r Nant); *y tri chyntaf; y tri chedyrn*. The rule is not always observed in writing and speaking, e.g. *y tri cyntaf, y tri cedyrn*. (An explanation of the inconsistency is offered in TC 66.)

Today it is the soft mutation that is heard in an adjective after *tair:* *tair dda* (like *tair merch dda); tair wen* (like *tair cath wen*).

Pedwar, Pedair: The radical always follows in nouns: *y pedwar peth, y pedair gwraig*. If the noun is omitted between *pedair* and the adj. the mutation is still retained in the adj., e.g. *pedair fach* (for *pedair merch fach), pedair fawr*.

Pum: Followed by the radical: *pum tŷ, pum ceiniog. Exceptions:* the nasal mutation follows *pum* in *blynedd* and *blwydd* and often in diwrnod: *pum mlynedd, pum mlwydd (oed), pum niwrnod* (as well as *pum diwrnod*).

Chwe: Followed by the spirant mutation: *chwe cheffyl* 'six horses'; *chwe phennill* 'six verses'; *chwephunt* '£6'; *chwe thŷ* 'six houses'; but *chwe blwydd, chwe blynedd* (as the spirant mutation is confined to *p-, t-, c-*). On the use of *pump* and *chwech* see § 57 (b).

Saith, Wyth: In N. Wales *saith* and *wyth* normally take the soft mutation of *p-, t-, c-: saith/wyth geiniog* (formerly); *saith/wyth dref; saith/wyth bunt*. In S. Wales they take the radical: *saith/wyth ceiniog; saith/wyth tref; saith punt*. But *m-* is nowhere mutated after these two numerals: *saith mis* '7 months'; *wyth mil/mam* 'eight thousand/mothers'. Today, *t-* does not mutate after them even in N. Wales: *saith tref* '7 towns'; *wyth tŷ* '8 houses'; *saith telyn* '7 harps'. Nor do *b-, d-, g-* change after *saith/wyth*.

Like *pum, saith* and *wyth* take the nasal of *blynedd* and *blwydd* and sometimes of *diwrnod: saith mlynedd, wyth mlwydd, saith niwrnod*. The unusual mutation in *saith muwch* (Gen. xli. 27) is an archaism, as *saith* at one time was followed by the nasal of *b* and *d* in other words.

Naw, Deg, Deuddeg, Pymtheg, Deunaw, Ugain, Can: No mutation except of *blynedd, blwydd, diwrnod*—nasal as above. Before *m-* the following three, *deg, deuddeg, pymtheg* become respectively *deng, deuddeng, pymtheng*, e.g., *naw mlynedd, deng mlynedd, deng mlwydd, canmlwydd, can mlynedd, deng milltir, pymtheng munud*. As well as *deng niwrnod* one often hears *deg diwrnod*.

Deng sometimes occurs before vowels: *deng ewin, deng awr;* but also, *deg ewin* and *deg awr* are heard.

> 'Aeth angau â'i *bymthengiaith,*
> Obry'n awr, heb yr un iaith!' (E.O. BE 19)

'Death took away his fifteen tongues; (he is) now below, without any tongue'.

An old nasal of *g-* is preserved in *dengwaith* (see on *gwaith* after numerals, § 56) and *dengair: Y Dengair Deddf* 'The Ten Words of Law (i.e. Commandments)'.

§ 63. Mutation after ordinals: (see also § 59). *Cyntaf* does not normally precede a noun as an ordinal, but when it does, there is no mutation: *cyntaf peth.*

There has been no consistency with regard to mutation or non-mutation after *ail.* The modern tendency is to have soft mutation in the noun: *ail ddydd, ail beth, ail law,* etc.

The other ordinals take the soft of fem. nouns and the radical of masc. nouns: *yr unfed bennod ar ddeg; y drydedd ferch; y bedwaredd wlad, y bumed waith; yr unfed tŷ ar ddeg; y trydydd pren; y pedwerydd brenin; y pumed tro,* etc.

§ 64. Distributives are formed by using cardinal numerals preceded by *bob yn* (formerly by *bob* alone) with lenition of the numerals, e.g. *bob yn un* 'one by one'; *bob yn ddau* 'two by two'; *bob yn bedwar* 'four by four'.

The ordinal *ail* 'second' is used in *bob yn ail* 'alternately' and in *ar yn ail* 'alternately'. (See § 102, iii).

§ 65. Fractions. These can be expressed thus: *hanner* 'half'; *traean* 'third'; *chwarter (cwarter), pedwaran* 'fourth'; *pumed (rhan)* 'fifth'; *deuparth* 'two thirds'; *canfed* 'hundredth'; *canran* 'hundredth, percentage', etc. Alternate expressions are *un rhan o ddwy* 'half'; *tair rhan o bedair* 'three quarters', etc.

PRONOUNS

PERSONAL PRONOUNS

§ 66. Personal pronouns in Welsh are distributed thus:

I. Independent: (a) Simple. (b) Reduplicated. (c) Conjunctive.

II. Dependent: (a) Prefixed (genitive). (b) Infixed (genitive and accusative). (c) Affixed (auxiliary).

§ 67. Forms of the Independent Personal Pronouns:

(a) Simple

Singular	Plural
1. mi, fi	ni
2. ti, di	chwi
3. ef *(masc.)*	hwy, hwynt
hi *(fem.)*	

(b) Reduplicated

Singular	Plural
1. myfi	nyni
2. tydi	chwychwi
3. efe, efô,	hwynt-hwy
fe, fo *(masc.)*	
hyhi *(fem.)*	

(c) Conjunctive

Singular	Plural
1. minnau	ninnau
2. tithau	chwithau
3. yntau *(masc.)*	hwythau, hwyntau
hithau *(fem.)*	

The forms under (b) are accented on the final syllable.

§ 68. Examples of the uses of the Independent Pronouns:

(i) Object of verb:

Credwch *fi!* 'Believe me!'; Dyro *hwy* iddo! 'Give them to him!'; A welsoch chwi *hi?* 'Did you see her?'; Oni welsoch chwi *yntau* (hefyd)? 'Did you not see him too?'; Fel yr edwyn y Tad *fyfi* 'As the Father knoweth me'; 'Y Tad cyfiawn, nid adnabu'r byd *dydi*' 'O righteous Father, the world hath not known thee'; 'ac yn awr y diddenir *ef,* ac y poenir *dithau*' 'now he is comforted and thou art tormented'. Luke xvi. 25; the use of *dithau* instead of *di* implies a contrast—'thou, on the other hand'); 'Canys nid apwyntiodd Duw *nyni* i ddigofaint' 'For God hath not appointed us to wrath'; 'Oni ddewisais i *chwychwi?*' 'Have I not chosen you?' The reduplicated forms are somewhat more emphatic than the simple.

(ii) Before a relative clause (§§ 76, 83) as antecedent:

'*Myfi* sy'n magu'r baban' 'It is I who nurses the baby'; '*Ti sydd yn dweud hynny*' 'It is you who is saying that'; '*Hi* a roddodd y pethau i mi' 'It was she who gave me the things'; '*Hwynt-hwy* a wnaeth y gwaith' 'It was they who did the work'; '*Efô* a ŵyr, *Efô* a ŵyr, *Efô* (J.M.-J. 171) 'It is He who knows . . . it is He'.

(iii) As the complement before forms of the verb *bod* 'to be' (§ 141):

'*Myfi* yw'r winwydden, chwithau yw'r canghennau' 'I am the vine, ye are the branches'; *Ef* yw perchen y tir 'It is he who is the owner of the land'; 'Arglwydd y lluoedd, *efe* yw Brenin y gogoniant' 'The Lord of hosts, he is the King of glory'; '*Ti* oedd y meistr, *ninnau* oedd y gweision' 'You were the master, and we were the workmen'.

In replies we often have the pronoun without the remainder of the sentence, e.g. Pwy yw'r cadeirydd? *Fi* 'Who is the chairman? I (am)'; Pwy a ddewiswyd? *Ti* 'Who was chosen? You'.

Note that the pronoun is emphatic in the examples under (i) and (ii) above.

(iv) Before a verb, or *a* + verb, with no emphasis on the pronoun:
Mi af yno yfory 'I shall go there tomorrow'; Ac *efe* a gododd 'And he arose'; *Hwythau* a ddywedasant 'They (on their part) answered'; eithr *chwi* a olchwyd 'but you have been washed'.

'*Mi* ganaf gerdd i'r henwlad' 'I shall sing a song to the old land'; '*Di* fegi bendefigion' 'Thou wilt rear noblemen'; '*Ti* enillaist yn hollol' 'Thou hast won completely' (J.M.-J. 1, 66, 89). '*Hwy* gânt fynd y ffordd a fynnon' 'They may go the way they will' (HB 78).

The pronominal forms in the above examples before verbs or *a* + verbs are not true pronouns, and are now considered to be particles. Also there is a tendency to use *fe* or *mi* as an impersonal particle before the verb instead of a pronoun agreeing in person with the verb:
Fe welaf 'I see'; *Fe* wnawn ni hynny 'We shall do that'; *Fe* aethant 'They went'; *Mi* gewch eich talu 'You will be paid'; *Fe* gollwyd y cwbl 'Everything was lost' (§ 121); *Fe* welir 'It will be seen'. Note that the soft mutation follows the above forms. In the Welsh of the Bible (1588) *efe a* is used instead of *ef a*.

(v) In the vocative case:

Ti, gyfaill, gwrando! 'You, friend, listen!'; *Chwi*, sydd wrth y drws, a ydych yn clywed? 'You, who are by the door, can you hear?'

(vi) In apposition to a noun (i.e. the conjunctive forms):
Daeth Dafydd *yntau* ir dref 'David too came to the town'; Caiff y plant *hwythau* ddyfod 'The children too will be allowed to come'; Collwyd llyfrau'r ferch *hithau* 'The girl's books were lost also'.

(vii) After uninflected prepositions, or after conjunctions (§§ 195, 228):

gyda *mi* 'with me'; ewch â *mi* 'take me (go with me)'; wedi *hwy* 'after them'; fy mrawd a *minnau/finnau* 'my brother and I'; chwi neu *ni* 'you or we'; ai *tydi* ai dy frawd 'whether you or your brother'; ai'ch mam neu *ynteu chwi* 'either your mother or (else) you'.

Ynteu (an earlier form of *yntau*) can be used as a conjunction ('then, else'): Pwy, *ynteu*, a ddaw? 'Who, then, will come?'; Ai cysgu y mae, *ynteu* gorffwys? 'Is he sleeping, or else resting?'

(viii) The subject of an independent phrase *(absolute* construction) § 252: Daeth ef â thorth i'r tŷ, a *minnau* newydd brynu un! 'He brought a loaf to the house, though I had newly bought one!'; A *hi*'n cerdded mor ofalus, ni wnaeth ddim sŵn 'With her walking so carefully, she made no sound'.

NOTE.   According to EWG 89 the pronouns noted under (i) above are called *Dependent Substantive Pronouns,* but it is more reasonable to call them *Independent Pronouns,* as in GCC 31.

§ 69. Forms of the Dependent Personal Pronouns:

(a) Prefixed

	Singular		Plural
1.	fy 'my'		ein 'our
2.	dy 'thy'		eich 'our'
3.	ei 'his/her'		eu 'their'

(b) Infixed

Genitive			Accusative	
S.	Pl.		S.	Pl.
1. 'm 'my'	'n 'our'		1. 'm 'me'	'n 'us'
2. 'th 'thy'	'ch 'your'		2. 'th 'thee'	'ch 'you'
3. 'i, 'w, 'his/her'	'u, 'w 'their'		3. 'i, -s 'him/ her'	'u, -s 'them'

(c) Auxiliary or *Affixed*

Simple			Conjunctive	
S.	Pl.		S.	Pl.
1. i, fi	ni		1. finnau, innau	ninnau
2. di, ti	chwi		2. tithau, dithau	chwithau
3. *(masc.)* ef, efô fo, fe *(fem.)* hi	hwy, hwynt		3. *(masc.)*yntau *(fem.)* hithau	hwythau,

§ 70. Usages of the Prefixed Pronouns:

Before nouns and verb-nouns: *fy mam* 'my mother'; *dy dŷ* 'thy house'; *fy ngweld* 'seeing me'; *ein cadw* 'keeping us'.

Before a vowel *fy, dy* often become *f', d': f'enaid* 'my soul'; *d'adar* 'thy birds'.

An adj. may come between the pronoun and the noun or verb-noun: *f'annwyl* frawd 'my dear brother'; *ein mwyn* gyfeillion 'our gentle friends'; *ei wir* weld 'truly seeing him'.

A prefixed pronoun is always in the genitive case, although the corresponding pronoun in English, following a participle, is in the accusative case, e.g., *seeing me.*

§ 71. Mutations after prefixed pronouns:

fy, nasal mut.: brawd—*fy m*rawd; gweld—*fy ng*weld
dy, soft mut.: tŷ—*dy dŷ*; ci—*dy g*i; llaw—*dy l*aw
ei (masc.), soft: tad—*ei d*ad; lle—*ei l*e; gardd—*ei a*rdd
ei (fem.), spirant: pen—*ei ph*en; caru—*ei ch*aru; troed—*ei th*road
(pl.) *ein, eich, eu,* radical after each: *ein* brawd, *ein* tŷ, *eich* ci, *eu* plant. Before a vowel the aspirate *h-* follows *ei* (fem.) *ein* and *eu: ei h*arian; *ein hannwyl chwaer; *eu h*ofnau.

NOTE. In natural spoken Welsh *ei* is pronounced as *i.* There is a growing tendency to pronounce it so in verse-speaking, singing, etc.

§ 72. Usages of the Infixed Pronouns:

The forms *'m, 'th,* in the genitive case, are used after the following words: *a* (conj.), *â* (prep. and conj.), *gyda, tua, efo* 'with', *na* (conj.), *i* (prep.), *o* (prep.), *mo* (from *ddim o*), e.g.:

fy mrawd a*'m* chwaer 'my brother and my sister'; gyda*'th* dad 'with thy father'; tua*'m* gwlad 'towards my land'; efo*'th* gi 'with thy dog'; na*'m* bwyd na*'m* diod 'neither my food nor my drink'; yn fwy na*'th* gyflog 'more than thy wages'; i*'m* tŷ 'to my house'; o*'th* gartref 'from thy home'; ni welais mo*'th* lyfrau 'I have not seen (anything of) thy books'; i*'m* gweld 'to see me'.

In speaking, the prefixed pronouns are very often used instead of the infixed, e.g.: fy mrawd *a fy* chwaer; *gyda dy* dad; dos *i dy* le!

The infixed *'i, 'n, 'ch* and *'u,* in both genitive and accusative cases (i.e. before nouns, verb-nouns and verbs) can follow a vowel or a diphthong, e.g. enw*'i* fab 'his son's name'; torri*'ch* gwallt 'cutting your hair'; oni*'ch* gwelodd? 'did he not see you?'; golchi*'n* dillad 'washing our clothes'; oriau*'n* bywyd 'the hours of our life'; bwyta*'u* bwyd 'eating their food'.

'w is always genitive and can be used only after the prep. *i* 'to', e.g. i*'w* dŷ ef, 'to his house'; i*'w* mam hi 'to her mother'; i*'w* gweld hwy 'to see them' (though *'w* is genitive, *them* in English is accusative); *'m* and *'th* are used in the accustive after the relative pronoun and various particles preceding verbs, e.g.: Pwy a*'m* gwelodd i? 'Who (is it) who saw me?'; Hi a*'th* dywys 'She will guide thee'; *Fe'm* gwelwyd 'I was seen'; *Ni'th* gosba 'He will not punish thee'; *Oni'm* credant? 'Will they not believe me?'; Pa le *y'th* welais? 'Where did I see you?'; *Pe'm* curech i *fe'ch* cosbid 'If you were to beat me you would be punished'; Paham *na'th* gredodd di? 'Why did he not believe thee/you?'

Expressions such as *lle y'm; lle y'th; yna y'm; yno y'th,* are sometimes contracted, respectively, to *lle'm, lle'th, yna'm, yno'th.*

-s is used only as the object of a verb suffixed to *ni, na, oni, pe,* e.g. *nis* gwelsoch (ef); am *nas* rhoddasoch (ef/hi/hwy) iddynt; "a'r eiddo ei hun *nis* derbyniasant ef" (John i. 11); "*pes* adwaenasent, ni chroeshoeliasent Arglwydd y gogoniant" (1 Cor. ii. 8).

Note the difference between *nis gwn* 'I do not know it' and *ni wn* 'I do not know'.

§ 73. Mutations after the infixed pronouns:

The soft mut. follows *'th,* genitive *'i* (masc.) and *'w* (masc.), e.g. o*'th* dŷ; ni*'th* drawodd; ef a*'i* geffyl; ni welsoch mo*'i* gynt; i*'w* fam.

The spirant mut. follows genitive *'i* (fem.) and *'w* (fem.), e.g., hi a*'i* thad; o*'i* phentref hi; mae hi wedi rhwygo*'i* chnawd 'she has torn her flesh'; af i*'w* chodi hi 'I will go to lift her'.

In all other cases the infixed pronoun is followed by the radical, e.g. i'*m* gwlad; gyda'*m* merch; o'*n* tref; a'*ch* plant; i'*w* gwlad hi/hwy.

Note that when '*i* (masc. and fem.) is the object of a verb it is followed by the radical: Fe'*i* gwelais ef; Pwy a'*i* cred hi?

Before a vowel the aspirate *h*- is joined to it after '*i* (fem.), '*n*, '*u* whether they be genitive or accusative, e.g., hi a'*i h*oen 'she and her lamb'; ein haur a'*n h*arian; gwrthododd hwy, a'*u h*anfon yn ôl 'he refused them and sent them back'. (Cf. the corresponding prefixed forms, *ei* (fem.), *ein, eu*, § 71).

As '*th* and '*ch* are themselves aspirate it would be superfluous to add another aspirate before a vowel, so we have, e.g. i'*th ofal* 'to thy/your care'; â'*ch arian* 'with your money'.

Before a vowel *h*- is added also after '*w* (fem.) gen. and accus.: e.g. i'*w hafon hi* 'to her river'; i'*w hachub hi* 'to save her'.

When '*i* (masc.) is the object of a verb (i.e. in the accusative) it is followed by *h*- before a vowel, e.g., fe'*i h*achubwyd ef 'he was saved/one saved him'; ei dad a'*i h*anfonodd ef '(it was) his father who sent him'.

§ 74. Usages of the Affixed Pronouns (auxiliary):

(i) After personal forms of verbs and prepositions. The first sing. present of most verbs and the first sing. of prepositions end in -*f*, and the form of the affixed pronoun may be either *i* or *fi*, e.g. yr wyf *(f)i;* gennyf *(f)i;* gwelaf *(f)i*. If the verb or preposition (2nd sing.) ends in -*t*, the pronoun takes the form *ti* instead of *di*, e.g. deui*t ti;* wrthy*t ti*. In the other persons the forms shown in § 69 (c) are used: rhedodd *ef/hi;* wrtho *fo/fe;* gwelais *i;* gwelsom *ni;* ohonom *ni;* byddwch *chwi;* trosoch *chwi;* y maent *hwy;* ganddynt *hwy*.

(ii) To emphasise or affirm a prefixed or infixed pronoun:

fy ngwlad *i; ei* dad *ef;* i'*ch* cartref *chwi;* fe'*th* welodd *di;* ni*s* gwelais *hi; eu* hachos *hwy;* a'*u* tref *hwynt*.

The conjunctive forms are used to add emphasis or else to imply contrast: gwelodd *yntau*'r dyn 'he, too, saw the man'; dechreuodd weiddi ond ni ddywedais *innau* air 'he began to shout but I, on my part, said not a word'; Da *chwithau!* peidiwch â mynd allan! 'Please, don't you too go out!'; Ond mynd allan a wnaethant *hwythau* 'But they, on the other hand, went out'.

Syntactically a sentence is complete without an auxiliary pronoun, but it is frequently required to clarify the meaning: e.g. the gender of the object is not denoted in *fe'i gwelwyd*, but it is in *fe'i gwelwyd ef/hi* 'he/she was seen'.

In speaking, the voice can emphasise the affixed pronoun: *ein* gwaith *ni; eu* bai *hwy*. But in ordinary speech it is very often used without any intention of adding emphasis.

POSSESSIVE PRONOUNS

§ 75. These have been called Possessive Adjectives, but since they are no longer used as adjectives qualifying nouns it is more appropriate to call them Possessive Pronouns.

Forms:	*Singular*	*Plural*
1.	eiddof	eiddom
2.	eiddot	eiddoch
3.	eiddo *(masc.)*	eiddynt
	eiddi *(fem.)*	

In poetry, even up to the twentieth century, and in prose of the early modern period such as editions of the Bible (including that of 1955) the older forms, *mau* and *tau,* occur instead of *eiddof* and *eiddot:* 'y geiriau *mau* fi nid ânt heibio ddim' (Mark xiii. 31); '*Tau* gestyll teg eu hystum' (IGE 24); 'Pell wyf o wlad fy nhadau,/Och sôn! ac o Fôn gu *fau*' (GO 60).

The forms *eiddof, eiddot,* etc. ar used (a) unpreceded by the article: 'Chwilio'r celloedd oedd *eiddi'* (R.G.D. 47); 'Canys *eiddo* 'r Arglwydd y ddaear' (1 Cor. x. 26); 'Canys *eiddot* Ti yw y deyrnas' (Mat. vi. 13).

(b) preceded by the article, like a noun: 'A phan glybu *'r eiddo ef,* hwy a aethant i'w ddal ef' (Mark iii. 21); 'At ei eiddo ei hun y daeth, a *'r eiddo ei hun* nis derbyniasant ef' (John i. 11); (at the end of a letter) *Yr eiddoch* yn gywir.

Eiddo can also be a noun meaning 'property': Fe gollodd ei holl *eiddo.* Mae ganddo lawer o *eiddo.*

THE RELATIVE PRONOUN

§ 76. (i) The relative pronoun *a* is either the subject or the object in a relative clause:

(a) Subject

Ef yw'r dyn *a* ddaeth ('who came') i'm gweld. Pwy *a* ddywedodd ('who said') hynny? Newyddion da *a* ddaeth yma heddiw.

(b) Object

Hwn yw'r llyfr *a* brynais ('which I bought'). Beth oedd y golau *a* welwyd ('which was seen')? Credai hi bopeth *a* ddywedai ef.

The relative *a* may be omitted before forms of the verb *bod* 'to be' (§ 140) in a relative clause:

'Eithr cyfododd rhai o sect y Phariseaid y rhai *oedd* yn credu' (Acts xv. 5); hwn yw'r bachgen *fydd* yn mynd i'r coleg; dyma'r tŷ *fu* ar werth.

(ii) The negatives *na(d)* and *ni(d)* 'who . . . not, which . . . not, whom . . . not' are used as negatives both as subjects and objects:

'Y dwylaw *na* ddidolir rhagor' (R.W.P. 100).

'Gwyn ei fyd y gŵr *ni* rodia yng nghyngor yr annuwiolion, ac *ni* saif yn ffordd pechaduriaid, ac *nid* eistedd yn eisteddfa gwatwarwyr (Ps. i. 1).

Mae ef yn ŵr *nad* ofna neb 'He is a man who does not fear anyone'.

Nis and *nas* occur also, but always in the accusative case: Clywsant bethau *nas* deallent; 'Cywreindeb *nas* gŵyr undyn' (J.M.-J. 75). 'Eithr y rhai hyn sydd yn cablu'r pethau *nis* gwyddant' (Jude. 1. 10).

In modern writing na, (nad, nas) have largely displaced ni (nid, nis) as negative relatives.

A relative clause in which the relative is either nominative or accusative is called a Proper Relative Clause (§ 245).

For the omission of the antecedent of a relative clause see § 87, and for the relative verbal form *sydd* see § 143.

§ 77. Mutation after relative pronouns.

The rel. pron. *a* takes the soft mutation: yr hwn *a fu;* y sawl *a w*elodd; y byd *a dd*aw.

After *ni, na* the spirant mut. of *c, p, t* follows, and the soft mut. of *b, d, g, ll, rh, m:*
y sawl *ni ch*red; . . . *na ph*rynodd; . . . *na th*orrodd; . . . *ni f*u; . . . *na dd*aw; . . . *na a*ll; . . . *ni f*ynnant; . . . *na l*wyddodd; . . . *ni r*ydd.

Initial *b* in forms of *bod* sometimes remains unmutated: rhai *na b*uont; peth *ni b*ydd marw.

If an infixed pron. comes between the relative and the verb, mutation or non-mutation after the pronoun depends on its person and gender as shown in § 73: yr hwn *a'i g*welodd ef/hi: y sawl *a'i h*anfonodd ef/hi; ei dad *a'i c*anfu; y dynion *nas c*redasant ef/hi/hwy; y ferch *a'th w*elodd di; Pwy *a'th g*red di?

§ 78. Agreement of the nominative relative pron. and the verb. The rule today is that the verb after the rel. pron. *a* in a rel. clause is always in the *third person singular:*
Dyma'r *llyfr a dd*aeth ddoe. Dyma'r *llyfrau a dd*aeth ddoe.

(The antecedent *llyfr* is singular and the other antecedent *llyfrau* is plural, but the rel. pron. *a* is singular in each sentence, and the verb agrees with it.) This is always the rule in natural spoken Welsh.

In the past another rule was often followed in written Welsh, viz. that the verb agreed in number and person with the *antecedent.* Scholars toward the end of the 19th century showed that such a rule was artificial and had been adopted by analogy with other European languages. The Welsh Bible provides countless examples, e.g.

'Rhag yr annuwiolion, *y rhai a'm gorthrymant;* rhag fy ngelynion marwol, *y rhai a'm hamgylchant'* (Ps. xvii. 9).

However, the two constructions are often to be seen side by side, e.g. 'bendithiwch *y rhai a'ch melltithiant,* gwnewch dda i*'r sawl a'ch casânt,* a gweddïwch dros *y rhai a wnêl* niwed i chwi, ac *a'ch erlidiant* (Mt. v. 44).

On the other hand, when *ni* or *na* is the subject the verb should agree with the antecedent:

'Y lle bûm yn gware gynt / Mae *dynion na'm hadwaenynt'*(G.O. 60). (Where I played of yore / There are men who (would) know me not); 'yr wyf yn dywedyd i chwi, fod *rhai* . . . *ni phrofant* angau' (Mk. ix. 1).

Exceptions to this rule are sometimes found: 'y *llygaid na all agor'* (R.W.P. 100); 'i wneuthur y *pethau nid oedd* weddaidd' (Rom. i. 28).

§ 79. The relative pronoun may be in cases other than the nominative and accusative, viz.:

(a) in the *genitive,* when it is followed by a verb + a genitive pronoun (prefixed or infixed) + a noun or verb-noun.

(b) *governed by a preposition,* when it is followed by a verb + a preposition referring to the antecedent.

(c) *in the adverbial case,* when the relative clause follows a noun denoting place, time, cause or manner.

When a relative is in any of these cases, the clause is called an Oblique Relative Clause (§ 245). Examples are given in the next paragraph.

§ 80. In modern writing it is the particle *y* or *yr* that is used as a genitive relative (*y* before a consonant and *yr* before a vowel or *h*):

Dyna'r tŷ y chwythwyd ei do ymaith 'That is the house the roof of which was blown away'. Pwy yw'r *ferch y torrwyd ei braich?* 'Who is the girl whose arm was broken?' Pa le mae'r *plant yr aethoch i'w ceisio?* 'Where are the children whom you went to seek?'

Formerly the form *a,* as well as *y, yr,* was used in this construction: 'Mai'r Ioan *a* dorrais i *ei ben* yw hwn' (Mk. vi. 16).

This form is seldom used in the genitive today except sometimes when it depends on a verb-noun: y peth *a* allodd ef *ei wneud;* yr hyn *a* ddymunwn *ei gael.*

The negative forms are *ni, nid, na, nad:* 'y pethau *nid* ydys yn *eu* gweled (Heb. xi. 1); 'cyfwng *na* ellir *ei* rychwantu' (T.H.P.-W. *Ysgrifau* 48) 'the gap that can not be spanned'.

§ 81. The particles *y* and *yr* are the forms of the relative governed by a preposition, with *na, nad* as negatives in the construction today: yr ysgol *yr* awn *iddi;* y desgiau *y* cedwir y llyfrau *ynddynt* (lit. 'the desks that one keeps the books in them'); y gwledydd *y* clywsem *amdanynt* 'the lands we had heard about them, i.e., of which we had heard';

rhyw lyfr *na* chlywodd neb *amdano* 'some book of which no one has heard'; tref *nad* oedd neb yn gwybod *amdani* 'a town of which no one knew anything'.

§ 82. When the relative is in the adverbial case it follows the noun (denoting time, place, *etc.*), and its forms are *y, yr, na, nad:*
Yma y bu er y *dydd y* ganed ef. Dyna'r *adeg y* deffrois. Dyna'r *lle y* gwelais hi. 'Mae'r esgid fach yn gwasgu / Mewn *man na* wyddoch chwi' (Folk Song). Dyna'r *modd y* clywais i am y peth.

The adverbial relative can be preceded by a verb-noun or an adverb instead of a noun:
Yn gorwedd ar y llawr *y* cafwyd ef 'It was lying on the floor that he was found'. 'Canys *felly y* carodd Duw y byd'. *Unwaith y* buont hwy yma. *Yno yr* arhosodd y bechgyn. Dyna *sut na* chefaist ti'r arian.

§ 83. The verb *bod* has a special relative form in the 3 s. pres. indic. in a relative clause, viz. *sydd*, with variants *y sydd, sy, y sy*. The antecedent of *sydd* may be singular or plural:
Hwn yw'r dyn *sydd* yn *(sy*'n) canu. Pwy yw'r plant *sydd* yn *(sy*'n) adrodd? 'This is the man who sings. Who are the children who are reciting?'

Since *sydd* is a relative form it can not be preceded by a rel. pronoun. In a negative clause *sydd* is replaced by nad/nid + yw/ydynt:
(Affirmative) Wele ddyn *sy*'n gweithio. Pwy yw'r rhai *sy*'n credu?
(Negative) Wele ddyn *nad yw*'n gweithio. Pwy yw'r rhai *nad ydynt* yn credu?

Ni(d) and *na(d)* are the negative forms that precede all other verbal forms:
'Gwyn ei fyd y gŵr *ni rodia* . . . ac *ni saif* . . . ac *nid* eistedd . . . (Ps. i. 1).

§ 84. By today the form *piau* 'who owns' has acquired a relatival meaning, although its original meaning was 'to whom is?': 'Myfi *biau* dial' (Heb. x. 30). Ifan *biau*'r tŷ hwn '(It is) Ifan who owns this house'.

Piau is generally lenited to *biau* in literary Welsh today, but formerly it was written, and is still heard in the spoken language, without mutation: Pwy *piau*'r llyfr hwn? Fi *piau* hwn. 'Pwy yw'r gŵr *piau*'r goron' (DGG. 141).
As it is relatival it does not require *a* before it, except when the object is an infixed pronoun: Rhowch yr arian i'r sawl *a'i* piau 'Give the money to the one who owns it'. Cofiwch mai'ch gwlad *a'ch* piau.

The noun object after *piau* now has soft mutation (like all verbs), but in such examples as *Myfi biau dial* (not *ddial*) the radical is historically correct because the noun following *piau* was originally its *subject*. Corresponding to the 3 s. present *piau* there is a 3 s. imperfect *pioedd* which is now considered to be antequated although it is still heard in some dialects in S. West Wales: 'efe *bioedd* y ddaear' (Job xxii. 8).

§ 85. In older Welsh, and especially in the Scriptures, we find *a'r a* instead of *a* used as rel. pron., and even *a'r y sydd* instead of *(y) sydd:* 'hebddo ef ni wnaethpwyd dim *a'r a* wnaethpwyd' (John i. 3); 'na llun dim *a'r y sydd* yn y nefoedd uchod, nac *a'r y sydd* yn y ddaear' (Deut. v. 8); 'byd oll . . . / *a'r y sydd* a erys hwn' (W.LL. 214) 'The whole world . . . that exists, he awaits'.

Negative, *a'r na(s):* 'nid oes dim cuddiedig, *a'r nas* datguddir' (Mt. x. 26).

The *a'r* in such expressions is no longer meaningful and is obsolete.

§ 86. Many pronouns and nouns are used as antecedents of a relative pronoun or particle: *yr hwn, yr hon, yr hyn, y sawl, y neb, y rhai, yr un, y gŵr, peth, (pa) beth bynnag, pwy bynnag, pryd bynnag, pa le bynnag.*

(i) The antecedent may be an essential part of the sentence: 'A phan ddaeth *y rhai a* gyflogasid . . . hwy a gawsant bob un geiniog (Mt. xx. 9); *Yr hwn a* ddaeth at y drws ddoe yw'*r sawl a* wnaeth y drwg; 'gwnewch dda i'*r sawl a*'ch casânt, a gweddïwch dros *y rhai a* wnêl niwed i chwi' (Mt. v. 44); digwyddodd *yr hyn a* ofnais; 'a *pha beth bynnag a* wnêl, efe a lwydda' (Ps. i. 3); *Pwy bynnag a* weli di yno, rho'r tocyn iddo 'Whomsoever you (will) see there, give the ticket to him'.

(ii) The antecedent may be in apposition to another word or words in the principal clause: Ewch drwy'r drws, *yr un* sydd ar y chwaith; Mae gennyf lestri eraill, *y rhai a* gefais gan fy mam; Rhedodd yr athro ar ôl y plant, a daliodd un ohonynt, *yr hwn* oedd yn gloff.

In the last example *a* is omitted before the verb *oedd*. This is frequently done before forms of the verb *bod: yr hon fydd;* y gŵr *fu* yno; *pwy bynnag fo* yno. The soft mutation of *b-* to *f-* in such cases shows that *a* is understood. In speaking this elision has spread to the use of other verbs in relative clauses, and it became a fairly common practice among writers of prose as well as poetry, especially in the nineteenth century: Beth 'welodd hi? Pwy 'ddwedodd wrthych? 'Grug y mynydd yn eu blodau, / edrych arnynt hiraeth 'ddug' (Ceiriog). (The apostrophe is seldom used to mark the elision).

Modern writers of standard Welsh, especially of prose, avoid the elision of the relative *a*.

The relatival expression may supply some additional information about the antecedent: 'Ac ef—*peth nad* oedd gyfiawn—/lleidr a'i dug yn lledrad iawn' (L.G.C. *Llên Cymru* T.G.J. 18). Pan aeth y bachgen i'r tŷ gwelodd y lleidr, *yr hwn* oedd yn bygwth ei dad.

A noun can be repeated to make it an antecedent of a rel. clause:
Penderfynwyd codi *capel—capel y* byddai'r pentrefwyr yn falch *ohono.*
Bu'n chwilio'n hir am *waith—gwaith a* ddygai gysur i'w deulu.

§ 87. (i) In proverbial and other traditional expressions the antecedent is often implied: *a brŷn dir* a brŷn gerrig 'who buys land buys stones'; *a laddo* a leddir 'who kills shall be killed'; *A fo* gorau i ryfel, gorau i heddwch 'what is best for war is best for peace'; 'Bod fis heb ddim bwyd a fyn, / am *a laddo* ym mlwyddyn' (I.D. 41) 'It will go for a month without food, because of what it kills in a year'); Doed *a ddêl* 'Come what may (come)'; Dyna'r gwir, am *a wn* i 'That's the truth for (all) that I know'.

(ii) The antecedent is frequently not expressed after the following words: *dyma, dyna, ond, ag, nag: Dyma a* welais i. Nid *dyna* a ddywedodd ef. Fe wariodd gymaint *ag a gafodd. Y mae yma fwy nag a* fu erioed. 'Beth yw dy waddol, yr eneth ffein ddu? / Dim ond *a welwch,* O! syr, mynte hi' (Folk-song).

In some dialects *hynny* replaces *cymaint ag:* Fe gewch *gymaint ag / hynny* / sy gennyf 'You shall have as much as / all that / I have'.

The relative particle *y* is often elided after *lle: Dyna'r lle'th (lle y'th)* welwyd 'that is the placed where you were seen'.

INTERROGATIVE PRONOUNS

§ 88. The interrogative pronouns are *pwy* and *pa. Pwy?* 'Who?' is used of persons only, and *Pa?* 'What?' is followed by a noun or pronominal form etc. which undergoes soft mutation.

(i) The interrogative may be followed by some form of the verb *bod:*
Pwy yw hwn? *Pa beth (Beth) yw* eich enw? *Pa un oedd* eich mab? *Pwy oedd* ei wraig? Llyfr *pwy yw* hwn? *Pa ysgol yw* hon? *Pwy wyt ti? Pa fath ydynt hwy?*

Note that the interrogative in the above examples is the *complement* (or together with the verb, the *predicate*) of the sentence.

(ii) The interrogative may precede a relative clause:
Pwy a ddaw gyda ni? (i.e. *Pwy yw'r sawl a ddaw* gyda ni?)
Pwy a wnaeth hyn? *Beth a wnewch* chwi yno? *Pwy ni chred* hyn?
Pa beth na roddwn i'w gael yn ôl? A *phwy sy'n* dweud hynny?

The spoken practice of omitting *a* before the rel. clause is often followed in writing, particularly before the verb *bod:*
'*Pwy g*lywodd am bechadur / Mewn unrhyw oes na gwlad . . .?' (T.W. 17); *Pwy oedd* yn y tŷ? (§ 76, i).

(iii) When the interrogative is governed by a proposition it is followed by the particle *y, yr:*

'*I ba beth y* byddaf brudd?' (Folk-song).
Trwy ba awdurdod y gwnaethoch hyn?
Gyda phwy yr aethoch i'r dref?

(iv) Adverbial interrogative expressions such as *pa fodd, pa ffordd, paham, pa sawl* also are followed by *y, yr* or *na, nad:*
'*Pa fodd y* cwympodd y cedyrn!' (2 Sam. i. 19).
'*Paham* hefyd *yr ydych* yn fy ngalw i, Arglwydd, Arglwydd, ac *nad ydych* yn gwneuthur yr hyn yr wyf yn ei ddywedyd?' (Luke vi. 46).
'*Pa sawl gwaith y* mynnwn gasglu dy blant ynghyd!' (Mt. xxiii. 37).
§ 217, vi.

Note: The Interrogative Pronouns are also used in indirect questions; v. §§ 223-5; 249, iv.

A recent corruption of the construction is the use of the verb-noun *bod* after *pam (paham)* instead of *y(r)* + verb:

Pam bod/fod dynion yn credu hyn? (instead of *Pam (y) mae* dynion . . .).
Pam eich bod? (instead of *Pam yr ydych?*, or colloquially *Pam 'rych chi?* *Pam 'rydych ('rydach) chi?*).

DEMONSTRATIVE PRONOUNS

§ 89. In the singular these have masculine, feminine and neuter forms:

Singular:	Masculine	Feminine	Neuter
	hwn, hwnnw	hon, honno	hyn, hynny

In the plural there are no differences of gender:

Plural: hyn, hynny

The forms *hwn, hon* and pl. *hyn* refer to persons or things near at hand, or are referred to as if they were so. *Hwnnw, honno* and *hynny* pl. refer to persons or things out of sight or associated with some other time. *Hyn* s. and *hynny* s. refer to an abstraction, such as circumstance, incident, size, etc.

These pronouns can be used as substantives and as adjectives:

(i) Substantivally:
Bachgen yw (ydyw) *hwn* 'This is a boy'. *Hon* yw ei merch hi 'This (girl) is her daughter'. Nid yw *hyn* yn wir 'this (statement, belief, etc.) is not true'.

Hwnnw oedd mab y brenin 'That (boy) was the king's son'. Ni roddais ddim i *honno* 'I did not give anything to her (i.e. the female already mentioned)'. Ni chredai ef mo *hynny* 'He would not believe that'.

Dafydd yw enw *hwn* 'This (boy's) name is Dafydd'. Beth fydd canlyniad *hynny?* 'What will the consequence of that be?'

Adverbs can be added to these pronouns: *hwn yma, hon yna, hyn yna, hwn acw:* y tŷ *hwn yma;* y fuwch *hon yna;* y dynion *hyn yna;* y cae *hwn acw.*

In speaking such expressions are often contracted, e.g. *honna* for *hon yna;* *hwncw* for *hwn acw,* and in S. Wales *hwnco,* for *hwn acw/yco: nacw* in N. Wales for *hon acw; honco* in S. Wales for *hon yco.*

(ii) Adjectivally:

Y pentref *hwn;* y wraig *hon;* y wlad *honno;* y gŵr *hwnnw;* y dynion *hyn;* y pethau *hynny.*

The masc. neuter *hyn* is rarely adjectival in standard modern Welsh except in a few traditional expressions, e.g. *y pryd hyn; y pryd hynny, y peth hyn, y modd hyn.* (In the dialects, however, the neuter is extensively used instead of the masc. or fem. e.g. *y fferm hyn; y ford/bwrdd hyn.*)

The article must precede a noun followed by an adjectival pronoun: *Yr afon hon.* 'Pwy yw y *Brenin gogoniant hwn?'* (Ps. xxiv, 10; here *Brenin gogoniant* is a loose compound). Y pethau *hynny.*

Formerly a prefixed pronoun was sometimes used instead of the article before a noun: *'fy* mab *hwn'* (Luke xv. 24); *'dy* ddrygioni *hwn'* (Acts viii. 22).

§ 90. The plural pronouns *hyn* and *hynny* are not now used as substantives, but are combined with the pronominal *rhai* (§ 98): *y rhai hyn; y rhai hynny.* These are mostly contracted thus: *y rhain; y rheiny/ y rheini.*

In these the article should always be shown in writing:
Pwy yw *'r rhai hyn?* Y mae *'r rheini*'n goch. A welsoch chwi *'r rhain?* Gwywodd pob un o'r *rheiny; (un o rhain* and *y mae rheiny/rheini* are signs of slovenly writing).

Rhain and *rheiny/rheini* should not be made adjectival. Expressions such as the following are corrupt colloqualisms, and should be avoided in writing: *y dyddiau rhain* (for *y dyddiau hyn*) and *'Y Ddau Hogyn Rheiny'* (for *Y Ddau Hogyn Hynny).*

§ 91. Demonstrative pronouns, *hyn* and *hynny,* are combined with prepositions to form adverbs: *ar hynny* 'thereupon'; *wedi hynny* 'thereafter'; *wedi hyn, wedyn* 'after this'; *er hynny* 'nevertheless'; *am/gan/oblegid/oherwydd/o achos hynny* 'Therefore'.

These demonstratives also occur in various idiomatic expressions: *hwn-a-hwn* 'so-and-so, this (man) and that'; *hon-a-hon* 'so-and-so, this (woman) and that'; *ar hyn o bryd* 'at the present time'; *hyn o daith* 'this present journey'; *hyn o lythyr* 'this letter'; *ar hyn o dro* 'on this occasion'; *hyn o fyd* 'this present world, the world such as it is'; *yn hyn-ny o beth* 'in such a matter as that'.

For the use of *yr hwn, yr hon, y rhai* as antecedents in a relative clause see § 86.

PRONOMINALIA

§ 92. Alternatives. Pronominalia denoting alternatives may be either substantival or adjectival and either definite or indefinite:

(i) Substantival and definite: *y naill . . . y llall* 'the one . . . the other'; Yr oedd *y naill* gartref, a'*r llall* wedi mynd i ffwrdd; Credaf fod *y naill* yn *fawr* ond bod *y llall* yn fach.

Plur. *y naill . . . y lleill* 'the one (group) . . . the others'.

yr un . . . y llall 'the one . . . the other': Cymerodd ef *yr un* coch, a chymerais innau'*r llall.*

y rhai . . . y lleill 'the ones . . . the others': Gadewch *y rhai* sydd ar y llawr ond gellwch fwyta'r *lleill.*

Substantival and indefinite: *un . . . arall* 'one . . . another': Peidiwch â rhoi mwy i *un* nag i *arall.*

Plur. *rhai . . . eraill* 'some . . . others': Bydd *rhai* yn gweithio, ac *eraill* yn cysgu.

(ii) Adjectival and definite: *y naill* + noun . . . + noun + *arall:*
Daliwyd *y naill leidr* ond dihangodd y *lleidr arall.*
Y mae'r *naill beth* yn wir, ond ni allaf gredu'r *honiad arall.*

Adjectival and indefinite: *un/rhyw* + noun . . . noun + *arall:*
Os yw hyn yn iawn i *un dyn,* mae'n iawn i *ddyn arall.*
Os caiff *rhyw fachgen* ddyfod i mewn, rhaid gadael i bob *bachgen arall* ddyfod.
Gan fod *rhyw blant* yn ddrwg fe gosbwyd y *plant eraill* gyda hwy.

§ 93. *Y naill* may be used without being followed by *arall/y llall:*

Ar *y naill* law yr oedd y graig yn serth.
Rhowch *y naill* hanner o'r afal iddo.
Aethant yn gyflym i'*r naill* du 'They went quickly to one side'.
Rhowch y llyfrau o'*r neilltu!* 'Put aside the books'.

Also, a demonstrative pronoun or noun can replace *y naill* in the first of the alternatives:
'*Câr* yn cuddio *arall,*—Hawdd i'*r llaw* gyhuddo'*r llall*' (T.A. 267).
Ambell *dro* mi rodiwn gyda'r lan, a *thro arall* mi eisteddwn i ddarllen.
Bu ef yn siarad am *hwn a'r llall* gan sôn am *hyn a'r llall.*

Before a noun *naill* can mean 'one': bachgen *naill-fraich* 'one-armed boy'; plentyn *naill-lygad* 'one-eyed child'; chwaer *naill-ran* 'half-sister'.

There is soft mut. in the noun after *naill,* except in the compounds
neilltu 'one side' and *neillparth* 'one part'.

In another (fairly modern) construction *naill ai* is followed by *neu* or
neu ynteu: Mae'r stori *naill ai'n* wir *neu*'n gelwydd 'The story is either
true or false'. *Naill ai* yr wyt yn wan *neu (ynteu)* mae'r baich yn drwm
'Either you are weak or (else) the burden is heavy'.

§ 94. Un. In addition to the use of *un, yr un,* shown in § 92(i) and as
an antecedent in a rel. clause, § 86, it occurs in other constructions:

(i) Mae eu tŷ hwy'n llai na'ch *un* chwi. Mae'r llyfr yn *un* mawr. Yr
oedd hi'n *un* deg/dlos. (§ 62).
In these examples *un* is used to avoid repetition of a noun.

(ii) synonymous with *rhywun* 'someone':
'Ac wele *un* gwahanglwyfus a ddaeth' (Mt. viii. 2).
Ai ti oedd yn y tŷ, ai *un* arall oedd yno?

(iii) like other numerals with *o* + genitive:
un o'r plant; *un ohonoch; un o*'r saith.

(iv) synonymous with *unrhyw* 'any' in negative and interogative
sentences:
Nid oes *un* dyn byw yma. Nid oes *un* fam nad yw'n caru ei
phlentyn.

In negative sentences we may have *yr un* instead of *un:*
Nid oes yno'r *un.* Daeth adref heb ddal *yr un* pysgodyn. 'He came
home without having caught a single fish'.

(v) meaning 'similar': Mae'r plentyn yr *un* ben â'i dad (§ 62).

(vi) meaning 'the one and the same':
yn yr *un* tŷ; o'r *un* dref; yn yr *un* lle ag ef (§ 62).
'Yr *un* yw Ef o hyd' (D.J. CAN 242).

(vii) meaning 'very' (followed by a demonstrative pron.):
yn yr *un* lle *hwnnw* 'in that very place'; ar yr *un* awr *honno* 'in that very
hour'.

(viii) meaning 'only':
'Credaf yn Nuw Dad . . . ac yn Iesu Grist ei *un* Mab ef' (Apostles
Creed).

(ix) in expressions denoting standard of price, measurement etc.:
ceiniog *yr un*; ffenestri dwylath *yr un;* arhosodd yr ymgeiswyr yno am
hanner awr *yr un* (§ 9 (iii)).

(x) in distributives:
o *un* i *un;* bob yn *un* ac *un;* bob yn *un* (§ 64).

(xi) in compounds (a) proper: *unfryd, unllais, unfarn;* (b) improper:
unwaith; unrhyw; unman; untro; undyn; unlle (§ 186).

(xii) in adverbial expressions such as *un prynhawn, un noson, un*

diwrnod. In an older construction, still common, *rhyw* is similarly used
(§ 96).

(xiii) with *pa* in an interrogative pron. (§ 88): *pa un? p'un? p'run?*

§ 95. Fy Hun, Dy Hun, etc. (Reflexive Pronouns). The forms *hun,
hunan* (sing.) and *hunain, hun* (plur.) are used with prefixed or infixed
pronouns. *Hunan, hunain* are mostly hard in S. Wales, and *hun* (sing.
and plur.) mostly in N. Wales.

(i) They are largely auxiliary and can follow:

(a) a prefixed or infixed pronoun:

fy nhad *fy hun* 'my own father'; *eich* gwlad *eich hun(ain);* i'm tŷ *fy
hunan;* â'i harian *ei hun* 'with her own money'; i'w hardaloedd *eu
hunain* 'to their own districts'; y mae'n *ei* ganmol *ei hun* 'he is praising
himself'; paid â'th ddangos *dy hunan* 'don't show thyself'; fe'i gwêl *ei
hun* 'he sees himself'.

(Note that *yn ei gartref ei hun* is correct, and that *yng nghartref ei hun* is
incorrect.)

(b) the personal form of a preposition:

wrthyf fy hun 'alone, by myself' (not *wrth fy hun); daeth ati ei hun* 'she
came to herself'; *arnoch eich hun; iddynt eu hunain.*

(c) an independent or an auxiliary pronoun:

Myfi fy hun sydd yma. Y mae'r llun fel *ti dy hunan.* Yr oedd hi'n siarad
â *hi ei hun.* Daethant *hwy eu hunain.* Sylwais *i fy hun* arno. Cewch
chwi'ch hunain ei weld. (§§ 66-68, 74).

After a personal form of a verb the auxiliary pronoun my be
omitted: *Deuthum fy hun* 'I myself came'; *Gwelsoch eich hun* pwy oedd
yno 'you yourselves saw who was there'.

(d) a noun:

Gwelais y *dyn ei hunan* 'I saw the man himself'. Daeth y plant *eu hunain*
yma 'The children themselves came here'.

In this construction *ei hun* etc. may be adverbial, meaning 'by
himself/herself' or 'alone':

Croesodd yr *eneth* y ffordd *ei hun* 'the girl crossed the road by herself'.
Bu farw'r rhieni gan adael y *plant* yn y tŷ *eu hunain* 'the parents died
leaving the children all alone in the house'.

(ii) These forms are now used as objects (a) of imperative verbs:
Dangoswch eich hunain! Adnebydd dy hun! 'Know thyself!'

(b) of verbs in other moods and verb-nouns:

Gollyngodd ei hun i'r llawr 'he let himself to the floor'. *Taflasant eu
hunain* i'r dŵr 'they threw themselves into the water'. Nid yw ef yn
niweidio'i hun 'he does not injure himself'.

According to Sir John Morris-Jones and some other later
grammarians the use of *fy hun* etc. as the object of a verb-noun is a

colloquial corruption. However, examples from as early as the thirteenth century have been found in prose, and the usage is now accepted by many scholarly writers (e.g. mae ef yn *twyllo'i hun*).

§ 96. Rhyw. As a noun *rhyw* means 'kind, species, sex', but we are here concerned with the pronominal adjective *rhyw* 'some, (a) certain': Yr oedd *rhyw* deulu o'r enw Prys yn byw yno. Ein hathro ni oedd *rhyw* löwr caredig a oedd wedi colli'i iechyd.

Together with the following noun, *rhyw* forms a compound, either strict or loose, and the noun element therefore is mutated: *rhywbeth, rhywbryd, rhywfaint, rhywle, rhywdro, rhyw eiriau, rhyw ddiwrnod, rhyw brynhawn, rhyw flwyddyn.*

The second element may be a pronoun or numeral: *rhywrai, rhywun, rhyw ddau fachgen.*

As well as being definite, *rhyw ddyn* can be indefinite, i.e. either 'a certain man' or 'some man (unknown)', the difference being shown by the context, or in speaking by the tone of voice. The indefinitude is obvious in such expressions as *rhyw ddau neu dri, rhyw ychydig, rhyw lawer.* Either contempt or compassion can be implied by others, e.g., *rhyw bregethwr bach, fel rhyw blentyn, rhyw dipyn o fwyd.*

Rhyw is used with verb-nouns to imply that the action is inexact: *Rhyw gysgu*'r oeddwn i 'I was sleeping, more or less'; Yr oedd hi'n *rhyw esgus mynd.*

The interrogative *pa ryw un* is often contractd to *p'run.*

§ 97. Amryw *(am + rhyw),* **Cyfryw** *(cyf + rhyw),* **Unrhyw** *(un + rhyw).*

(i) Nowadays *amryw* is used only with plural nouns: *amryw bethau* 'several things'; *amryw ddyddiau.* Formerly it could be followed by a singular noun: *amryw fesur* 'divers measures'.

To express 'various, divers' we now use *amrywiol; amrywiol lyfrau* or *llyfrau amrywiol. (Gwahanol* means both 'different' and 'various': *llyfrau gwahanol* 'different books', *gwahanol lyfrau* 'various books').

Amryw can also be substantive like E. 'miscellany, miscellaneous'.

(ii) Like E. 'such' *cyfryw* is mostly adjectival but sometimes substantive: *y cyfryw bethau; a'r cyfryw rai; y cyfryw un;* 'Rwy'n hoffi ffrwythau—afalau a'r *cyfryw; y cyfryw wlad.*

N.B. *cyfryw* does not mutate after the article *y* even before a fem. s. noun: *y cyfryw ferch* 'such a girl'.

Cyfryw may be followed by *â, ag* 'as': 'Bu rai ohonynt hwy *gyfryw ag* a adawsant enw ar eu hôl' (Ecclus. xliv. 8); y *cyfryw* ŵr *â* hwnnw; y *cyfryw* wraig *â* honno.

(iii) In general *unrhyw* is adjectival: *unrhyw beth; unrhyw ddynion* 'any men'; *unrhyw ddiwrnod* 'any day'. It is a loose compound in *o'r un rhyw* 'of the same kind'. It means 'selfsame' in 'mae'r un a'r *unrhyw* ysbryd' (1 Cor. xii. 11).

§ 98. Rhai. If a plural is required corresponding to *un*, § 94, (i, iii), *rhai* is the form used:

(i) to avoid repeating a noun:
Dyma'ch esgidiau chwi, ond ni wn pa le mae fy *rhai* i 'Here are your shoes, but I do not know where mine are'. Mae fy nillad i yn *rhai* gwynion 'My clothes are white ones'.

(ii) before *o* + a genitive: *rhai* o'r disgyblion; *rhai* ohonynt 'some of them';
also independently: Mae *rhai* yn credu hyn, 'some (people) believe this'.

(iii) as an 'alternative' pronoun, § 92 (i).

(iv) as antecedent of a relative clause, § 86.

(v) as substantive demonstrative pronouns, § 90: Pwy oedd y *rhai* ar y bont? 'Who were the ones on the bridge?'

(vi) adjectively to denote a small number: *rhai geiriau; rhai lleoedd.* In fairly rare examples it follows the noun: *'gwragedd rai'* (Luke viii. 2).

A noun following *rhai* does not mutate, and such expressions as *rhai geiriau* are not compounds (cf. §§ 100 (iii); 101 (iv); 102 (ii)).

§ 99 . Maint. As well as being a masc. common noun *maint* is used in the following constructions:

(i) in interrogative sentences:
Pa faint o ddŵr sydd yn y badell? 'How much water is there in the pan?' *Pa faint o* bobl oedd yno? 'How many people were there?'

Pa is often omitted before *faint: Faint o* blant sydd yma? *Faint o* arian sy gennych? Ni ŵyr ef *faint o* gyfoeth sy ganddo 'He does not know how much wealth he has'.

As well as a noun, a comparative adj. may follow *Pa faint: Pa faint gwell* fyddwch chwi o hyn? *Faint callach* wyt ti'n awr?

It can also be followed by bynnag: *Pa faint bynnag* ('however much') o waith a wna, ni fydd ddim gwell. *Faint bynnag* a wnaf drosto, ni chaf ddim diolch. Nid oedd hynny'n ddigon, *faint bynnag* oedd.

In question such as *Faint yw hwn?* words referring to price, measurement, amount etc. are implied.

(ii) as an equative adj. after *er* 'in spite of':
'Ond *er maint* ei allu a dyfned ei ddichellion, *er maint* o emprwyr . . . sy

tan ei faner . . . *Er maint,* er cryfed . . . yw'r mawr hwn. . .' (B.Cw. 17) 'However great is his power and however deep his deceits, despite the number of emperors under his banner . . . However great and powerful is this mighty one . . .'

Instead of *er maint* the usual form in this construction is *er cymaint: er cymaint yw ei allu.* (The colloquial form *er cyn gymaint* is tautologous).

(iii) as a fem. s. noun with the article *y* omitted, but with the soft. mut. preserved:

Yr oedd yno *faint* a fynnem o fwyd. Fe gei di *faint* sy gennyf. The full form *y veint (= y faint)* was commonly written in Medieval Welsh. The fem. gender is clearly shown in *yr un faint* 'the same size'.

(iv) after a preposition:

Ni allem aros yno *gan faint* y gwres 'We could not stay there because the heat was so great'. *'Â maint* y gwres nid rhyfedd gweled / y dŵr yn berwi dros fy llyged' (HB 107), 'Because the heat was so great it was no wonder to see the water boiling over my eyes'.

§ 100. Peth. The noun *peth* like E. 'thing' has a variety of meanings which need not be discussed here. As a pronoun it has several uses:

(i) as an interrogative: Pa beth? Beth? (§ 88).

(ii) as antecedent of a relative (§ 86).

(iii) to express 'a little, some', either with or without a noun:

Y mae *peth dŵr* yn y badell. Y mae ganddo *beth arian.* A gawsoch chwi fwyd? Do, fe gawsom *beth.* Dywedodd *beth celwydd.*

As the radical initial of the noun shows, *peth* does not form a compound here with the noun. (Cf. §§ 98 (vi); 101 (iv); 102 (ii); 108 (i); 110 (iii)).

(iv) followed by *o,* meaning 'some of, part of':

Y mae *peth o*'r gwaith yn dda. Darllenais *beth o*'r llyfr. Aeth y ci at y llaeth ac yfodd *beth ohono.*

(v) adverbially (with soft mut. *beth*):

'Yn wir, ni fedrais innau nad wylais *beth* o dosturi' (B.Cw. 28) 'Indeed, I could not but weep somewhat from compassion'. Mae ef yn dalach *beth* na hi. 'A challach ystwythach dyn / O beth ydoedd byth wedyn' (BE 40) 'a somewhat wiser, mor flexible man was he ever after'.

Uses (iii) and (v) are combined in 'Arhosodd yma *beth* amser'.

(vi) In a few idioms:

O dipyn i *beth* (= o dipyn i dipyn) 'litle by little'. Mae'n *druan o beth* ei bod hi'n dioddef 'It is a sad thing that she is suffering'. Mae'n *dipyn/llawer o beth* ei fod ef wedi llwyddo o gwbl 'It is quite a good thing that he has succeeded at all'.

§ 101. Llawer. Constructions with *llawer* correspond to those with *peth* (iii—v) above:

(i) with *o* + indefinite noun:
Yr oedd *llawer o ddynion* yn y tŷ 'There were many men in the house'.
Cafodd *lawer o helbul* 'He had much trouble'.

(ii) with *o* + definite noun:
Mae *llawer o'r* plant yn cysgu 'Many of the children are asleep'.

A pronominal form of *o* may replace *o* + noun:
Gwelais *lawer ohonynt* yn rhedeg 'I saw a good number of them running'.

(iii) with no noun following:
Dysgodd *lawer* i mi 'He taught me much'. Mae *llawer* yn credu hyn 'Many (people) believe this'. Nid oes *llawer* i'w ddweud 'There is not much to be said'.

(iv) with a singular noun following:
'*Llawer gwir,* gwell ei gelu' (proverb) 'many a truth is best hidden', *Llawer troed; llawer peth.* (Cf. *peth* and *pob* § 102).

(v) adverbially (with soft mut. *lawer*):
Mae Eryri'n llai *lawer* na'r Alpau. Nid arhosai *lawer* gartref.

Forming an adverb with a noun denoting measurement, manner etc.
'Duw, wedi iddo lefaru *lawer gwaith* a *llawer modd* . . .' (Heb. i. 1).

It can modify a comparative adj.: *llawer gwell; llawer mwy.*

It is also adverbial when preceded by *o:* Mae'r ffenestr hon yn lanach na'r llall, *o lawer* 'this window is cleaner by far than the other'.

(vi) the plural, *llaweroedd,* can replace *llawer* in each of the above constructions except (iv) and (v): Mae *llaweroedd* yn credu ynddo. *llaweroedd o bethau; llaweroedd ohonynt;* Daeth gwrandawyr *laweroedd* i'r cyngerdd.

Note. *Llawer* may be preceded by *rhyw* except when it is followed immediately by a noun: *rhyw lawer ohonynt; yn rhyw lawer gwell.* It is often followed by *iawn* in the sense of 'very': *llawer iawn o bethau.*

§ 102. Pawb, Pob. (i) *Pawb* is substantive and is now considered to be plural generally:
'Ac yr oedd *pawb* yn dwyn tystiolaeth iddo' (Luke iv. 22).
Dewch ymlaen, *bawb* ohonoch!

In old expressions and proverbs it is still regarded as a singular:
'*Pawb* at y peth y bo' (Lit. 'Each one to what he may be'). 'Rhydd i bawb ei farn' ('Every one has a right to his opinion'). '*Pawb* drosto'i hun' ('Each one for himself').

After a plural verb or a verb-noun *pawb* is adverbial:
'a chymerasant *bawb* eu gwŷr' (2 Kings xi. 9). Yr oeddynt yn dychwelyd *bawb* i'w cartrefi.

(ii) *Pob* is adjectival, and is followed by a noun or pronoun etc.: *pob peth; pob un; pob creadur; pob merch:* 'Fy amser i ganu yw Ebrill a Mai / A hanner Mehefin, chwi wyddoch *bob rhai*' (Folk-song).

Like *peth, rhai* and *llawer, pob* is followed by the radical initial. As well as *pob peth, pob man, (o) bob tu* 'from every side' we have the improper compounds *popeth, pobman, (o) boptu. Rhyw* and *cyfryw* often follow *pob: pob rhyw beth* 'every kind of thing'; *pob cyfryw beth* 'every such thing'.

(iii) In the form *bob* it is commonly used adverbially and in adverbial idioms:
bob nos; bob dydd; bob blwyddyn; bob yn un/bob yn un ac un 'one by one'; *bob yn ddau* 'two by two'; *bob yn ail/bob eilwers* 'alternately'; *bob yn dipyn* 'bit by bit'; *bob yn bunt* 'a pound (£) at a time'; *bob (yn) eilddydd* 'every other day'; *bob ail fis* 'in alternate months'.

Pob + noun can be adjectival, qualifying a preceding noun: *esgidiau pob-dydd* 'every-day shoes'; *Siôn pob-gwaith* 'Jack-of-all-trades'; *côt/cot bob tywydd* 'all-weather coat' (in which the mutated form *bob . . .* qualifies the fem. noun *côt/cot*).

For 'the children had a penny each (each a penny)' we have *cafodd y plant geiniog bob un* or *cafodd y plant bob un geiniog*. In the dialects we also have . . . *bob i geiniog* and *bob o geiniog*.

§ 103. Holl, Oll. (i) *Holl* is an adjective used before a noun or as the first element of a compound adjective, and as such takes the soft mutation: *holl* bobl y byd 'all the people of the world'; *holl* drigolion y ddaear; dy *holl* gyfoeth; *hollalluog* 'almighty'; *holliach* 'completely healthy'; *holl-bwysig* 'all-important'; *hollgyfoethog* 'all-powerful'.

Holl + noun may form a compound noun: *hollfyd; hollallu; hollbresenoldeb. Yn hollol* is an adverbial phrase.

Mae'r ateb *yn hollol* gywir. Rhaid i chwi orffen y gwaith *yn hollol*. Mae hyn yn wir *hollol;* Gwyn *hollol* yw ei liw.

An exceptional use is seen in the following: 'Mae y gair *yn hollol*, fod yn eich plith chwi odineb' (1 Cor. v. 1).

(ii) *Oll* is now adverbial, but it could formerly be substantive. It is found, (a) after a definite noun or a personal pronoun or personal preposition: *y pethau hyn oll; 'Nyni oll* a grwydrasom fel defaid' (Is. liii. 6); y mae cartrefi *ganddynt oll*.

In negative clauses in such expressions as *dim oll, neb oll* and *un cnawd oll* (Mt. xxiv. 22) the meaning of *oll* is 'at all'. An extension of this usage is seen in negative sentences as 'Ni fuoch yma *oll*' ('You have not been here at all').

(b) in an adjectival or adverbial phrase:
yr oedd yr wybren *yn las oll* 'the sky was all blue'; y mae'r llestri'n aur

oll; gwerthodd *gymaint oll* ag a feddai 'he sold as much altogether as he possessed'.

Oll is often used to modify a superlative adj.: *gorau oll; mwyaf oll;* (§ 52 (iii)).

Note. One may say *yr holl ddynion* or *y dynion oll.* An expression such as *yr (h)oll o'r dynion* is incorrect.

§ 104. Cwbl. *Cwbl* may be (i) a substantive:

Dyna'r *cwbl!* 'That is all!' Dywedodd y *cwbl* wrtho. Mae'r *cwbl* hyn yn wir. Yr oedd y *cwbl* o'r afalau yn ddrwg. Wedi'r *cwbl!*

The article, *y/yr/'r,* is invariably used with *cwbl* today, but in older writing the article is sometimes omitted: 'a *chwbl* sydd ynof' (Ps. ciii. 1).

(ii) an adjective: *taliad cwbl* 'complete payment'; *cwbl werth* 'whole value'.

(iii) an adverb: Yr oedd y lle yn *gwbl* dywyll. Mae hi'n *gwbl* fyddar. Yr ydym yn *cwbl* gredu.

In this construction *cwbl* + adj. or verb-noun form a compound.

Other adverbial forms are *o gwbl* and *yn gwbl:* Ni welais ef *o gwbl* 'I did not see him at all'. Gwadodd y peth *yn gwbl* 'He denied the thing completely'.

§ 105. Sawl. (i) *Y sawl* may be the antecedent of a rel. clause (§ 86), either singular or plural: 'i'r *sawl* a'ch casânt' ('to those who hate you'); *y sawl* a'ch caro ('the one who loves you').

(ii) *Pa sawl,* followed by a singular noun, is an interrogative: *Pa sawl* torth sy gennych? *Pa sawl* gwaith y bu ef yma? (§ 88 (iv)).

Pa is often omitted before *sawl* (cf. *Pa beth? Beth?*): *Sawl* un sydd yna? *Sawl* ceiniog sydd mewn punt?

(iii) There is a tendency to substitute *sawl* for *llawer* or *amryw:* Mae ganddi *sawl* brawd 'she has several brothers'.

§ 106. Ychydig. The soft. mut. follows *ychydig* in a noun which may be singular or plural. Except for this it is used like *llawer:*

(i) with *o* + an indefinite noun: *ychydig o bethau* ('a few things'); *ychydig o ddŵr* ('a little water').

(ii) with *o* + a definite noun or personal preposition: *ychydig o'r plant; ychydig ohonynt; ychydig o'r bwyd.*

(iii) with no noun following: 'llawer sydd wedi eu galw, ac *ychydig* wedi eu dewis' (Mt. xx. 16); *ni welaf ond ychydig* ('I see only a little').

(iv) followed by a sing. or plur. noun: *ychydig win; ychydig lyfrau; ychydig orffwys.*

(v) adverbially: Yr wyf wedi blino *ychydig*. Rhaid iti orffwys *ychydig*.

It may modify a comparative adj. (without mut.): *ychydig gwell; ychydig mwy*. It is more usual to put *yn* between ychydig and the adj.: *ychydig yn well; ychydig yn fwy*.

Note. In each of the above constructions *ychydig* can be preceded by *rhyw*: *rhyw ychydig (o) bethau; rhyw ychydig gwell; yn well o ryw ychydig*. *Rhyw* here has the modifying effect of 'some, somewhat'. When *iawn* follows *ychydig* it has the effect of 'very': *ychydig iawn* 'a very little'.

In negative sentences there are other comparable usages with comparative adjectives, such as: *(yn) fawr gwell* 'hardly better'; *nemor gwaeth* 'hardly worse'; *(yn) ronyn elwach* 'not a whit more profitable'; *(yn) fymryn llai* 'not a bit less'; *(yn) ddim tlysach* 'not (at all) prettier'; *(yn) damaid gwell* 'not the least better'.

§ 107. Digon. *Digon* can be substantive, adjectival or adverbial.

(i) substantive:

Y mae *digon* o fwyd ganddo. Mae hi wedi cael *digon*.

Digonedd means 'abundance, very large number/quantity':

Yr oedd *digonedd* o arian ganddo. Mae *digonedd* o afalau ar y goeden.

(ii) adjectival:

Nid yw'r darn hwn yn *ddigon* 'This piece is not enough'.

Digonol is an alternative form: Pwy sydd *ddigonol* i'r gwaith? 'Who is sufficiently qualified for the task?'

(iii) adverbial:

Nid yw hynny'n *ddigon* da 'that is not good enough'. Gweithiodd yn *ddigon* caled 'he worked sufficiently hard'.

§ 108. Gormod, Gormodd. *Gormod/gormodd* is used in the same ways as *digon,* except that it does not modify an adj. The literary form today is *gormod,* as a rule, but the older form *gormodd* is still heard in dialects.

(i) substantive: *gormod o waith* 'too much work'; *gormod o'r plant* 'too many of the children'; mae *gormod(d)* yn waeth na rhy ychydig 'too much is worse than too little'.

In an older construction *gormod* is followed immediately by a noun with radical initial: 'i'r unrhyw *ormod rhysedd*' (1 Peter iv. 4); *gormod poen* yw hynny. It can also follow a verb-noun: *siarad gormod; cysgu gormod*. A suffix is added to *gormod* to give *gormodedd* 'excess'; cf. *digonedd*.

(ii) adjectival: Mae'r baich yn *ormod(d)* iddo.

As an adj. *gormodol* (cf. *digonol*) is frequently used: Mae'r pris yn *ormodol* 'the price is excessive'.

(iii) adverbial: 'Na chwsg *ormod!*' Paid â siarad yn *ormodol*.

§ 109. Rhagor. *Rhagor* may be either a noun or an adverb:

(i) as noun (= 'difference, more'):

Y mae eisiau *rhagor* o fwyd arno 'He needs more food'. 'Canys y mae *rhagor* rhwng seren a seren mewn gogoniant' (1 Cor. xv. 41).

A former construction of *rhagor i*, as in 'ys *rhagor i* bedair blynedd ar ddeg' (2 Cor. xii. 2), has been replaced by *rhagor na(g)*, which is treated as if it were a comparative adj. + *na(g):*
Gwelais *ragor nag* un yno. Y mae ganddo *ragor* o synnwyr *na'i* frawd. Bu'n aros yma am *ragor na* mis.

(ii) as adverb:

Bydd y genedl hon yn ffyddlon, *rhagor* unrhyw genedl ar y ddaear 'This nation will be faithful, more than any nation on earth'.

Derivatives of *rhagor:* *rhagorol* (adj.), *rhagoriaeth* (noun), *rhagorach* (comp. adj.), *rhagori* (verb-noun), *rhagoraf* (verb).

§ 110. Dim. (i) As a noun *dim* 'anything' is commonly used in negative sentences or equivalent phrases:

Ni welais *ddim*. 'Heb Dduw, heb *ddim'*. Nid oedd *dim* yno.

It means 'thing' in *pob dim:* 'Y mae yn dioddef *pob dim*, yn credu *pob dim* . . . ' (1 Cor. xiii. 7).

It can be preceded by the article and followed by an adj.:
Ni fu ond *y dim* rhyngddo a syrthio (Lit. 'There was only a whit between him and falling', i.e. 'he almost fell'). Nid wyf yn credu'r *dim lleiaf* ('the least thing') a ddywedwch.

It may be predicative: 'nid wyf fi *ddim'* (1 Cor. xiii. 2). Nid yw hynny'n *ddim* i mi.

(ii) Because of the frequent use of *dim* in negative sentences, it acquired the meaning of 'nothing, none'. Thus in reply to such a question as *Beth sydd yn dy law?,* instead of the full *Nid oes dim* one hears *'Does dim* (where the *'D* stands for *Nid*), or more commonly *Dim* (cf. French *rien).*

As there was no word in Welsh for 'nothing', it was natural to give that meaning to *dim* in expressions such as *creu rhywbeth o ddim* 'creating something out of nothing'. In the dialects it became customary to say *dim ond* for 'nothing but, only', and the usage spread to folk-poetry and to the work of standard poets, e.g.,

'Dim ond heno tan yfory, *dim ond* fory tan y ffair' (Folk-verse).
'Dim ond calon lân all ganu' (Gwyrosydd, CAN 829).
'Dim ond lleuad borffor/Ar fin y mynydd llwm' (Hedd Wyn 157).

(iii) An indefinite noun may follow *dim:*
Nid oes ganddynt *ddim bwyd.* Nid oedd *dim cysur* yn ei eiriau.

If the noun is definite it must have *o* before it after *dim:*

Nid oedd dim o'r bwyd ar ôl. Ni chaiff Dafydd *ddim o arian ei dad*. (As shown in § 7 *Note*, *arian* followed by a dependent genitive in the last example is definite).

The preposition *o* may be pronominal (or personal) in form:
Aeth Nia i chwilio am ei brawd ond ni welodd *ddim ohono* 'Nia went to look for her brother but she saw nothing of him'.

In sentences of the type *Ni chymerodd ef ddim o'r bwyd* or *Ni chymerodd ef ddim ohono* the word *ddim* may be stressed in speaking so as to mean 'anything at all'. But on the other hand it may be that *ddim (o)* here merely supports the negative, so that the two sentences mean no more than *Ni chymerodd ef y bwyd* and *Nis cymerodd ef*. When no stress is intended in speaking *ddim o* is often contracted to *mo* and *ddim ohono* to *mohono or mono*. (Corresponding forms in other persons are *mohonof, mohonot, mohoni, mohonom, mohonoch, mohonynt,* or *monof* etc. (§ 191)). These contracted forms frequently appear in writing:
'Meddyliai Gwen am Ddeio'r Go/na welai *mono* mwy' (W.J.G. *Caneuon* 30).
'Na alw *monom*, Grist, yn ddrwg a da' (T.H.P.-W., *Cerddi* 39).
'Nac ysbeilia *mo*'r tlawd' (Prov. xxii. 22).

(iv) The negative element is stressed also when *ddim* is used adverbially: 'a'r hwn a ddêl ataf fi, nis bwriaf ef allan *ddim*') (John vi. 37). Ai ti oedd yno? Nage *ddim*. Nid af fi *ddim* yno, beth bynnag.

Colloquially the negative *ni(d)* is not heard as a rule except in negative replies, but the mutation caused by the elided *ni* is retained in the verb: *'Ddaw e' ddim* (for *Ni ddaw ef ddim); 'chreda' i ddim* (for *ni chredaf fi ddim)*. In *'dwy' i ddim* the final *'d* of *nid* is retained. (See §§ 106 (v) Note; § 221).

§ **111. Neb.** Like *dim*, *neb* is used very frequently in negative sentences.

(i) It means 'anyone' in the following examples:
Nid oedd *neb* yn y tŷ. Ni ddywedaf wrth *neb*. Ni welais *neb*.

(ii) Like *dim* it acquired a negative meaning 'no one':
Pwy oedd yno? *Neb* (for *nid oedd neb*). A welodd rhywun di? Naddo, *neb*. From this usage arose the expression *neb ond* 'no one but':
*Neb ond ti a wnâi'*r fath beth (for *Ni wnâi neb ond ti* etc.).
'*Neb ond Ti*, Waredwr f'enaid/Dygaist Ti yn llwyr fy mryd' (J. Lloyd, Treffynnon).

(iii) It has the straight meaning of 'anyone' in phrases other than negative:
Dos ymaith cyn i *neb* dy weld. Llosgodd y llythyr rhag i *neb* ei ddarllen. Onid oes *neb* yn gwybod 'Does not anyone know?' Mae

ganddo gymaint o hawl â *neb*. 'Os ewyllysia *neb* ddyfod ar fy ôl i' (Luke ix. 23).

(iv) *Neb* can be followed by *o* + a plur. or collective noun (or its equivalent): *neb o'r dynion; neb o'i deulu; neb o'n cenedl; neb ohonom; neb ohonynt*.

(v) As shown in § 86 *y neb* can be the antecedent of a relative clause: 'a'*r neb* sydd yn ceisio sydd yn cael' (Mt. vii. 8). Os delir *y neb* a wnaeth y drwg, fe'i cosbir.

(vi) Formerly *neb* was used adjectivally, and traces of this remain in such phrases as *neb rhyw ddyn* 'any kind of man'; *neb cyfryw* 'anyone of the kind'; *nemor* (from *neb mawr); nepell* (from *neb pell*):

Nid oedd *nemor neb* yno 'there was hardly anyone there'. *Nid* yw'r ysgol *nepell* o'r pentref 'The school is not far from the village', (In recent writing the construction is often corrupted in such sentences as *Yr oedd y tŷ nepell o'r afon*).

§ 112. (Ei) Gilydd (Cilydd).

There was at one time a noun *cilydd* 'fellow', which underwent soft mutation under the same conditions as any other noun with initial *c-*, e.g. after the pronouns *ei*, *'i*, *'w* (§ 69). After *pob un, pawb, un, neb* it would be necessary to add *ei* ('*i*) *gilydd* to complete the phrase as in:

Gwelai pob un ei gilydd 'Each one saw the other'. *Nid oedd neb yn fwy na'i gilydd* 'No one was greater than the other'.

The word *cilydd* disappeared from the language, but *ei gilydd* survived with the new meaning 'each/the other' instead of 'his/her/its fellow'. Later it was felt that *pawb/pob un* etc. were not always necessary before *ei gilydd,* and as early as the 1620 edition of the Bible there are many examples of the omission of these words:

'Eithr hwy a ofnasant yn ddirfawr ac a ddywedasant wrth *ei gilydd*' (Mk. iv. 41). 'Byddwch heddychlawn a'*i gilydd* (Mk. ix. 50).

The next step was to make the form of the pronoun preceding *gilydd* agree in person with the verb, pronoun etc. at the beginning of the sentence. Thus in the 1746 edition of the Bible the two examples quoted appeared 'amended':

'Eithr hwy a ofnasant . . . ac a ddywedasant wrth *eu gilydd*'; 'byddwch heddychlawn â'*ch gilydd*'.

New plural forms then came into use: *ein gilydd, eich gilydd, eu gilydd*. It was Sir John Morris-Jones, towards the end of the last century, who showed the spuriousness of these forms and rejected them, although he did not insist that *pawb* should be restored before *ei gilydd*. He was fairly readily followed in writing *ei gilydd* even after a plural verb etc., as no change of pronunciation was involved, both *eu* and *ei* being pronounced *i* in natural spoken Welsh. By today most writers feel that the other plur. forms are essential and that sentences such as the following must be regarded as correct: *Dywedwch wrth eich gilydd* and *Rhaid inni fynd gyda'n gilydd.*

Notice the following idioms: *rhywbryd neu'i gilydd* 'some time or other'; *rhywun neu'i gilydd; un dydd ar ôl ei gilydd* 'one day after another'; *o ben bwygilydd* 'from end to end'; *mynd i'w gilydd* 'to shrink, curl up'; Mae'r rhain yn dda, *at ei gilydd* 'taken as a whole'. The colloquial adverbial form *pentigili,* heard in south-west Wales, comes from *pen at ei gilydd* 'from end to end, altogether'.

THE VERB

§ 113. The Welsh verb has three moods: the indicative, the subjunctive and the imperative. The indicative has four tenses: present, imperfect, past and pluperfect. The subjunctive has two: present and imperfect, while the imperative has only present tense. In general each tense has six personal forms and one impersonal form. Welsh has no 'passive' forms but impersonal forms (and other constructions) are used to denote passive voice.

A negative sentence is formed by placing a pre-verbal particle *ni(d), na(d), na(c)* at its beginning; §§ 76 (ii); 77-78; 221.

When the subject is a noun, the verb is always in the *third person singular,* i.e. the verb is singular even when the noun subject is plural, e.g., *Chwardd y plentyn* 'the child laughs'; *chwardd y plant* 'the children laugh'; *canai'r bardd/beirdd* 'the bard/bards was/were singing'.

Where there is no noun subject the person and number are marked by the form of the verb, e.g., *gwelaf; ceri; rhedai; rhoddem; aethant.* An affixed pronoun may be added to these forms (*gwelaf fi, rhedai ef,* etc., § 74 (i), but an affixed pronoun is auxiliary and not the subject of the verb. This applies also to a pronoun or particle placed before the verb, e.g., *mi af, fe welsant,* § 68 (iv).

§ 114. *Present Indicative.* The present indicative is used in seven ways:

(i) To denote the simple or true present:

A *weli* di'r aderyn yn awr? *Gwelaf,* ond ni *chlywaf* ef yn canu 'Do you now see the bird? I do (see), but I do not hear it sing'.

Only a few verbs are used in their simple compact forms to denote the true present, e.g., *gweld, clywed, credu, tybied, bod, gwybod, adnabod, gallu, medru.* This tense is usually expressed by a periphrastic construction of *bod* + *yn* + verb-noun, e.g., *Yr wyf yn siarad* 'I am speaking'. *Mae hi'n cysgu* 'She is sleeping'. *Y maent yn rhedeg* 'They are running'.

(ii) To denote the present generally, but without reference to a particular time:

'Gwyn y *gwêl* y frân ei chyw' ('The crow sees her chick to be white').
'Ni *ad* efe i'th droed lithro; ac ni *huna* dy geidwad. Wele ni *huna* ac ni *chwsg* ceidwad Israel' (Ps. cxxi. 3, 4).

The time is general when certain verbs are used parenthetically (and mostly with soft mut.) to convey opinion, feeling etc., e.g., *debygaf, gredaf, goeliaf, welaf, ddywedwn (i), meddaf.*

Pwy, *debygwch* chwi, a welais? 'Who(m), do you think, I saw?'
Hyn, *meddaf,* sy'n iawn 'This, say I, is right'.
Nid aur, *gredaf* fi, yw hwn 'This, I believe, is not gold'.
Dyna, *goeliaf* fi, yr hyn a ddigwyddodd 'That, I believe, is what happened'.

(iii) To denote future time. This usage is very common as verbs, with the exception of *bod* and its compounds, have no future tense forms (§§ 140, 155—161):

A *wnei* di hyn? 'Will you do this?' *Gwnaf,* yn y man 'I will, presently'. Fe'ch *gwelwn* yfory, ac fe *gewch* y llythyr os *daw* ef 'We shall see you tomorrow, and you shall have the letter if it comes'.

(iv) As in other languages the dramatic present is used in telling of past events:

Yr oedd yr anifail yn ffoi; ond fe *red* yntau ar ei ôl, a chyn iddo gyrraedd ei ffau fe *neidia* arno 'The animnal was fleeing; but he runs after it, and before it reaches its lair he *jumps* on it'.

(v) To denote a condition, state or act that is continuous up to the time of speaking:

Yr *wyf* yma ers awr 'I am (have been) here for an hour'. Y *mae* ef yn byw yma byth er hynny 'He is (has been) living here ever since then. *Mae* hi'n ddall o'i geni 'She is blind from (her) birth'. Mi *wn* i hynny cyn d'eni di 'I know (have known) that (since) before you were born'.

(vi) To denote a habitual act or one that continues up to the time of speaking. As a rule it is the consuetudinal forms of *bod* with the verb-noun that form this construction:

Byddaf yn mynd yno bob haf 'I go there every summer'. *Bydd* ef *yn galw* yma fel rheol 'He calls here as a rule'.

The simple present tense forms, *wyf, wyt,* etc. are also used in the same way:

Yr *wyf yn mynd* allan yn aml 'I often go out'. *Mae* ef *yn gorffwys* bob prynhawn 'He rests every afternoon'.

Other verbs in their compact forms are used to express habitual action:

Fe *ddaw* heibio bob hyn a hyn 'He comes round from time to time'. Mi *gaf* rywbeth ganddo o hyd 'I receive something from him continually'. *Cynhelir* eisteddfod yno bob blwyddyn 'An eisteddfod is held there annually'.

(vii) The present tense of *bod*, with a future meaning, sometimes replaces the future tense (especially in speaking) when the context shows that reference is made to the future:

Mae ef *yn siarad* yma yfory 'He is speaking here tomorrow'. *Mae* cyngerdd yno ymhen mis 'There is a concert there in a month's time'. *Mae*'r pren hwn *yn gwywo* os na ddaw glaw 'This tree is withering if no rain comes'.

§ 115. *Imperfect.* There is no difference in form between the imperfect indicative and the imperfect subjunctive, except in a few irregular verbs *(bod, dyfod, mynd, gwneuthur)*.

The imperfect indicative is used:

(i) to indicate that an action or state was continuous at some period (in the mind of the speaker) in the past:

Fel y *deuai* ei lygaid yn gyfarwydd â'r tywyllwch fe *welai* ym mha le'r *oedd* 'As his eyes became accustomed to the darkness he could see where he was'. Tra *gorweddai* hi yno meddyliodd am y peth 'While she was lying there she thought about the matter'.

(ii) to denote a habitual action in the past:

Deuai yno bob dydd a *dygai* fwyd iddynt 'He came there every day and would bring them food'.

(iii) to express the subject's will, desire or willingness:

Gofynnodd imi a *awn* i gydag ef 'He asked me whether *I would go* with him'. Dywedodd hi *na wnâi hi* hynny 'She said that *she would not* do that'. *Ni fynnent hwy* siarad *'They did not wish* to talk'.

The time here is either general or indefinite.

(iv) to imply ability or possibility, mostly with verbs such as *gweld, clywed, teimlo, gwerthfawrogi* and the two verbs *medru* and *gallu* (which contain the implication):

Wedi syllu mi *welwn i*'r ynys 'After gazing I could see the island'. *Gwrandawai*'n astud, ond *ni chlywai* ddim 'He listened intently, but could hear nothing'. *Ni chlywem* yr oerfel 'We could not feel the cold'.

The action in the above examples is continuous in the past.

(v) in indirect speech after a past verb where the future would be used in direct speech:

Dywedodd y *deuai* yma yfory 'He said he would come here tomorrow'. *Tyngais* na *wnawn* hynny byth 'I swore that I would never do that'.

These examples could appropriately be included under (iii) also, but not the following, in which the simple present *wyf, wyt,* etc. become *oeddwn, oeddit,* etc. in indirect speech:

(direct) Pwy *wyt* ti? (indirect) Gofynnodd pwy *oeddwn* i.
(direct) Pa le *mae* ef? Holais pa le yr *oedd* ef.

In the same way we have the imperfect to replace the simple present:

(direct) Beth a *weli* di? Gofynnais beth a *welai* ef.

(vi) to express the future from the standpoint of the past:

Gwyddwn y *cawn* i fwyd 'I knew that I would have food'.
Mynnodd aros er na *châi* weld dim 'He insisted on staying although he would not be allowed to see anything'. Tybiais y *deuent* yn ôl 'I thought that they would return'.

(vii) In a main clause followed by a conditional clause or its equivalent:

Mi *roddwn* arian iddi pe bai angen 'I would give her money if there were need'. Fe *ddeuai* oni bai ei fod yn sâl 'He would come if he were not ill'. Ni *chanai* hi ar wahân i hynny 'She would not sing apart from that'. Nid *aent* i unman heb wahoddiad 'They would not go anywhere without an invitation'.

§ 116. *Past.* This tense is used in two ways:

(i) to denote an action in the past, as is done in relating a story, or in telling of a sequence of events:

Edrychodd ('he looked') yng nghyfeiriad y sŵn; *gwelodd* ('he saw') rywbeth yn symud, ac ar unwaith *neidiodd* ('he jumped') yn ôl i'w guddfan.
Gwelais ('I saw') swllt ar y llawr a *phlygais* ('I bent down') i'w godi.

(ii) to denote an action which has been completed by the time of speaking. This is called the *Perfect tense:*

Gwelais ef yn y dref droeon 'I have seen him in the town several times'. Fe *ddaeth* y llythyr o'r diwedd 'The letter has come at last'. Ni *fûm* i mewn llys erioed 'I have never been in a court'. A *welsoch* chwi'r llyfr hwn? 'Have you seen this book?' Do, ac fe'i *darllenais* 'Yes, and I have read it'.

In the periphrastic construction we have *yr wyf wedi bod* for *bûm; y mae wedi dyfod* for *daeth; y mae heb gyrraedd* for *ni chyrhaeddodd,* etc.

§ 117. *Pluperfect.* (i) The pluperfect tense denotes an action or state that was already past at a past time spoken or thought of:

Ni *welswn* ei debyg cyn hynny 'I had not seen the like of it before then'. *Cyraeddasai* hi o flaen ei llythyr 'She had arrived before her

letter'. 'Pa sawl gwaith y *mynaswn* gasglu dy blant ynghyd?' 'How
often would I have gathered thy children together?' (Luke xiii. 34).

In the periphrastic construction:

*Nid oeddwn wedi gweld; yr oedd hi wedi mynd; nid oeddynt hwy wedi
gweithio; yr oedd hi heb gychwyn.*

(ii) Like the imperfect it is used in a main clause followed or
preceded by a conditional clause or its equivalent (§ 115, vii):

Ni *roeswn* i ddim iddo oni *buasai* am ei dad 'I would not have given
him anything had it not been for his father'. Pe *buasai'r* meistr yn
bresennol *cawsai'r* gwas ei arian. 'If the master had been present the
manservant would have had his money'.

(iii) The plueperfect is used with interjections to express a wish or
regret with regard to the past:

'*O na buaswn* farw drosot ti, Absolom, fy mab, fy mab!' (2 Sam. xviii.
33). '*O! na threuliaswn* yn ddi-goll / O dan iau Crist fy mebyd oll!'
(Pedr Fardd CAN 220).

Note. There is a tendency to use the pluperfect for the imperfect in
constructions (ii) and (iii) above:

Pe *buasech* yn gofyn fe *gawsech* y tŷ (for *Pe baech . . . fe gaech . . .*).
Dywedodd na *fuasai (= fyddai)* byth yn gwneud hynny.

One may hold that the mood of the verb in (ii) and (iii) is
subjunctive rather than indicative, but the two moods do not differ in
verbal forms for the pluperfect.

§ 118. *Present Subjunctive.* (i) The present subjunctive is used to
express a wish or curse:

Na ato Duw! 'God forbid!' Byw *fyddo*'r Teyrn! 'May the Monarch
live!' *Melltigedig fyddont!* 'May they be accursed!' '*Caffwyf* ffafr yn dy
olwg di, fy arglwydd' (Ruth ii. 13). 'Y nefoedd a'i *helpo*'.

(ii) It is used if the action of the verb is indefinite in time:

(a) in a relative clause:

Ni ellir credu popeth *a ddywedo*. 'Nid ofni rhag . . . y saeth *a ehedo* y
dydd; na rhag yr haint *a rodio* yn y tywyllwch; na rhag y dinistr *a
ddinistrio* ganol dydd' (Ps. xci. 5-6). 'Y neb *y maddeuer* ychydig iddo, a
gâr ychydig' (Luke vii. 47).

(b) in an adverbial clause after *lle (y), pan, tra, oni, cyn y, wedi y, nes
y, fel y* (denoting purpose or comparison), *fel na, modd y, megis y, rhag
na, am y:*

'*Lle y* bo'r dolur y bydd y llaw' (§ 82). '*Pan fyddo*'r môr yn berwi . . .
Ond *pan fo*'r môr heb awel . . .' (J.J.W. 101). 'Ond cariad pur sydd
fel y dur/Yn para *tra bo* dau' (Folk-song). '. . . dangoswch farwolaeth

yr Arglwydd *oni ddelo'* (1 Cor. xi. 26). 'Mae'n rhaid i ni barhau *nes y caffom* gan Noah wrando' (LlTA 172). 'Mae'r Feinir a'i bryd ar ei fawredd . . . *modd y caffo* hi'r blaen ar lawer o'i chymdogesau' (B.Cw. 30). 'yna pawb a'i stori . . . os gwir, os celwydd, nis gwaeth, *am y bo* ('provided it is') hi'n ddigrif' (B.Cw. 23). 'mae llawer o'r dynion newyddion yma heb bris am y byd . . . *am y caffont* fod gyda Noah yn yr Arch' (LlTA 161). 'Canys ofni yr wyf, *rhag* . . . na'ch *caffwyf* yn gyfryw rai' (2 Cor. xii. 20).

(iii) It occurs in a negative noun-clause following a main clause expressing wish or command:

'a chaniatâ *na syrthiom* y dydd hwn mewn un pechod, ac *nad elom* mewn neb rhyw berygl' (Ll.G.G.). Gofelwch *na ddywedoch* hyn wrth neb! 'Edrychwch *na thwyller* chwi' (Luke xxi. 8).

Here is an example of the same construction in an affirmative clause, by analogy:

'a chaniatâ . . . *y byddo* i'r sawl sy'n gweithio gyfranogi'n helaeth o gynhaeaf y tir' (BBN 19).

Note. When the action referred to by the command or entreaty is affirmative it is a verb-noun, and not a noun-clause, that is mostly used: *Cofiwch alw! Gorchmynnodd iddo fynd. Caniatâ imi ddyfod.*

The negative command etc. is now mostly conveyed by *peidio â:* Dywedodd wrthi am *beidio â mynd* 'He told her not to go'. Crefodd hi ar iddo *beidio â dweud* 'She begged him not to tell'.

(iv) In a construction which is now obsolete the present subjunctive could be used in a negative noun-clause with its verb indefinite in time:

'Da yw *na fwytaer* cig, ac *nad yfer* gwin' (Rom. xiv. 21).

In the 1975 Welsh translation of the New Testament the version of the above reads thus:

'Y peth iawn yw *peidio â bwyta* cig *nac yfed* gwin'.

A comparable modernization of syntax is seen on comparing two versions as follows:

'Ni all *na ddêl* rhwystrau' (old) and 'Y mae achosion cwymp yn rhwym o *ddod'* (new) (Luke xvii. 1.)

§ 119. *Imperfect subjunctive.* This tense is seen,

(i) in a conditional clause after *pe (ped, pes):*

Pe bawn i'n ei weld, fe gâi gurfa 'If I were to see him he would get a thrashing'.
Ni fyddai'n werth byw *pe bai* hynny'n wir 'It would not be worth living if that were true'.

Ped edrychech o'r ffenestr uchaf, fe welech y môr 'If you were to look from the highest window you would see the sea'.
Pes gwelwn, fe'i credwn 'If I were to see it, I would believe him'.

In a negative conditional clause we have *pe na:*

Pe na chawn y swydd, mi awn adref yfory 'If I were not to get the job, I would go home tomorrow'.
Pe nad arhosai hi, nid arhoswn innau 'If she would not stay, neither would I'.

We also have *oni* in a negative conditional instead of *pe na:*

Byddai'r plentyn yn llefain *oni châi* sylw 'The child would cry if he would not get attention'.
Oni bai am hynny, fe fyddent yma gyda ni 'Were it not for that, they would be here with us'.

(ii) with interjections to express a wish or regret with regard to the present or the future:

'*O! na bawn* i fel y nant!' (Ceiriog). *O! na ddeuai*'r bore! (Cf. § 117 (iii)).

§ 120. *Imperative.* The imperative mood expresses:

(i) a command (mostly in the second person singular and plural):
Gwna hyn! Rhowch y llyfrau i mi!

(ii) guidance or advice:
Dilynwch yr heol hyd at yr eglwys, ac yna *trowch* i'r dde. *Byddwch* wych! '*Byddwch* lawen a hyfryd . . . *Llewyrched* felly eich goleuni . . .' (Mt. v. 12, 16).

(iii) a wish or entreaty:
'*Bydded* goleuni'. '*Gwneler* Dy ewyllys'.

(iv) When the command etc. is negative *na(c)* is placed before the word:

Na ladd! Nac arbed! Na chymerwch! 'Ac *nac arwain* ni i brofedigaeth'. *Na hidiwch!*

In the periphrastic negative *peidio â/ag* is placed before the verb, and this is the construction now used in speaking:

Paid â mynd! Peidiwch ag aros! Peidier â thaflu cerrig! (cf. §§ 118 (iii) Note, and 181).

§ 121. *Impersonal Forms.* When no reference is made to any doer of the action of the verb the impersonal form of the verb is used:

Dywedir bod pethau'n gwella 'It is said (one says) that things are improving'. *Nid addolir* yn y capel hwn yn awr 'No one worships (one does not worship) in this chapel now'. *Eir* ar hyd y ffordd hon i

Gaerdydd 'One goes along this road to Cardiff'. *Telid* arian iddynt 'Money would be paid to them'. *Nid aethpwyd* i mewn i'r ddinas 'No one went into the city'.

The doer of the action of an impersonal verb can be indicated by the use of the prepositon *gan* + a noun or of a pronominal form of *gan:*

Lladdwyd y ffermwr *gan darw* (lit. 'there was the killing of the farmer by a bull'). *Ni chenir* y dôn hon *gan y côr. Adroddwyd* yr hanes *ganddo ef. Pregethir ganddynt* nos yfory.

If the verb is transitive its impersonal forms may have an object:

Gwelir y môr. Rhoddwyd bwyd iddynt. *Gwerthid esgidiau* yno. *Cosbir chwi.* Fe'*m gwelwyd.*

Grammatically these impersonal forms are *active,* but if the impersonal form has an object the verb may be translated into English as if it were *passive:*

Gwelir y môr 'The sea *is seen'* (more literally 'one sees the sea'). Fe'*m gwelwyd* 'I was seen'.

Thus, although the Welsh verb has no passive voice, the passive can be implied when the impersonal form has an object. But if it has no object a verb in the active voice is essential in English when translating:

Pregethir ganddynt 'They will preach' (or, more literally, 'there will be preaching by them'). *Eir i mewn* 'one (they) will enter'.

By paraphrasing, the action may be made passive in English:

Cesglir yn y cyfarfod 'a collection will be made in the meeting'.

§ 122. *Verb-noun.* Because the verb-noun is a combination of a verb and a noun it has two functions, as a verb and as a noun. See below §§ 177-82. (A full discussion of the verb-noun constructions appears in *Cystrawen y Frawddeg Gymraeg* (Melville Richards), pp. 44-64).

§ 123. *Subject and Object—Mutations.* The rules in Modern Welsh are as follows:

(i) When the *subject* (not preceded by the article or any other word) comes immediately after the verb, there is no mutation:

Daeth *cardotyn* at y tŷ. Fe dyfai *pren* yno. Rhedodd *merch* dros y ffordd. Gwaeddodd *rhywun* arno. Bydd *llawer* yma.

(ii) When the *object* (not preceded by the article or any other word) comes immediately after (a) the verb, or (b) the verb + an auxiliary pronoun, or (c) the subject, it undergoes soft mutation:

Gwelais *geffyl.* Gwelant hwy *longau.* Deil y dynion *bysgod.* Cafodd Ifan *fraw.* Rhodded y beirniad *wobr* iddo!

(iii) The object is not mutated when it follows immediately after an impersonal form of a verb:

Gwelir *tonnau*'r môr. Rhoddwyd *gwobrau* iddynt. Rhodder *tâl* iddo.

Exceptions: The Independent Personal Pronouns (§ 67) are mutated as objects of impersonal forms:

Gwelir *fi*. Dilyned y plant *fi!* Cosbir *dithau*.

(iv) The object of a *verb-noun* immediately following it does not mutate:

Yr oedd ef yn *dysgu canu*. Bydd hi'n *ennill cyflog*. Paid â *rhoi trafferth* iddo.

[The same grammatical relationship exists between a noun + noun *(geiriau cân* 'the words of a song') and a verb-noun + noun *(dysgu cân* 'learning a song'), and in each case the second element is in the genitive case; so that the 'object' of a verb-noun is in the genitive case.]

(v) Where the subject or object of a verb follows the article, a numeral, or an adjective etc., the rules of initial mutation after these parts of speech apply, as shown in §§ 8, 42, 62, 186 (i) (a).

(vi) After an interpolation soft mutation occurs in the subject, the object of an impersonal verb and the object of verb-noun:

(a) the interpolation being an adverb or its equivalent:

Daeth *yno blant*. Rhuthrodd *o'r tŷ rywbeth* mawr. Gwerthid *hefyd lyfrau* yno. Yr oedd yn dwyn *ar ei gefn faich* mawr.

(b) the interpolation being a preposition:

Mae *ganddo geffyl*. Yr oedd *iddo fab*. Cafwyd *ganddo wisgoedd* i'r llwyfan.

(vii) The subject of *oes* (even without interpolation) often has soft. mut.:

Nid *oes lawer* yma. A *oes rywbeth* ar ôl? (§§ 140-1).

Mostly, however, it is the radical that follows *oes:*

A *oes ceiniog* gennyt?

Formerly the mutation sometimes followed *oedd, bu,* etc.

THE REGULAR VERB

CANU 'to sing'

§ 124. *Indicative Mood*

	Present Tense			Imperfect Tense	
	Sing.	Pl.		Sing.	Pl.
1.	canaf	canwn	1.	canwn	canem
2.	ceni	cenwch	2.	canit	canech
3.	cân	canant	3.	canai	canent
	Impers. cenir			*Impers.* cenid	

Past Tense			Pluperfect Tense		
Sing.		*Pl.*	*Sing.*		*Pl.*
1.	cenais	canasom	1.	canaswn	canasem
2.	cenaist	canasoch	2.	canasit	canasech
3.	canodd	canasant	3.	canasai	canasent
	Impers. canwyd			*Impers.* canasid (canesid)	

Subjunctive Mood

Present Tense			Imperfect Tense		
Sing.		*Pl.*	*Sing.*		*Pl.*
1.	canwyf	canom	1.	canwn	canem
2.	cenych	canoch	2.	canit	canech
3.	cano	canont	3.	canai	canent
	Impers. caner			*Impers.* cenid	

Imperative Mood

	Sing.	*Pl.*
1.	_____	canwn
2.	cân	cenwch
3.	caned	canent

Verb-noun: canu   *Verbal adjectives:* canadwy, canedig

When the following terminations: *-i, -wch, -ir, -id, -ais(t), -ych,* are added to a stem containing *a,* this *a* becomes *e* (by the change called *affection,* see Appendix B (i)), e.g. *tal-, teli; car-, cerwch; rhann-. rhennid; tafl-, teflir; can-, cenais(t); gwasg-, gwesgych.*

In the dialects this rule is generally disregarded (e.g., *tali, canwch, canais, talir*). This disregard is spreading to the literary language, as seen in the 1975 translation of the New Testament, e.g., 'Safwch yn gadarn . . . Daliwch ati i weddîo. Cyfrannwch at reidiau'r saint . . .' (Rom. xii. 12-13); 'Os ydych yn fy ngharu i, fe gadwch fy ngorchymynion i'. (John xiv. 15).

Note that *aw* and *ha* of the stem are regularly changed to *ew* and *he* before the terminations mentioned, e.g., *gwrandaw-, gwrandewi; gadaw-, gadéwch; parha-, parhéir; addaw-, addewais(t); glanha-, glanheais(t).* Good speakers observe the rule in these last cases.

In the impersonal form pluperfect both *canasid* and *canesid* are written.

§ 125. *Indicative present, 3 singular.* In many verbs the 3. sing. pres. indic. is the same in form as the stem of the verb: e.g., *câr (caraf); cred (credaf); gwêl (gwelaf); rhed (rhedaf); cwymp (cwympaf); gwad (gwadaf).*

In many other verbs there are vowel changes in the 3 sing. pres. viz.: (i) (a) the changes called *affection* (Appendix B i):

a becomes ai

1 *sing.*	3 *sing.*	1 *sing.*	3 *sing.*
paraf	pair 'causes'	caffaf (caf)	*caiff 'will have'
safaf	saif 'stands'	dyrchafaf	dyrchaif 'raises'
			*future in meaning

a becomes ei

1 *sing.*	3 *sing.*	1 *sing.*	3 *sing.*
taflaf	teifl 'throws'	ymaflaf	ymeifl 'grasps'
daliaf	deil 'holds'	cadwaf	ceidw 'keeps'
galwaf	geilw 'calls'	llanwaf	lleinw 'fills'
archaf	eirch 'commands'	gallaf	geill 'can'

(By now *gall* has largely replaced *geill*)

a becomes y (clear sound)

1 *sing.*	3 *sing.*
gwasgaraf	gwesgyr 'scatters' (*also* gwasgara)
bwytâf	bwyty
parhaf	pery 'lasts' (with two changes)

ae becomes ai

1 *sing.*	3 *sing.*
cyrhaeddaf	cyrraidd 'reaches'

(*cyrraidd*, formerly used in poetry, is now obsolete, having been replaced by *cyrraedd*).

e becomes y (clear sound)

1 *sing.*	3 *sing.*
atebaf	etyb 'answers' (with two changes)
gwelaf	gwŷl 'sees'

(This form also is obsolete; modern *gwêl*).

o becomes y (clear sound)

1 *sing.*	3 *sing.*	1 *sing.*	3 *sing.*
collaf	cyll 'loses'	torraf	tyr 'breaks'
rhoddaf	rhydd 'gives'	cyfodaf	cyfyd 'rises raises'
ffoaf	ffy 'flees'	cyffroaf	cyffry 'stirs'
deffroaf	deffry 'awakes'	cloaf	cly 'locks'

With **a—o** in the stem we have **e—y** in the 3 sing., and with **o—o** in the stem we have **e—y** also (cf. *gwesgyr, pery, etyb*).

1 *sing.*	3 *sing.*	1 *sing*	3 *sing.*
agoraf	egyr 'opens'	anfonaf	enfyn 'sends'
dangosaf	dengys 'shows'	arhosaf	erys 'stays'
adroddaf	edrydd 'reports'	datodaf	detyd 'undoes'
ataliaf	etyl 'prevents'	gosodaf	gesyd 'puts'
ymosodaf	ymesyd 'attacks'		

aw becomes au

1 *sing.*	3 *sing.*
tawaf	tau 'is silent'

(*tau* is used now in poetry only).

(b) In the following list there is no vowel change in the 3 sing.:
talaf, tâl; gadaf, gad; tarddaf, tardd; chwarddaf, chwardd; malaf,
mâl; dihangaf, dianc; dialaf, dial; barnaf, barn; rhannaf, rhan;
gwadaf, gwad; canaf, cân; chwalaf, chwâl; lladdaf, lladd; gwanaf,
gwân; gwasgaf, gwasg; casglaf, casgl; crafaf, craf; naddaf, nadd;
brathaf, brath; claddaf, cladd; cynhaliaf, cynnal; darparaf, darpar;
deallaf, deall; gwatwaraf, gwatwar; sathraf, sathr; gallaf, gall (*also*
geill); adferaf, adfer; arbedaf, arbed; arferaf, arfer; atebaf, ateb (*but
mostly* etyb); credaf, cred; cymhellaf, cymell; cymeraf, cymer;
cyfaddefaf, cyfaddef; dychwelaf, dychwel; eisteddaf, eistedd;
goddefaf, goddef; gomeddaf, gomedd; gwelaf, gwêl; goddiweddaf,
goddiwedd; gwerthaf, gwerth; medaf, med; gorffennaf, gorffen;
medraf, medr; meddaf, medd; gwaredaf, gwared (*also formerly*
gweryd); rhedaf, rhed; ymdrechaf, ymdrech (*also* ymdrecha);
ymddiriedaf, ymddiried; ymwelaf, ymwêl.

(ii) the changes called *mutation of vowels* (Appendix B (ii)).

ei becomes ai

1 *sing.*	3 *sing.*	1 *sing.*	3 *sing.*
peidiaf	paid 'desists'	ceisiaf	cais 'seeks'
neidiaf	naid 'leaps'	meiddiaf	maidd 'dares'
treiddiaf	traidd 'penetrates'	beiddiaf	baidd 'dares'

y (obscure) becomes w

1 *sing.*	3 *sing.*	1 *sing.*	3 *sing.*
cysgaf	cwsg 'sleeps'	dygaf	dwg 'takes, brings'
llyncaf	llwnc 'swallows'	tyngaf	twng 'swears'

o becomes aw

1 *sing.*	3 *sing.*	1 *sing.*	3 *sing.*
boddaf	bawdd 'drowns'	coddaf	cawdd 'offends'
holaf	hawl 'questions'	molaf	mawl 'praises'
nofiaf	nawf 'swims'	profaf	prawf 'tests'
soddaf	sawdd 'sinks'	toddaf	tawdd 'melts'
poraf	pawr 'grazes'	toliaf	tawl 'reduces, cuts'

y (obscure) becomes y (clear)

1 *sing.*	3 *sing.*	1 *sing.*	3 *sing.*
crynaf	crŷn, cryn 'quakes'	cyrchaf	cyrch 'attacks'
dysgaf	dysg 'learns, teaches'	dilynaf	dilyn 'follows'
dyrnaf	dyrn (dyrna) 'threshes'	derbyniaf	derbyn 'receives'
esgynnaf	esgyn 'ascends'	disgynnaf	disgyn 'descends'
glynaf	glŷn 'adheres'	gwlychaf	gwlych 'wets'
gofynnaf	gofyn 'asks'	mynnaf	myn 'insists'
llyfaf	llyf 'licks'	plygaf	plyg 'folds'
prynaf	prŷn, pryn 'buys'	syflaf	syfl 'budges'
sychaf	sych 'dries'	syrthiaf	syrth 'falls'
tynnaf	tyn 'pulls'	tybiaf	tyb, tybia 'supposes'
yfaf	yf 'drinks'	chwenychaf	chwennych 'desires'

Many verbs form the 3 pres. sing. by adding -**a** to the stem; see below.

§ **126.** When a verb is formed from a noun or adjective, -*a* is added to the stem to form the 3 pres. sing.:

noun or adj.	1 *sing.*	3 *sing.*
gwên	gwenaf	gwena 'smiles'
gweddi	gweddïaf	gweddïa 'prays'
cosb	cosbaf	cosba 'punishes'
saeth	saethaf	saetha 'shoots'
gwaedd	gwaeddaf	gwaedda 'shouts'
bloedd	bloeddiaf	bloeddia 'yells'
llyw	llywiaf	llywia 'steers, governs'
gwasanaeth	gwasanaethaf	gwasanaetha 'serves'
dirmyg	dirmygaf	dirmyga 'despises'
du	duaf	dua 'blackens'
coch	cochaf	cocha 'reddens'
oer	oeraf	oera 'cools'
gwresog	gwresogaf	gwresoga 'warms, heats'
tawel	tawelaf	tawela 'calms, silences'
gwyn	gwynnaf	gwynna 'whitens'
llwyd	llwydaf	llwyda 'turns grey'
gwawd	gwawdiaf	gwawdia 'mocks'

A few exceptions appear in the list in § 125, i (b) in which the 3 sing. has the same form as the noun, e.g., *mâl, cân, deall, cred, brath.*

Verbs other than those formed from nouns and adjectives eventually acquired -*a* as a 3 pres. sing. termination, and by now there are many such which we do not associate with any noun or adjective, although some of them may have been so derived, e.g., *cerdda, rhodia, llefa, tycia, cilia, dymuna, traetha, haera, taera, preswylia, nodda, cuddia, fflamycha, tyrcha.*

Sometimes the endings are *-haf* and *-ha* instead of *-af* and *-a,* and with these endings the word is accented on the ultimate syllable, e.g.,

1 *sing.*	3 *sing.*	1 *sing.*	3 *sing.*
glanhaf	glanha 'cleans'	cryfhaf	cryfha 'strengthens'
mwynhaf	mwynha 'enjoys'	trymhaf	trymha 'makes/grows heavy'
pellhaf	pellha 'moves away'	trugarhaf	trugarha 'shows mercy'
llwfrhaf	llwfrha 'loses heart'	gwanhaf	gwanha 'weakens'
rhyddhaf	rhyddha 'frees'	cwblhaf	cwblha 'completes'
parhaf	parha 'continues'	byrhaf	byrha 'shortens'

To the same class belong some verbs in which *-h-* has been assimilated in pronunciation to a preceding consonant, and is therefore not shown in writing, e.g., *agosâf, agosâ; iachâf, iachâ; gwacâf, gwacâ; tecâf, tecâ; caniatâf, caniatâ; dwysâf, dwysâ; nacâf, nacâ.*

Exceptions: *bwytâf, bwyty* (the latter being accented on the penult); *parhaf* has either *parha* or *pery* in the 3 sing. (§ 125 (i) (a)).

In the dialects one hears *-iff* and *-ith* as terminations in the 3 pres. sing. or fut., e.g., *gweliff/gwelith* for *gwêl; crediff/credith* for *cred.* Although such forms have appeared in non-dialect writing they are not accepted as literary forms.

§ 127. *Third Person Plural.* In every tense in the 3 plural there has been a tradition to include *-nt* in the terminations (and also in pronominal prepositions, §§ 191-4), e.g., *canant, gwelent, prynasant.* This is merely a literary practice, as the final *-t* is never heard in natural speech. Nasal mutation took place in such terminations many centuries ago, so that *-nt* became *-nnh,* and the rhymes of poets from an early date shows that the change was accepted. The final *-t* was, however, restored in the 1588 Welsh Bible, and it was this translation that became the standard of literary Welsh. But poets, even to this day, have clung to the oral as well as the literary tradition.

'Bugeiliaid pan *ddaethon'* / I Fethlem dref dirion,
  Hwy *gawson'* un cyfion mewn côr' (Old carol).
'Ac â newydd ganeuon / A thanbaid enaid y *dôn'* (J.M.-J. 66).

The auxiliary pronouns (§ 74) have been, and still are, commonly used after verbs and at one time, e.g., the Welsh for 'they see' would be written *gwelant wy.* With the nasal mutation of *-nt* this became *gwelannh-wy,* which became recorded as *gwelan-nhwy.* Thus new forms of the pronoun came to be spoken and written, viz., *nhwy* and *nhw.*

§ 128. *Imperfect.* In the second person singular the termination is now *-it,* but note that *-a-* *in the penult is not affected to -e-* (§ 124). This is because the old termination was *-ut* or *-ud,* which did not cause affection. For the same reason we have *-asit* (from *-asut*) in the 2 sing. pluperf. Colloquially the 2 sing. imperf. termination is now *-et,* for *-it,* and in the pluperf. *-set*, for *-asit (caret ti, carset ti)*. The form *-et* is sometimes used in poetry:

'Oni *hoffet* fyw ar ddiliau . . .?' (Eifion Wyn, i, 37).

In the 3 plur. *oeddynt* an old ending *-ynt* is retained, but *oeddent* is often written, to conform with *-ent* in other verbs.

§ 129. *Past Tense.* (i) The usual termination of the 3 sing. past is now *-odd*, but formerly there were others, one of which, *-wys. (-ws)*, is still heard in S. Wales dialects, and another, *-es*, is still written in a few verbs, e.g., *rhoddes, rhoes, troes, torres, cloes*. The usual termination in these, however, is *-odd: rhoddodd, rhodd, trodd, torrodd, clodd.*

At the beginning of the modern period *cafas (= cafodd)* was a form regularly written and a variant of it, *cas*, is commonly heard in some S. Wales dialects.

An old termination is preserved in *cymerth (= cymerodd)* and *cant (= canodd)*. The authorhsip of poems collected in old manuscripts is shown by writing 'a'i cant' after the poet's name at the end of the poem. We still have in literature two old forms in this tense (without terminations) viz., *dug (= dygodd)* and *dywad (= dywedodd)*.

(ii) In the plural the terminations *-asom, -asoch, -asant*, are contracted to *-som, -soch, -sant* if the stem ends in *-aw-, -ew-, -al-, -el-, -oe-, -yw-*, (but not *-ywi-*): *gadawsom, trawsoch, cawsant, rhewsant, gwelsom, dychwelsant* (also *dychwelasant*), *talsant* (also *talasant*), *clywsoch* (but *llywiasoch*), *troesom, rhoesoch, cloesant*. See also the irregular verbs (§§ 140; 155—162).

(iii) In the impersonal form the endings are sometimes *-ed, -ad* instead of *-wyd: rhoed, rhodded, doded, ganed, poened;* but the ending *-wyd* also appears in these verbs (except *rhoed*): *rhoddwyd, dodwyd, ganwyd, poenwyd. Cad* formerly *cahad, caffad*, occurs rarely in poetry, but this form has very largely been superceded by *caed*.

In a few irregular verbs *-pwyd* occurs instead of *-wyd: aethpwyd, daethpwyd, gwnaethpwyd, ducpwyd;* but for these the more 'regular' forms are generally used: *aed, deuwyd, gwnaed, dygwyd* (§ 162). The forms *dywetpwyd, dywespwyd, clywespwyd* are now obsolete, but one may still hear *fe wespwyd (= fe ddywedwyd)* in S. Wales.

An old form sometimes met with in poetry is *llas (= lladdwyd)*.

§ 130. *Pluperfect.* In the plural the endings *-asem, -asech, -asent* are contracted by losing *-a-* under the same conditions as in the past tense (§ 129 (ii)).

§ 131. *Subjunctive Mood.* (i) The endings in the pres. subjunctive had an initial *-h-* at one time, and this resulted in provection when added to final *-b-, -d-, -dw-, -g-* of the stem. There are traces of this in a few

words occurring in some stereotyped or proverbial expressions such
as:

Na *ato* Duw! Duw *cato* ni! Cas gŵr ni charo'r wlad a'i *maco*. A *gatwer*
a geir wrth raid.

(*ato* from *gad* + *ho* = *gado* 'may allow'; *cato* from *catwo* from *cadw* +
ho = *cadwo* 'may keep'; *gatwer* from *catwer* = *cadwer* 'may be kept').

(ii) The second person singular subjunctive is seldom used now
except in poetical language:

'Pan *fych* mewn poen afiechyd . . .' (R.G.D. 68).
'Di, rhed—a'th dynghedu'r wyf,
Na *fethych* cyn na *fythwyf*' (T.G.J. *Caniadau* 25).
'Yno, o *delych*, unawr . . .' (T.G.J. *Caniadau* 67).

In the various editions of the Bible *-ech* appears as a variant of *-ych*:
'A phan *weddïech* . . . Ond tydi, pan *weddïech* . . .' (Mt. vi. 5, 6; but cf.
CN *pan weddïych*).
'canys pa le bynnag yr *elych* di, yr af finnau; ac ym mha le bynnag y
lletyech di, y lletyaf finnau . . . Lle y *byddych* di . . .' (Ruth i. 16, 17).

§ 132. *Imperative Mood.* (i) As there is no form for the first pers. sing.
in the imperative mood, the subjunctive mood is used to express a
wish in this person:

'I Gaer . . . Y Fflint—a *welwyf* yn fflam!' (L.G.C. FN 103).

(ii) In very many verbs the 2 sing. imperative is the same as the 3
sing. indicative, e.g., *dysg, cred, cân, gad, barn, cladd, dychwel, gwerth,
gwena, gweddïa, gwaedda, gwresoga, gwasanaetha, mynega.* The rule
therefore, is this: if the 3 sing. indic. ends in *-a*, so does the 2 sing.
imperative.

On the other hand, if the 3 sing. indic. shows the change called
affection (§ 125, i (a)), the vowels in the 2 sing. imperat. are those of
the radical, or unaffected, stem, e.g.,

3 *indic. sing.*	2 *imperat. sing.*	3 *indic. sing.*	2 *imperat. sing.*
deil	dal!	saif	saf!
pair	pâr!	ceidw	cadw!
etyb	ateb!	tyr	tor!
deffry	deffro!	dengys	dangos!
gwrendy	gwrando!	tau	taw!

If the change called *mutation* appears in the vowels of the 3 sing.
indic. we have the same change in the vowels of the 2 sing. imperat.,
e.g., *paid, cais, prawf, dysg, plyg, yf, tyn, prŷn* or *pryn, myn, dilyn, gofyn.*
The indic. *tyb* has an alternative *tybia*, but the imperat. has *tybia*
only.

(iii) The usual termination in the 3 plur. imperat. is *-ent,* but *-ant* is found in the Bible (probably by false analogy with the indic.).

For the forms and uses of verb-nouns and verbal adjectives see §§ 170—184.

CONTRACTED FORMS

§ 133. Verbs having stems ending in *-o-* or *-a-* have contracted forms, e.g., *trof* for *tro-af,* *mwynhaf* for *mwynha-af.* In words like *mwynhaf* and *parhau* the accent falls on the final syllable (§§ 126, 136).

The two verbs **trof** and **mwynhaf** are conjugated below as paradigms:

INDICATIVE MOOD

Present Tense

Sing.	Plur.	Sing.	Plur.
1. trof 'I turn'	trown	mwynhaf	mwynhawn
		'I enjoy'	
2. troi	trowch	mwynhei	mwynhewch
3. try	trônt	mwynha	mwynhânt
Impers. troir		*Impers.* mwynheir	

Imperfect Tense

1. trown	troem	mwynhawn	mwynhaem
2. troit	troech	mwynhait	mwynhaech
3. trôi	troent	mwynhâi	mwynhaent
Impers. troir		*Impers.* mwynheir	

Past Tense

1. trois	troesom	mwynheais	mwynhasom
2. troist	troesoch	mwynheaist	mwynhasoch
3. troes, trodd	troesant	mwynhaodd	mwynhasant
Impers. trowyd, troed		*Impers.* mwynhawyd	

Pluperfect Tense

Sing.	Plur.	Sing.	Plur.
1. troeswn	troesem	mwynhaswn	mwynhasem
2. troesit	troesech	mwynhasit	mwynhasech
3. troesai	troesent	mwynhasai	mwynhasent
Impers. troesid		*Impers.* mwynhasid	

SUBJUNCTIVE MOOD

Present Tense

1. trowyf	trôm	mwynhawyf	mwynhaom
2. troech	troch	mwynheych	mwynhaoch
3. tro	trônt	mwynhao	mwynhaont
Impers. troer		*Impers.* mwynhaer	

Imperfect Tense

(the same forms as in the indicative mood)

IMPERATIVE MOOD

1. ⸺	trown	⸺	mwynhawn
2. tro	trowch	mwynha	mwynhewch
3. troed	troent	mwynhaed	mwynhaent
Impers. troer		*Impers.* mwynhaer	

VERB-NOUN

troi   mwynhau

VERBAL ADJECTIVES

troedig, troadwy, tro   mwynhaol

In some of the above forms there is no contraction, and *-ha-* or *-he-* comes before the ending. In these cases *-ha-* or *-he-* forms the penultimate syllable and is regularly accented, e.g., *mwynhéais, mwynháo, mwynháer.*

§ 134. The following verbs are conjugated like *mwynhaf:* glanhaf, parhaf, cryfhaf, mawrhaf, gwanhaf, cadarnhaf, pellhaf, gwacâf *etc.* (§ 126; the verbs *bwytâf* and *parhaf*, with 3 sing. indic. irregular forms *bwyty* and *pery* respectively, are included in the above class).

In some verbs the *-a-* or *-e-* (by affection) of the stem ending combines with a following vowel to form a diphthong which is accented, e.g., *bwytéi, casáwn, neséwch, agoséir, bwytáem.*

The *-haf* class of verbs do not have verbal adjectives in *-edig* and *-adwy*, except *bwytadwy* and *bwytedig*, but adjectives ending in *-ol* or *-us* are formed from several of them, e.g., *parhaol, parhaus, cryfhaol, caniataol, boddhaol, boddhaus, nacaol, cadarnhaol, iachaol;* also *bwytéig* 'voracious' from *bwytâf.*

As stated above (§ 126), *-h-* is not written in the stem of some verbs of this class. In their verb-nouns the acute accent is used to mark the stress on the final syllable, e.g., *casáu, brasáu, tecáu, caniatáu, gwacáu, gwastatáu.*

§ 135. The following verbs are conjugated like *trof:* rhof, datrôf, cnof (cnoaf), clof (cloaf), ffoaf, deffroaf, cyffroaf, paratôf (paratoaf), crynhôf (crynhoaf), datglôf (datgloaf).

Rhof is a variant of *rhoddaf,* which is conjugated fully and regularly except that the 2 sing. imperat. is *rho* (not *rhodd),* and that in the 3 sing. indic. we have *rhydd, rhy* and *dyry (= dy + ry).* A form corresponding to the latter is *dyro (= rho),* 2 sing. imperat.

Although we have *-oaf* as ending in the 1 sing. indic. in some of the verbs in this class, the conjugation apart from this follows *trof,* e.g., *deffrown* and *deffrois* (both accented on the ultima) and *deffroesom.* The accent is regular (on the penult) in *deffry, cyffry, detry, detgly* 3 sing. indic. (§ 125, i(a)). In *paratoa* and *crynhoa, -a* is added to the stem in the 3 sing. indic. and 2 sing. imperat.

§ 136. There is contraction too when the endings *-wn, -wch* follow *-aw, -ew, -yw* in the stem-ending: gadawn (gadáw-wn), gadewch (gadéw-wch), tewch (téw-wch), clywn (clyw-wn). Contraction also occurs in the verb-noun *cau* (cae-u), but the forms are full in the conjugation of the verb: *caeaf, caei, cae, caewn, caewch, caeant* (pres. indic.), *caeent* (3 plur. imperat.), *caeer* (impers. subj. and imperat.). There is no contraction in *gweddiïr, beïd.* Through contrtaction the following verb-nouns are accented on the final syllable: *dileu* (verb *dileaf), cyfleu, dyheu* (cf. the adjectives *cyfleus, chwareus, amheus;* but contrast *beius* (two syllables) and *difeius* (three syllables)).

§ 137. Caf. (i) The present conjugation of *caf* is based on two forms of the stem, viz., *caff-* and *ca(h)-:*

Indic. pres. sing. 1 *caf,* 2 *cei,* 3 *caiff;* plur. 1 *cawn,* 2 *cewch,* 3 *cânt;* impers. *ceir (cair).*

Indic. imperf. sing. 1 *cawn,* 2 *cait,* 3 *câi;* plur. 1 *caem,* 2 *caech,* 3 *caent;* impers. *ceid (caid).*

Indic. past sing. 1 *cefais, ces,* 2 *cefaist, cest,* 3 *cafodd, cadd, cafas, cas;* plur. 1 *cawsom,* 2 *cawsoch, cawsant;* impers. *cafwyd, cad, caed.*

Pluperf. sing. 1 *cawswn,* 2 *cawsit,* 3 *cawsai;* plur. *cawsem,* 2 *cawsech,* 3 *cawsent.*

Subjunct. pres. sing. 1 *caffwyf,* 2 *ceffych,* 3 *caffo;* plur. 1 *caffom,* 2 *caffoch,* 3 *caffont;* impers. *caffer.*

Subjunct. imperf. sing. 1 *caffwn, cawn,* 2 *caffit, cait,* 3 *caffai, câi;* plur. 1 *caffem, caem,* 2 *caffech, caech,* 3 *caffent, caent;* impers. *ceffid.*

Imperative, the only forms are sing. 3 *caffed, caed;* plur. *caffent, caent;* impers. *caffer.*

On *cafas, cas, cad, caed* see § 129, (i), (iii).

Verb-noun: *cael, caffel, caffael.* There are no verbal adjectives.

(ii) The indicative of *caf* is used thus:

(a) to denote present general time: *Ni chaf fod hynny'n wir* 'I don't find that that is true'.

(b) to denote future time: *Caf y dillad yfory* 'I shall have the clothes tomorrow'.

(c) to denote the consuetudinal present or imperfect: *Fe gâi rywbeth ganddo o hyd* 'He would get something from (would be given something by) him continually'. *Cawn ni groeso yno bob amser* 'We get a welcome there always'. *Cânt hwy fynd adref pryd bynnag y mynnont* 'They are allowed to go home whenever they wish'. (§ 114, ii, iii, vi).

(d) in periphrastic constructions (see § 182, iii, iv).

Caf often means 'I am (shall be) allowed' as well as 'I (shall) have'.

§ 138. Gadawaf, gadaf.

At one time *gadawaf* 'I leave, leave behind' and *gadaf* 'I leave, let, permit' were two separate verbs, but they are now regarded as one, with the *gadawaf* forms having largely superseded those of *gadaf*. The conjugation of *gadawaf* is regular (§ 136).

Indic. pres. sing. 1 *gadawaf*, 2 *gadewi*, 3 *gedy;* plur. 1 *gadawn*, 2 *gadewch*, 3 *gadawant;* impers. *gadewir*.

Indic. imperf. sing. 1 *gadawn*, 2 *gadawit*, 3 *gadawai* etc.

Subjunctive pres. sing. 1 *gadawyf*, 2 *gadewych, gadawech*, 3 *gadawo;* plur. 1 *gadawom*, 2 *gadawoch*, 3 *gadawont*.

In the imperat. sing. 2 *gad* (from *gadaf*) is used; 3 *gadawed;* plur. 1 *gadawn*, 2 *gadewch*, 3 *gadawent.* Impers. *gadawer*.

Pluperf. *gadawswn, gadawsit* etc.

The conjugation of *gadaf* is regular, but its forms are rarely used except in the imperat. sing. and plur. 2 *gad* 'leave, leave behind, let, permit' and *gedwch* 'let, permit' (see § 207 (ii)). In some dialects *gadwch* is heard for *gedwch*. The 3 sing. subj. *gato* is preserved in *Na ato Duw!* 'God forbid!'

Ymadawaf is conjugated like *gadawaf* except that it has *(nac) ymado* and *ymâd* in the 2 imperative.

Formerly the two forms of the verb-noun *gadael* and *gadel* belonged to the verb *gadaf*, but now the three forms *gadael, gadel* and *gado* (from *gadaw*) are regarded as forms of the verb-noun of *gadawaf*. Correspondingly *ymadael, ymadel* and *ymado* are forms of the verb-noun of *ymadawaf*.

Usually *gadawaf* takes an object:

    Gadawodd ef y dref. Gadewais fy mab yno. Ni'ch gadawaf.

With *ymadawaf,* however, the object must be governed by the preposition *â, ag:*

   Ymadawodd â Chymru. Ymadewais ag ef. Nid ymedy â'i gartref.

Ymadawaf can also be used without an object governed by *â, ag:*
   'Y gogoniant a *ymadawodd* o Israel' (1 Sam. iv. 21).

§ 139. Codaf, cyfodaf. The conjugation is regular except that *cyfyd*
as well as *cwyd* occurs as the 3 sing. pres. indic. of *codaf:*

Indic. pres. sing. 1 *cyfodaf,* 2 *cyfodi,* 3 *cyfyd;* plur. *cyfodwn* etc. 1 *codaf,*
2 *codi,* 3 *cwyd, cyfyd;* plur. *codwn* etc.

Imperative, sing. 2 *cyfod, cod* (not *cwyd*), 3 *cyfoded, coded;* plur. *cyfodwn,
codwn* etc.

The forms of *codaf* are now mostly used in preference for those of
cyfodaf. Verb-noun: *cyfodi, codi.* All the form of this verb may be
transitive, e.g., *c*(yf)*odaf 'I raise, rise'; c*(yf)*odais 'I raised, rose'.*

IRREGULAR VERBS

THE VERB **BOD**

§ 140.   *Indicative Mood*

Present Tense

Sing.	Plur.
1. wyf, ydwyf	ŷm, ydym
2. wyt, ydwyt	ych, ydych
3. yw, ydyw, y mae, mae, oes	ŷnt, ydych

        Relatival form: y sydd, sydd, y sy, sy
        Impersonal form: ys, ydys
        Conjunctive forms: mai, taw

Future and Consuetudinal Present Tense

Sing.	Plur.
1. byddaf	byddwn
2. byddi	byddwch
3. bydd	byddant

      Impers. byddir

Imperfect Tense

Sing.	Plur.
1. oeddwn	oeddem
2. oeddit	oeddech
3. oedd, ydoedd	oeddynt (oeddent)

      Impers. oeddid

Consuetudinal Imperfect Tense

	Sing.	Plur.
1.	byddwn	byddem
2.	byddit	byddech
3.	byddai	byddent

Impers. byddid

Past Tense

	Sing.	Plur.
1.	bûm	buom
2.	buost	buoch
3.	bu	buant, buont

Impers. buwyd

Plueperfect Tense

	Sing.	Plur.
1.	buaswn	buasem
2.	buasit	buasech
3.	buasai	buasent

Impers. buasid

Subjunctive Mood
Present Tense

	Sing.	Plur.
1.	bwyf, byddwyf	bôm, byddom
2.	bych, byddych, -ech	boch, byddoch
3.	bo, byddo	bônt, byddont

Impers. bydder

Imperfect Tense

	Sing.	Plur.
1.	bawn, byddwn	baem, byddem
2.	bait, byddit	baech, byddech
3.	bai, byddai	baent, byddent

Impers. byddid

Imperative Mood

	Sing.	Plur.
1.	—	byddwn
2.	bydd	byddwch
3.	bydded, boed, bid	byddent

Impers. bydder

Verb-noun: bod

§ 141. *Indicative Present, Third Person Singular.*

(i) In simple affirmative sentences the form *y mae, mae* comes first in the sentence:

Y mae Ifan yn saer. *Y mae*'r ferch yma. *Mae* plant yma. *Mae* ef yn gweithio. *Mae* Mair yn y tŷ. *Y mae*'r cŵn yn cyfarth.

The word *yn* which precedes a noun or adjective in such sentences as *Y mae Ifan yn saer* or *Mae'r bwyd yn brin* is called the 'predicative *yn*', because it is related to the 'predicate', i.e. what is 'predicated' about the subject. One may say that the *yn* is predicative in a periphrastic construction such as *Mae Ifan yn gweithio,* but to differentiate between these two uses of predicative *yn,* the latter may be called the 'pre-verb-noun *yn*'. In a sentence like *Mae Mair yn y siop* the *yn* is the preposition *yn* 'in', § 213.

In the above examples the subject may be definite (*Ifan, 'r ferch, ef*), or indefinite (*plant*).

(ii) In negative sentences the form of the verb is either *yw/ydyw* or *oes* preceded by *nid:*

(a) *Nid yw/ydyw,* if the subject is definite:

Nid yw Ifan yn saer. *Nid yw*'r ferch yma. *Nid ydyw ef* yn gweithio.

(b) *Nid yw/ydyw,* if the subject is indefinite and followed by *yn* (whether predicative or pre-verb-noun):

Nid yw bwyd *yn* brin yno. *Nid ydyw* cig *yn* dda i faban. *Nid ydyw* dynion *yn* credu hynny. '*Nid yw* neb wedi golau cannwyll, *yn* ei chuddio hi â llestr' (Luke viii.16).

(c) When the meaning is 'there is (are) not' we have a verb, not a copula, and *nid oes* is used with an indefinite subject (i.e. a noun or one of the pronominalia *neb, nemor neb, dim neb, llawer, digon* etc.):

Nid oes dynion yn byw yn yr anialwch. *Nid oes plant* gan Gwen. *Nid oes nemor neb* yn yr eglwys. *Nid oes digon* o bobl yn gweithio yn y pwll. *Nid oes llawer* ohonynt yn wir feirdd.

Yr un is regarded as either definite or indefinite, and so it can be preceded by either *nid oes* or *nid yw:*

'Canys *nid oes yr un* ohonom yn byw iddo'i hun, ac *nid yw*'r *un* yn marw iddo'i hun' (Rom. xiv. 7).

Instead of *nid oes dim/neb ond* we often have *nid oes ond:*

Nid oes ond ychydig ohonynt yn canu. *Nid oes ond un* o'r blodau wedi agor.

Oes instead of *wyf* is exceptional in 'myfi nid *oes* gennych bob amser' (John xii.8).

(iii)(a) In questions introduced by the particles *a, onid,* with a definite subject, and also in direct replies, the form of the verb is *yw/ydyw:*

A ydyw Ifan yn saer? *Ydyw.* *A ydyw*'r plant yn yr árdd? *Ydynt.*
Onid yw ef yn gweithio? *Ydyw.* *Onid yw*'r ferch yma? *Nac ydyw/yw.*

Note that though *yw/ydyw* is 3 sing. even before a plural subject, the reply in that case is 3 plural. In the direct reply the affirmative form is *ydyw* (or *ydynt* in the plural) and not *yw*.

(b) When the subject is indefinite in a question introduced by *a* or *onid* the form of the verb is *oes,* and in the reply either *oes* or *nac oes:*

A oes rhywun yn y cae? *Oes.* *A oes* tamaid gennyt? *Nac oes.*
Onid oes anifeiliaid yn pori yn y cae hwn? *Nac oes.*
A oes llawer o bobl yn byw yn y pentref? *Oes.*

(c) When the subject is an indefinite noun and followed by *yn* (as in the negative sentences in ii(b)) the form of the verb is *yw/ydyw* in questions and *ydyw* (or *ydynt)* in direct replies:

A ydyw pobl yn gallu clywed o gefn y neuadd? *Ydynt.*
A ydyw golud yn well nag anrhydedd? *Nac yw/ydyw.*

When the question begins with *onid* an affirmative reply is usually expected:

Onid yw tlodi yn amlwg yn y wlad? *Ydyw.*
Onid yw lliwiau'r hydref yn hardd? *Ydynt.*

The subject may be a verb-noun:

A ydyw crogi yn atal llofruddio? *Onid yw maddau* yn well na digio? (The latter question could be put thus: 'Mae maddau yn well na digio, onid yw?')

§ 142. (i) In a sentence like *Saer yw Ifan, Saer* is the complement, *yw* is the copula and *Ifan* the subject. If the complement (a noun, pronoun or adjective) comes first in the sentence, the copula *(yw/ydyw)* comes between it and the subject:

Bachgen *yw*'r plentyn. Glas *yw*'r blodau. Athro *ydyw* Gwilym.

The subject may be implied, or it may be a pronoun:

Glas *yw.* Gwyn *ydyw* hwn. Carreg *yw hi.*

To make such sentences negative *nid* is placed before the complement:

Nid glas yw. *Nid* gwyn ydyw hwn. *Nid* carreg yw hi.

The construction is the same in questions where *pwy, pa beth, beth* etc. is the complement:

Pwy ydyw hwn? *Beth yw* ceiniog? *Pa beth yw* dy fwriad? *Pa faint ydyw* hyn? *Pa werth yw* arian iddo?

(ii) A verb-noun or an adverb or adverbial expression may come first if emphasis is desired, but the form of the copula must then be *mae/y mae:*

Cysgu y mae'r plentyn. *Yma y mae*'r llyfrau. *Heddiw mae*'r ffair.

(iii) (a) In adverbial clauses after *fel, fel ag, megis, megis ag, pryd, lle*

etc., and in questions after *pa bryd, pa le, ble, paham, sut* etc., the form
of the copula is *y mae:*

Gwnaf *fel y mae*'r llyfr yn dweud. Cymerwch ef *fel ag y mae* ef. Mae
ef yn gweithio *pryd y mae* eraill yn cysgu. Daethom at y fan *lle mae*
olion castell. *Pa bryd y mae* hi'n mynd? *Pa le mae*'r ysgol? *Paham y
mae*'r fam yn wylo? *Sut y mae'r claf?*

In the Bible and in poetry *Mae?* is sometimes written instead of *Pa le
mae?:*

'*Mae* Abel dy frawd di?' (Gen. iv.9).
'*Mae* Alaw? *Mae* Caw? *Mae* cant?' (G.O. 107).

(b) Sentences like the above are made negative by putting *nad yw (nid
yw)* to replace *y mae;* cf. § 141, (ii)):

Mae hwn mor drwm *fel nad yw*'n hawdd i mi ei godi. Mae ef yn
gweithio *pryd nad yw* eraill. Sefwch dan y pren, *lle nad (nid) yw*'r
haul yn gryf. *Paham nad yw*'r merched yn canu?

(c) *Nad oes* takes the place of *nad yw* under the same conditions as *nid
oes* is used in the examples under § 141, (ii)(c):

Paham nad oes dim arian gennyt (lit. 'Why is there no money with
you?, i.e. Why have you no money?'). *Pa fodd nad oes* neb i helpu?
'Why is there no one to help?'
'*lle nid oes* na gwyfyn na rhwd yn llygru' (Mt. vi. 20).

§ 143. (i) In a relative clause the forms *sydd, y sydd, sy, y sy,* are used
(see § 83) if the relative is in the nominative case. *Sydd* corresponds to
'who (which) is (are)', *who, which* being nominative forms, i.e. used
as subjects of clauses etc.

(a) *Sydd* is truly relative in the following examples:

Dyma'r dyn *sydd yn (sy'n)* canu. Pwy yw'r plant *sydd* yn yr ardd?
Fe gei bopeth *sy* gennyf. Tynnwch yr afal *sy'n* goch.

Also when the subject is placed first for emphasis, *sydd* comes
between it and the rest of the sentence, and thus a *mixed sentence* is
formed (§ 246):

(simple) Mae Dafydd yn y tŷ. *(mixed)* Dafydd *sydd* yn y tŷ 'It is
D. who is in the house'.
(simple) Yr wyf fi'n ysgrifennu. *(mixed)* Myfi *sy*'n ysgrifennu 'It is
I who is writing'.
Hyn sy'n deg/*Hyn sy deg* 'This is what is fair'.

(b) There is a similar construction (in so far as *sydd* is relative and
nominative) when the preposition *â/ag* follows *sydd* (see § 228(i)(d)):

'Gwyn ei fyd y gŵr ni rodia . . . ond *sydd â*'i ewyllys yng
nghyfraith yr Arglwydd' (Ps. i. 1, 2). Pwy yw'r bachgen *sydd ag*
afal yn ei law? Dyna hi! y ferch *sydd â* het wen.

(c) An extension of the above construction (b) is one in which other
prepositions follow *sydd:*

Beth *sydd arno* ei eisiau? (lit. 'What is there lacking on him?, i.e. What does he need?').

'Gwyn eu byd y rhai *sydd arnynt* newyn a syched am gyfiawnder' (Mt. v. 6). 'Gwasgar y bobl *sydd* dda *ganddynt* ryfel' (Ps. lxviii. 30). In this construction the relative is not the true subject.

(d) The construction with *sydd raid i* is exceptional:

Beth *sydd raid i* mi ei wneud? 'What must I do?'

Dyma'r amodau *sydd raid* i chwi eu derbyn 'These are the conditions that you must accept'.

The construction is normal in *Gwna yr hyn sydd raid!* or *Mae ef yn gwneud yr hyn sydd yn rhaid,* because here the relative is nominative and *raid/rhaid* is the complement (cf. *Hyn sy deg,* (i) (a) above).

(ii) *Sydd* occurs in an abnormal sentence, in which the subject comes first although it is not placed so for emphasis (§ 247):

Yr adeilad *sydd* uchel (= Mae'r adeilad yn uchel).

This is a very common construction in the Bible, but modern writers shun it, except sometimes in poetry.

'Duw *sydd* noddfa a nerth i ni' (Ps. xlvi. 1).

'. . . ei drugaredd *sydd* yn dragywydd' (Ps. c. 5).

(iii) The complement following *sydd* may, or may not, be preceded by the particle *yn/'n*. In each case there is initial lenition in the complement:

Ef *sydd* yn *ben 'He* is chief.' Hynny *sy decaf 'That* is fairest'.

§ **144.** *Negativity.* (i) Where *sydd* is used in an affirmative clause, the substitution of *nad yw* or *nid yw* for it makes the clause negative (§ 83):

Dyma un *nad yw*'n gweithio. A oes rhywun *nad ydyw*'n caru ei wlad?

'Paham y gweriwch eich arian am yr hyn *nid ydyw* fara?' (Is. lv. 2).

(ii) A simple way to make negative the affirmative examples in § 143(i)(b) is by substituting *heb* 'without' for *â/ag* after *sydd,* e.g., Pwy yw'r bachgen *sydd heb* afal yn ei law? Dyna hi! y ferch *sydd heb* het wen.

As for those in § 143 (i) (c), they can be made negative in two ways:

(a) taking that 'y bobl *sydd dda* ganddynt ryfel' means the same as the more regular 'y bobl *y mae'n dda* ganddynt ryfel' (§ 81), and giving this mental paraphrase a regular negative form, viz., 'y bobl *nad ydyw*'n dda ganddynt ryfel'.

(b) substituting *nad oes* for *sydd* in a clause such as 'y rhai *sydd* arnynt newyn . . .', so that it will read in its negative form 'y rhai *nad oes* arnynt newyn . . .'. Today it would be natural to write 'y rhai *nad oes* arnynt *ddim* newyn'. Similarly the negative form of 'Beth *sydd* arno ei eisiau?' would be 'Beth *nad oes* arno *mo'i* (= *ddim o'i*) eisiau?' This negative clause corresponds to the negative sentences in § 141 (ii) (c).

§ 145. (i) In a relative clause where the relative element is in either the genitive or adverbial case, or governed by a preposition, (§§ 79-82), the normal form used is *y mae*.

Dyna'r dyn *y mae*'r tŷ yn *ei* feddiant 'That's the man in *whose* possession the house is'. Hwn yw'r llwyn *lle mae* mwyar 'This is the bush *where* there are blackberries'. Beth yw enw'r wlad *y mae* ef yn byw *ynddi* 'What is the name of the country *in which* he lives'. (cf. § 142 (iii) (a)).

(ii) If the relative clause in the above pattern is negative, the verbal forms used are:

(a) *nad yw/ydyw* with a definite subject:
Dyna'r dyn *nad yw*'r tŷ yn *ei* feddiant. Beth yw enw'r wlad *nad ydyw ef* yn byw *ynddi?*

(b) *nad (nid) oes* with an indefinite subject:
Hwn yw'r llwyn *lle nad oes mwyar*. A oes byd *nad oes poen ynddo?*

§ 146. In a conditional clause where *os* precedes the verbal form the same rules apply as in negative clauses with *nid* (§ 141 (ii)):

(i) with definite subject:
Os yw ef yn credu hynny . . . *Os ydyw*'ch brawd yno . . .

(ii) with indefinite subject followed by *yn:*
Os yw plentyn yn gallu gwneud hyn . . . *Os yw pobl yn* meddwl.
Os ydyw bachgen yn gryf . . .

(iii) with an indefinite subject when the verbal form means 'there is (are)' or 'exists':
Os oes dynion yn byw yn yr anialwch . . . *Os oes plant* gan Gwen . . .
Os oes digon o bobl yn gweithio . . . *Os oes rhywun yn* dyfod . . .

NOTE: When the complement comes first, for emphasis, the same rules apply as in § 142:
Os bachgen yw'r plentyn . . . *Os glas yw*'r blodau . . . *Os athro ydyw* Gwilym . . . *Os hwn yw*'r gorau . . . (the emphasised complement being a noun, adj. or pronoun).
Os cysgu y mae'r plentyn . . . *Os yn yr ardd y mae*'r afalau . . . (the emphasised complement being a verb-noun or adverb).

§ 147. In an adverbial clause the subjunctive mood very often follows *pan* 'when', e.g., *pan fo,* but if it is desired to use the indicative the form is *pan yw:*
'*Pan yw* fy nhad a'm mam yn fy ngwrthod' (Ps. xxvii. 10).

§ 148. *Summary of the rules concerning the use of* YW, MAE, OES, SYDD:
Y Mae/Mae.

(i) In affirmative sentences, at the beginning of the sentence. § 141 (i).

(ii) In mixed sentences, after a verb-noun or adverbial expression placed first in the sentence for emphasis. § 142 (ii).

(iii) In an adverbial clause after fel, megis, pryd etc. § 142 (iii) (a).

(iv) In a relative clause where the relative is genitive, or governed by a preposition, or in the adverbial case. (§ 145 (i).

§ 149. *Yw/Ydyw.*

(i) In negative sentences after *nid,* (a) with a definite subject, (b) with an indefinite subject and predicative *yn* following. § 141 (ii) (a) (b).

(ii) In questions after *a, onid,* when the subject is definite, or with an indefinite subject followed by *yn.* § 141 (iii) (a) (c).

(iii) After the complement placed first. § 142 (i).

(iv) In a negative adverbial clause after *fel nad, pryd nad* etc. § 142 (iii) (b).

(v) In a negative relative clause after *nad, nid.* § 144 (i) (ii).

(vi) In a conditional clause after *os* with a definite subject, or with an indefinite subject followed by *yn.* § 146 (i) (ii) and *Note.*

(vii) After *pan,* if indicative is used instead of subjunctive. § 147.

§ 150. *Oes.*

(i) In simple negative sentences either with an indefinite subject not followed by predicative *yn,* or with an indefinite subject (a noun or pronominal, *neb, dim neb* etc.) followed by predicative *yn.* § 141 (ii) (c).

(ii) In questions after *a, onid* with indefinite subject as in (i) above. § 141 (iii) (b).

(iii) In negative adverbial clauses after *fel nad, pryd nad, lle nad* etc. §§ 141 (ii) (c), 142 (iii) (c).

(iv) In a negative relative clause with an indefinite subject. § 145 (ii) (b).

(v) In a conditional clause after *os.* § 146 (iii) and *Note.*

§ 151. *Sydd.*

(i) In a relative clause with the relative in the nominative case. § 143 (i) (a), (b), § 83.

(ii) In a relative clause with the relative governed by a preposition. § 143 (i) (b), (c).

(iii) In a relative clause before *raid i.* § 143 (i) (d).

(iv) In an abnormal sentence. § 143 (ii).

Other Forms of the verb BOD, *and the Particle* Y, YR

§ 152. (i) In the present and imperfect indicative **yr** precedes the verbal form *in every case where* **y mae** *is used* in the third singular:

Yr wyf fi (y mae ef) yn saer. Cysgu *yr oeddwn i.* Yn yr ardd *y maent hwy.* Onid yno *yr ydych* yn gweithio? Gwnaeth fel *yr oedd* ei dad wedi gorchymyn. *Yr oedd* hi'n gweithio pryd *yr oedd* eraill yn gorffwys. Pa le'*r wyt* ti? Sut *yr ydych* chwi? Ef oedd y bachgen *yr oedd* ganddo gi. Nid aeth ef at y tai *yr oedd* eu drysau'n gaeëdig. (Note that *yr* should not have been included in 'Canys pa un bynnag *yr* ydym . . .' (Rom. xiv. 8)).

(ii) In the other tenses, with forms having an initial **b-**,

(a) the verb form, not preceded by *y*, comes first in a simple sentence: *Bu* Ifan yn saer. *Byddaf* yn y dref yfory. *Buasai* hi yno o'm blaen i. *Byddai* Dafydd gartref bob amser.

(The particle *fe, mi* may be put before the verb, causing soft mut., *fe fu, mi fydd*. These have no significance of meaning, and are mainly used for the sake of euphony or of naturalness in speaking.)

(b) In every other case where we may have **y mae** in the 3 sing. present, we have **y** preceding forms with initial **b-**:

Gweithio y byddaf fi (y mae ef). Yn yr ardd *y buont hwy. Cerdded y byddai hi bob amser. Pa le y byddwch chwi?* Hwn yw'r bwthyn *y bu ei dad yn byw ynddo.* Dyna *sut y byddai hi'n* siarad. *'Lle y bo'*r dolur y bydd y llaw'.

Lle often stands for *lle y*; **§ 72**; *lle bo* = *lle y bo*.

The Relative Pronoun A *with forms of* BOD

§ 153. Because *sydd* is a relatival form itself, it can not be preceded by the rel. pronoun *a*. Every other form, of whatever tense, may be preceded by the rel. *a:*

Pwy yw'r plant *a fydd* yn mynd adref? Mair yw'r ferch *a oedd* bob amser yn ennill. Darllenais hynny mewn llyfr *a fu* gennyf rywdro. Ni wyddwn enw'r gŵr *a fyddai* gyda mi. Rhowch i'r plentyn ryw degan *a fo* wrth law. Rhoddid bwyd i'r rhai *a fyddai* yn newynog. Rhoddir y wobr i'r rhedwr *a fydd gyntaf (= a fydd yn gyntaf;* for the omission of *yn* cf. **§ 143** (iii)).

By an old custom, the rel. *a* can be omitted in the above examples: Pwy yw'r plant *fydd* . . . Mair yw'r ferch *oedd* . . . etc.

In negative clauses, of course, we have *na(d)* or *ni(d)*, but mostly *na(d)* now: *y plant na fyddant* . . .; y ferch *nad oedd* . . . **§§ 76, 77**.

§ 154. Whenever we have *yw/ydyw* in the present tense the corresponding forms in all other tenses are *fydd, fyddai, oedd, fu, fuasai, fo/fyddo*. Since *yw/ydyw* is *not* a form used in a relative clause, it can not be preceded by the rel. pronoun *a*. It can be preceded by the complement, § 142 (i).

Compounds of BOD

§ 155. The compound verbs commonly used are:

(a) *canfyddaf* (vb-n. *canfod* 'perceive'); *cyfarfyddaf* (vb-n. *cyfarfod* 'meet'); *darfyddaf* (vb-n. *darfod* 'end, happen'); *gorfyddaf* (vb-n. *gorfod* 'conquer' etc.);

(b) *gwn* (vb-n. *gwybod* 'know'); *adwaen* (vb-n. *adnabod* 'be acquainted, recognize'; *cydnabyddaf* (vb-n. *cydnabod* 'acknowledge').

The verbs in (a) above follow the conjugation of *bod* (with -*b*- softened to -*f*-) except in the present and imperfect indicative. Those in (b) above also follow *bod* in the same tenses, except that -*b*- is not changed.

Conjugation of verbs in (a)

Pres. Indic. *canfyddaf, canfyddi, cenfydd; canfyddwn, canfyddwch, canfyddant;* impers. *canfyddir.*

Imperf. *canfyddwn, canfyddit, -ai; -em, -ech, -ent;* impers. *canfyddid.*

Past *canfûm, canfuost, canfu; canfuom, canfuoch, canfuant;* impers. *canfuwyd.*

Pluperf. *canfuaswn, canfuasit, -asai,* etc.

Pres. Subj. *canfyddwyf, canfyddych, canfyddo; canfyddom, -och, -ont;* impers. *canfydder.*

Imperf. Subj. = Imperf. Indic.

Imperat. 2 sing. *cenfydd,* 3 sing. *canfydded;* 1 pl. *canfyddwn,* 2 pl. *canfyddwch,* 3 pl. *canfyddent;* impers. *canfydder.*

Darganfyddaf is conjugated like *canfyddaf* (vb-n. *darganfod* 'discover').

Similarly, *darfyddaf;* 3 pres. sing. *derfydd; cyfarfyddaf:* 3 pres. sing. *cyferfydd; gorfyddaf:* 3 pres. sing. *gorfydd.*

§ 156. The verb *darfod* has two meanings: (a) 'die, end, finish'; (b) 'happen'. The second meaning (b) is confined to the 3 pers. (§ 169).

(a) Oni rowch ddŵr i'r planhigion fe *ddarfyddant* 'If you do not give the flowers water they will die'. 'Byth *ni dderfydd* canmol Duw yn nhŷ fy nhad' ('The praise of God in my father's house will never *end'*). Mae'r poenau wedi mynd; *darfuant* yn llwyr 'The pains have gone; they have completely vanished'.

The verb in the 3 pers. can be followed by the preposition *am:*

Felly y *darfu am* yr anifail 'So the animal perished'. Fe *dderfydd amdanoch* os ewch allan i'r storm 'You will perish if you go out into the storm'.

(b) Pa beth a *ddarfu* i'w wraig? 'What happened to his wife?' Os *derfydd* i chwi gael gwybod, anfonwch lythyr 'If it will happen that

you will get to know, send a letter'. Ni *ddarfu* imi sylwi pwy oedd
yno 'I did not happen to notice who was there'.

A sentence like *Darfu i'r ceffyl redeg* can mean 'It happened that the
horse ran' or simply 'The horse ran'. Thus *darfu* has come to be used
as a kind of auxiliary verb, e.g., *Pa bryd y darfu iddo fynd?* (= *Pa bryd yr
aeth ef?*) 'When did he go?' This construction has become corrupt
colloqually; see § 169 (iii). *Daru* is generally heard in N. Wales for
darfu.

§ 157. (i) The verb *cyfarfod* is used in two constructions: (a) as an
intransitive verb followed by the preposition *â/ag* (the older construction) e.g., *Cyfarfyddaf â hwy* 'I shall meet them'; *Cyfarfûm ag ef* 'I
met him'.

(b) as a transitive verb taking an object: *Euthum i gyfarfod fy chwaer* 'I
went to meet my sister'; *Daeth hi i'm cyfarfod* 'She came to meet me'.

(ii) *Gorfod* can be an intransitive verb having two meanings:

(a) when followed by the preposition *ar* governing a noun or an
implied pronoun, it means 'conquer', e.g., *gorfu ef ar y gelyn,* lit. 'he
conquered over the enemy'; *gorfyddwn ni arnynt oll* 'we shall conquer
over all of them'; also not followed by *ar: Pa ochr a orfu?* 'Which side
won?'

(b) when the construction consists of *gorfod* + prep. *i* or *ar* + verb-
noun it means 'be obliged, be compelled', e.g., *Gorfu i Owen redeg*
'Owen was obliged to run'; *Gorfydd ar y bobl newynu* 'The people will
be compelled to starve'. The preposition may have a pronominal
form instead of governing a noun, e.g., *gorfu iddo redeg* 'he was obliged
to run'; *gorfydd arnynt newynu* 'they will be compelled to starve'.
(Gorfod i is more commonly used now than *gorfod ar.)*

Gorfod is used impersonally in 'felly y *gorfydd bod'* (Mt. xxvi. 54,
'thus it must be').

The verb-noun is sometimes used instead of a personal form, e.g.,
Gorfod iddo siarad yn y cyfarfod ddoe 'He had to speak at the meeting
yesterday'.

In periphrastic sentences *gorfod* ('be obliged') can take a verb-noun
as object:

Yr ydym yn gorfod mynd. Mae'r plant yn gorfod dysgu amryw bynciau.

§ 158. *Hanfod.* This verb, meaning 'be derived from, be descended
from, exist', is rarely used today, except as a verb-noun, *hanfod,* and in
the 2 sing. imperative, *henffych.* The term *henffych well* originally
meant 'mayest thou be better, mayest thou prosper', but it came to
be used loosely as a greeting, often shortened to *henffych!,* like E.
'hail!'

A spurious form *hanu* has arisen with a 3 sing. imperf. *hanai* for
hanoedd 'was derived'. A probable colloquial form of the latter would

be *hanodd,* and as *-odd* was taken to be the usual ending of the 3 sing. past some writers adopted it in that tense.

The adjective *hanfodol* 'essential' was formed from the verb-noun, and from the stem of the verb, *han-,* were formed the noun *haniaeth* 'abstraction' and the adjective *haniaethol* 'abstract'.

§ 159. *Gwybod*

Indicative Mood

Present Tense		Future Tense	
Sing.	*Plur.*	*Sing.*	*Plur.*
1. gwn	gwyddom	gwybyddaf	gwybyddwn
2. gwyddost	gwyddoch	gwybyddi	gwybyddwch
3. gŵyr	gwyddant	gwybydd	gwybyddant
Impers. gwŷs, gwyddys		*Impers.* gwybyddir	

Imperfect Tense		Past Tense	
Sing.	*Plur.*	*Sing.*	*Plur.*
1. gwyddwn	gwyddem	gwybûm	gwybuom
2. gwyddit	gwyddech	gwybuost	gwybuoch
3. gwyddai	gwyddent	gwybu	gwybuont, -ant
(gwyddiad)			
Impers. gwyddid		*Impers.* gwybuwyd	

Pluperfect Tense
Sing. 1. gwybuaswn, 2. gwybuasit, 3. gwybu, *etc. (regular)*

Subjunctive Mood
Present Tense

Sing.	*Plur.*
1. gwypwyf, gwybyddwyf	gwypom, gwybyddom
2. gwypych, gwybyddych	gwypoch, gwybyddoch
3. gwypo, gwybyddo	gwypont, gwybyddont
Impers. gwyper, gwybydder	

Imperfect Tense

Sing.	*Plur.*
1. gwypwn, gwybyddwn	gwypem, gwybyddem
2. gwypit, gwybyddit	gwypech, gwybyddech
3. gwypai, gwybyddai	gwypent, gwybyddent
Impers. gwypid, gwybyddid	

Imperative Mood

1. ——	gwybyddwn
2. gwybydd	gwybyddwch
3. gwyped, gwybydded	gwypent, gwybyddent
Impers. gwybydder	

Verb-noun gwybod   *Verbal adjectives* gwybyddus, gwybodus

§ 160. *Adnabod*

Indicative Mood
Present Tense

Sing.	Plur.
1. adwaen, adwen	adwaenom, adwaenwn
2. adwaenost, adweini	adwaenoch, adwaenwch
3. adwaen, adwen, edwyn	adwaenant

Impers. adwaenir, adweinir

Future Tense

Sing. 1. adnabyddaf, 2. adnabyddi, 3. adnebydd; *plur.* adnabyddwn, *etc.*

Imperfect Tense

Sing. 1. adwaenwn, 2. adwaenit, 3. adwaenai, *etc.*

Impers. adwaenid, adweinid

Past Tense

Sing.	Plur.
1. adnabûm	adnabuom
2. adnabuost	adnabuoch
3. adnabu	adnabuont, adnabuant

Impers. adnabuwyd

Pluperfect Tense

Sing. 1. adnabuaswn, 2. adnabuasit, 3. adnabuasai, *etc.*

Subjunctive Mood
Present Tense

Sing.	Plur.
1. adnapwyf, adnabyddwyf	adnapom, adnabyddom
2. adnepych, adnabyddych	adnapoch, adnabyddoch
3. adnapo, adnabyddo	adnapont, adnabyddont

Impers. adnaper, adnabydder

Imperfect Tense

Sing. 1. adnapwn, adnabyddwn, 2. adnapit, adnabyddit, 3. adnapai,
adnabyddai

Plur. 1. adnapem, adnabyddem, *etc.*

Impers. adnapid, adnabyddid

Also regular like adwaenwn, adwaenit, adwaenai, *etc. (indicative)*

The forms with -*nap*-, -*nep*- are today considered to be obsolete.

Imperative Mood

Sing.	Plur.
1. ——	adnabyddwn
2. adnebydd	adnabyddwch
3. adnabydded	adnabyddent

Impers. adnabydder

Verb-noun adnabod　　　*Verbal adjectives* adnabyddus, adnabyddedig

§ 161 (i) *Cydnabod*

Pres. Indic. and Future, sing. 1. cydnabyddaf, 2. cydnabyddi, 3. cydnebydd; *plur.* cydnabyddwn, *etc.*

Imperfect cydnabyddwn cydnabyddit, cydnabyddai, *etc.*

Past cydnabûm, cydnabuost, cydnabu, *etc.*

Pluperfect cydnabuaswn, cydnabuasit, cydnabuasai, *etc.*

Pres. Subjunctive cydnabyddwyf, cydnabyddych, cydnabyddo *etc.*
Impers. cydnabydder.

Imperf. Subjunct. = *Imperf. Indic.*

Imperative Mood: sing. 2. cydnebydd, 3. cydnabydded; *plur.* cydnabyddwn, *etc. Impers.* cydnabydder. *Verb-noun* cydnabod.

Verbal adjectives cydnabyddus, cydnabyddedig.

(ii) *Piau,* only forms: *Pres. indic.* 3 *sing.* piau; *Imperf. indic.* pioedd. See § 84.

OTHER IRREGULAR VERBS

§ 162. (i) *Af* ('I go') and *Gwnaf* ('I do, make'). These two verbs are conjugated in the same way except in the 2 sing. imperative and in the formation of the verb-noun. *Af* has no related verbal adjectives.

Indicative Mood

	Present Tense		Imperfect Tense	
Sing.		Plur.	Sing.	Plur.
1. af		awn	awn	aem
2. ei		ewch	ait	aech
3. â		ânt	âi	aent
	Impers. eir		*Impers.* eid	

In the same way gwnaf, gwnei, gwna, *etc.*

	Past Tense		Pluperfect Tense	
1. euthum	aethom	aethwn, elswn	aethem, elsem
2. aethost	aethoch	aethit, elsit	aethech, elsech
3. aeth	aethant	aethai, elsai	aethent, elsent
	Impers. aethpwyd, aed		*Impers.* aethid, elsid

Subjunctive Mood

	Present Tense		Imperfect Tense	
1. elwyf	elom	elwn	elem
2. elych	eloch	elit	elech
3. êl, elo	elont	elai	elent
	Impers. eler		*Impers.* elid

Imperative Mood

(af)		(gwnaf)	
1. ——	awn	1. ——	gwnawn
2. dos	ewch	2. gwna	gwnewch
3. aed, eled	aent, elent	3. gwnaed,	gwnaent,
			gwneled gwnelent

Impers. aer, eler   *Impers.* gwnaer, gwneler
Verb-noun myned, mynd   *Verb-noun* gwneuthur, gwneud
Verbal adjs. gwneuthuredig, gwneuthuradwy

In S. Wales dialects for the 2 sing. imperative one hears *cer, cere, cera,* instead of *dos,* and in all dialects in the plur. one hears *cerwch* for *ewch.* These and other dialect forms are sometimes used in recent writing, e.g., *es, eis* (for *euthum*), *gwnest* (for *gwnaethost*), *awd* (for *aethpwyd, aed*), *eith* and *aiff* (for *â*).

(ii) *Deuaf, Dof* ('I come'). There are many points of similarity in the conjugations of *deuaf (dof)* and *af,* but *deuaf* has more abbreviated forms.

Indicative Mood

Present Tense		Imperfect Tense	
1. deuaf, dof	deuwn, down	deuwn, down	deuem, doem
2. deui, doi	deuwch, dewch, dowch	deuit, doit	deuech, doech
3. daw	deuant, dônt	deuai, dôi	deuent, doent

Impers. deuir, doir   *Impers.* deuid, doid

Past Tense		Pluperfect Tense	
1. deuthum	daethom	daethwn	daethem
2. daethost	daethoch	daethit	daethech
3. daeth, doeth	daethant, daethont	daethai	daethent

Impers. daethpwyd, deuwyd, doed   *Impers.* daethid

Subjunctive Mood
Present Tense
Sing. 1. delwyf, 2. delych, *etc.* (like *elwyf* (i) above)

Imperfect Tense
Sing. 1. delwn, 2. delit, *etc.* (like *elwn* (i) above)

Imperative Mood

Sing.	Plur.
1. ——	deuwn, down
2. tyred, tyrd	deuwch, dowch, dewch
3. deued, doed, deled	deuent, doent, delent

Impers. deuer, doer, deler.
Verb-noun dyfod, dod, dywad (dŵad)   *Verbal adjective* dyfodol.

In the 2 sing. imperat. the forms *dabre, debre, degle* were formerly used. The usual form in S. Wales dialects is *dere,* which is also found in poetry. Other dialect forms are found in recent literatuire, e.g., *des, dois* (for *deuthum)* and *doist* (for *daethost).*

DEFECTIVE VERBS

§ 163. *Dichon.* The only form used is that of the 3 sing. pres. indic. It can mean either (a) 'can, is able':

'Ni *ddichon* pren da ddwyn ffrwythau drwg' (Mt. vii. 18), or

(b) 'it may be, perhaps':

Dichon fod gwir yn hynny 'It may be that there is truth in that'.
Dichon y daw glaw 'Perhaps rain will come'.

§ 164. *Dylwn* ('I ought'). The only surviving forms of this verb are those of the imperfect and pluperfect: *dylwn, dylit, dylai,* etc. and *dylaswn, dylasit, dylasai* respectively, and the two impers. forms *dylid* and *dylasid.* Though *dylwn* is in the imperfect tense as regards form, it is in the 'general present' in meaning, like English 'ought':

Fe *ddylai* hi wybod hynny, a hithau yn yr ysgol 'She ought to know that, being in school'.

Dylaswn is used in a pluperfect sense in the Bible, e.g.,

'myfi a ddylaswn gael fy nghanmol' (2 Cor. xii. 11), *'I ought to have* been commended'.

The difference between *dylwn* and *dyl(a)swn* has been largely lost in ordinary speech and in recent writing, with *dyl(a)swn* etc. taking the place of *dylwn* etc. In N. Wales -*i*- is heard in *dylia (= dylai), dyliech,* etc.

§ 165. *Ebr, ebe, eb.* These are the only forms of this verb. Like 'quoth' in English they are used in quoting spoken words. They always come immediately before the subject (noun or pronoun) regardless of its number or person:

'"Yn ara", *eb* yr angel, "un cwestiwn ar unwaith" . . . "Nid rhyfedd yn wir", *ebr* fi'. (B.Cw. 10). ("Slowly", quoth the angel, "one question at a time" . . . "No wonder indeed", quoth I).

'Bydd yn ofalus", *ebe*'r fam wrth y plentyn.

In N. Wales *ebra* is sometimes heard for *ebr.*

§ 166. *Meddaf* ('I say'). This verb has two tenses only, the present and the imperfect:

Pres. *meddaf, meddi, medd,* etc.; imperf. *meddwn, meddit, meddai,* etc.

The pres. is used to quote an expression of opinion, like E. 'say'.

The imperf. is used like *ebe, ebr* in narrative, and *medd* is often used in this way for *meddai:*

'Dos adref', *meddwn* i wrtho. 'Ni allaf fynd', *medd(ai)* yntau.

Pwy, *meddwch chwi,* yw beirdd mwyaf y ganrif?
Meddaf etc. can follow an indirect statement or a paraphrase:
    Ni allai fynd adref, *meddai* ef. Nid oes gobaith inni ennill, *meddant*
hwy. Dyma'r lle gwlypaf yn y wlad, *meddir.* (See § 114 (ii)).
The initial consonant of *meddaf* is never mutated.

§ 167. *Geni.* The only forms are the verb-noun *geni* 'be born' and the
following impersonal forms:
Indic. pres. *genir;* imperf. *genid;* past *ganwyd, ganed;* pluperf. *ganesid,*
ganasid; subjunctive pres. *ganer;* imperf. *genid;* verbal adj. *ganedig.*
    Gobeithiai ef mai merch a *enid* iddynt. *Genir* llawer o blant yno i
deuluoedd tlawd. Dyna'r tŷ y'm *ganed* i ynddo. Nid oedd y teulu
wedi mynd o Gymru pan *anwyd* y plentyn hynaf. Yn yr un tŷ y
ganesid ei fam.

§ 168. *Hwde, hwdiwch* ('take!'). *Moes, moeswch,* ('give!'). These
verbs are imperative only, 2 sing. and plur. In S. Wales there are
variants, *hwre* and *hwr(i)wch:*
    Hwre/hwde lymaid o laeth! *Hwdiwch/hwriwch,* dyma geiniog yr un i
chwi! *'Moes* i mi dair torth yn echwyn' (Luke xi. 5). *'Moeswch* i'r
Arglwydd, chwi feibion cedyrn' (Ps. xxix. 1). 'Melys, *moes* mwy!'

§ 169. VERBS IN THE 3 SINGULAR. These are followed by a preposition.
    (i) *Darfu i* (see under *darfod,* § 156):
Darfu iddo fynd allan 'He went out'. *A ddarfu i'r dyn siarad?* 'Did the
man speak?'
(The grammatical subject in each of the above sentences is a verb-
noun—*fynd* and *siariad*—but the doer is denoted by the personal form
of the preposition, *iddo,* and the noun, *dyn*).
    In addition to the past *darfu* the 3 sing. of the other tenses, except
the pres., is used in the same construction: future *derfydd,* imperf.
darfyddai, pluperf. *darfuasai.*
The verb-noun *darfod* can be similarly used instead of the verb:
    Cyn *darfod i'r siaradwr* godi, gwaeddodd rhywun o gefn y neuadd
'Before the speaker arose, someone shouted from the back of the
hall'. Meddai'r barnwr wrtho, 'Gan *ddarfod iti* gyffesu, ysgafn fydd
dy gosb'; 'The judge said to him, "Since thou hast confessed, thy
punishment shall be light"'.
    (ii) *Gorfu i/ar* ('it was necessary for'):
Gorfu i'r lleidr ffoi 'The thief had to flee'. Seee § 157 (ii). Other tenses;
gorfydd (future), *gorfyddai* (imperfect), *gorfuasai* (pluperfect).
    (iii) *Digwydd, damweinia (damwain) i* 'it happens to':
    Os *digwydd ichwi* ei weld, dywedwch wrtho fod y llyfr yn barod 'If

you happen to see him, tell him the book is ready'. *Digwyddodd i*'r bachgen syrthio 'It happened that the boy fell'. "Yr un peth a *ddamwain* i bawb" (Eccles. ix. 2).

The construction with these verbs has become corrupt by omitting the following prep. *i* and forms of persons other than the 3 sing., e.g., *Digwyddais fynd* instead of *Digwyddodd i mi fynd;* (Cf. E. 'I hapened to go' for 'It happened that I went'); *Darfu John gychwyn* for *Darfu i John gychwyn.*

(iv) *Tycia i* ('it avails'):

Ni thycia i chwi siarad 'it does not avail you to speak/it will not . . .' *Ni thyciodd i* neb ddilyn y ceffyl 'it availed no one to follow the horse'.

Other forms: *tyciai, tyciodd, tyciasai* and the verb-noun *tycio.*

If no person is mentioned, *i* is omitted after the verb:

'Ni *thycia* trysorau drygioni' (Prov. x. 2) 'Treasures of wickedness profit nothing".

(v) *Gwedda i* ('it becomes'): The only forms are *gwedda, gweddai* and the verb-noun *gweddu:*

Y mae'r wisg hon yn *gweddu i* ti. Ni *wedda* dawnsio i ferch fel hi. 'fel y *gweddai* i sancteiddrwydd' (Tit. ii. 3).

(vi) Formerly *methu gan* ('fails') and *synnu ar* ('be astonished') were used with a noun or a personal form of the prep. denoting the subject: '*Metha gan* y bobl ddianc' (Am. ii. 14). 'a *synnodd arno* wrth weled yr arwyddion' (Acts viii. 13) "and he wondered, beholding the miracles".

Today *methaf* or *methaf â* and *synnaf* are used like ordinary regular verbs:

Os yw ef yn credu hynny, y mae'n *methu.* 'Ni *fethodd* gweddi daer *â* chyrraedd hyd y nef' (Pantycelyn, CAN 80). '. . . ac a aeth allan yn eu gŵydd hwynt oll; hyd oni *synnodd pawb'* (Mk. ii. 12) ("... and went forth before them all; insomuch that they were all amazed"). Yr wyf yn *synnu ato (wrtho).*

THE VERB-NOUN

§ 170. (i) The verb-noun may consist of the stem of the verb without a suffix, or it may contain the stem (or sometimes some other form) together with a suffix.

(ii) When a suffix is added the change called *vowel mutation* takes place in the final syllable of some stems, e.g. *ai, au* become *ei, eu* (Appendix B (ii)):

Stem	*Verb-noun*	*Stem*	*Verb-noun*
gwaith	gweithio	golau	goleuo
naid	neidio	tenau	teneuo
plaid	pleidio		

(iii) In a few verbs the change called *vowel affection* takes place, viz. when *-i* is added to a stem containing *-a-*, e.g.,

Stem	Verb-noun	Stem	Verb-noun
par-	peri	taw-	tewi
(tranc-)	trengi	distaw	distewi
sang-	sengi		(Apendix B (i) (a))

(iv) If a suffixless verb-noun contains *-w-*, *-y-* (clear), or *-au-* in its final syllable, vowel mutation takes place when verbal terminations are added:

Verb-noun	1 Sing. Pres.
hebrwng	hebryngaf (*obscure* y)
gollwng	gollyngaf (,, ,,)
gostwng	gostyngaf (,, ,,)
canlyn	canlynaf (,, ,,)
dilyn	dilynaf (,, ,,)
derbyn	derbyniaf (,, ,,)
amau	amheuaf
dechrau	dechreuaf
glanhau	glanheuaf

(v) Adding a verbal suffix entails shifting the accent to the new penult, and in doing so *-nn-* and *-rr-* in an accented syllable become *-n-*(or *-nh-*) and *-rh-*. (Cf. the similar changes in adding plur. terminations to nouns, § 12 Note 1).

Verb-noun	1 Sing. Pres.
cynnau	cyneuaf
cynnull	cynullaf
cynnal	cynhaliaf
annog	anogaf
chwennych	chwenychaf (*obscure* y)
dannod	danodaf
cynnwys	cynhwysaf
cynnig	cynigiaf
cyrraedd	cyrhaeddaf

In *ennyn: enynnaf* there is a double change because of accent shift. In the following verbs, *-h-* precedes the accented syllable before the verbal ending: *aros: arhosaf; cymell: cymhellaf; amau: amheuaf; dianc: dihangaf; cynnal: cynhaliaf; cynnwys: cynhwysaf; cyrraedd: cyrhaeddaf.*

The aspirate *-h-* is not required in *cynnig: cynigiaf; annog: anogaf; cynnau: cyneuaf; dangos: dangosaf; ymddangos: ymddangosaf.*

(The traditional pronunciation of *dangos* is *dang-gos* (cf. *Bangor*), as preserved in S. Wales and as shown in the *cynghanedd* of early poets).

§ 171. Verb-nouns consisting of the stem without an ending: *achub, adrodd, amau, amgyffred, anfon, annog, arbed, arfer, arllwys, atal, ateb, cadw, cyfaddef, cyfarch, cyfarth, cyffwrdd, cymell, cynnau, cynnig, cynnull, cynnwys, cyrraedd, chwarae, dadlaith, dangos, dannod, datod, dadrys (datrys), deffro, dewis, dianc, dilyn, dioddef, disgyn, edrych, disgwyl, eistedd, ennill, erfyn, erlid, erlyn, estyn, ethol, gafael, galw, gorchymyn, gorwedd, gosod, gostwng, gwarchod, gwarchae, gwrthod, hel, lladd, ymddangos, ymddeol, ymladd, ymosod, ymwrthod* etc.

ENDINGS OF VERB-NOUNS

§ 172. -u: The ending *-u* is added to stems containing *a, ae, e, y* (obscure sound mutated from clear *y* or from *w;* see Appendix B (ii)): *caru, llamu, talu; baeddu, ffaelu, gwaelu, gwaedu, hiraethu, saethu; credu, cefnu, helpu, rhyfeddu, anrhegu; tynnu, mynnu, gwynnu, synnu; cysgu, dyrnu, mygu* etc.

The following stem endings have *-u* added to form verb-nouns: *-ych, -yg* and *-(h)a* (with contraction of *-(h)a* + *u* to *-(h)au* (§§ 133-134)): *bradychu, chwenychu, clafychu, tewychu; gwaethygu, mawrygu; glanhau, parhau, casáu, gwacáu (gwag + ha + u), nesáu (nes + ha + u).*

In *gwgu,* from *gwg,* and the borrowing *pwdu* (E. 'pout') there is no mutation, nor in some colloquial forms such as *llwgu (= llewygu), cwnnu (= cy(c)hwynnu), rhwdu (rhydu),. mwgu (mygu).*

Exceptions: (a) *-i* is added to a few stems containing *a* or *aw*, causing affection to *e* or *ew;* see § 170 (iii);

(b) *-i* is added to a few other stems, as noted below, § 174 (i) (iii).

§ 173. -o: (i) Some verbs of which the stem is a noun or adj. add *i* before the verb-noun ending *-o*, e.g., *glanio, ffurfio, teithio, gweithio; areithio, gwawrio, troedio, disgleirio, llywio, ceibio* (§ 170 (ii)) and borrowings such as *smocio, cnocio, cracio, teipio, pilio;*

(ii) Stems having *i, u, eu, ŵy,* in the final syllable have *-o* added to form the verb-noun, e.g., *britho, blino, cynefino, rhifo, crio, cribo, gweddïo, curo* ('knock'), *dymuno, addurno, llusgo, hudo, rhuo; ceulo, heulo, goleuo, euro; bwydo, rhwystro, cwyro, cwyno, mwydo, llwydo, anwylo, twyllo, arswydo.*

For the exception *lliwio* 'to dye, colour' there are colloquial forms with regular *-o, lliwo, llifo;* and the use of either *-o* or *-io* differentiates between *llifo* 'to flow' and *llifio* 'to saw, file'.

§ 174. -i: This is added (i) to stems ending in consonantal *w*, e.g., *berwi, enwi, chwerwi, meddwi, gwelwi, sylwi, llenwi.* It is added also to *-ew* (affected from *-aw,* § 170 (iii)): *tewi, distewi;* and to *-awn* in *cyflawni (cyflawn + i)* and to *-enw* in *cyflenwi (cyflanw + i).*

Exceptions. Some verb-nouns ending in consonantal -*w* have no additional ending: *cadw, llanw, marw, galw;* and unlike *tewi* there is no affection in *croesawu* with the ending -*u*.

(ii) to stems with *o* or *oe* in the final syllable, e.g., *rhoddi, torri, cyfodi, codi, llonni, ffromi, siomi, sorri, cronni, angori, arfogi, nodi; oeri, poeni, dihoeni, oedi, poeri, noethi, cyhoeddi;* and contracted forms: *troi, ffoi, paratoi, crynhoi, rhoi.*

(iii) in some exceptional forms: *medi, rhegi, mynegi, gweiddi* (from *gwaedd*).

§ 175. In addition to the three endings noted above (-*u*, -*o*, -*i*) which are very common, several other endings occur in a fairly small number of verb-nouns:

(i) -AEL, -EL, *cael, caffael, caffel* (§ 137 (i)); *gafael, gafel; dyrchafael* (as well as *dyrchafu*); *gadael, gadel* (as well as *gadu, gado* § 138).

(ii) -ACH, *caentach, cyfeddach, clindarddach, tolach, grwgnach.*

(iii) -AETH, *marchogaeth* (also *marchocáu*), *ymyrraeth* (also *ymyrryd*).

(iv) -OFAIN, *wylofain, cwynofain.*

(v) -FAN, *cwynfan, griddfan, ehedfan, hedfan* (also *ehedeg, hedeg*).

(vi) -AIN, *llefain, ochain, llemain (= llamu); ubain, diasbedain* (the last two with no conjugation).

(vii) -AD, *gwyliad* (today *gwylied, gwylio,* but *gwyl(i)ad* preserved in dialect).

(viii) -ED, *cerdded, yfed, clywed* (also *clybod*), *gweled* (*gweld*), *myned* (*mynd*); *ystyried, tybied, synied.* In the last three forms -*ied* is from -*iaid*.

(ix) -YD, *cymryd* (vb. *cymeraf*); *edfryd* (also *adferyd, adfer,* vb. *adferaf*); *gochelyd* (also *gochel* and formerly *gochlyd*); *ymogelyd* (formerly *ymoglyd*); *ymaflyd (ymafel); dychwelyd; (d)ymchwelyd; dywedyd* (from *dywedud;* also *dweud); syflyd; diengyd (= dianc); goddiweddyd* (formerly *go(r)ddiwes); agoryd (= agor); ymyrryd (= ymyrraeth).*

(x) -EG, *rhedeg, (e)hedeg.*

(xi) -ŴYN, *dwyn* (vb. *dygaf), ymddwyn* 'to behave', *ymddŵyn* 'to bear child' (vb. *ymddygaf).*

(xii) -AIN, *olrhain; darllain* (modern *darllen); dwyrain* 'to rise'. (From *dwyrain haul* arose the noun *dwyrain* 'east').

(xiii) -IAN, -AN, (a) pejorative in meaning, e.g., *gorweddian* 'to loll, lounge', from *gorwedd; sefyllian* 'to loaf', from *sefyll; clebran* 'to prattle'; *ymlwybran* 'to trudge' (*ymlwybro* 'to make one's way');

(b) added to loan-words, e.g., *lolian, hongian, trotian, loetran; mwmian (mwmlian); tincian).*

(xiv) -IAL, (variant of -IAN), *tincial, mwmial, mewial, myngial, sisial.*

(xv) -(H)A, in verb-nouns formed from nouns, e.g., *cneua, mwyara, lloffa* 'to glean' (lit. 'to hand'); *pysgota, adara, elwa, gwlana, cardota, coffa* (= *coffáu*); *atgoffa, gwra, gwreica, siopa* (= *siopio*), *bwyda* (= *bwydo*) 'to feed' (contrast *bwyta* 'to eat'); also in a few verb-nouns not formed from nouns; *rhodianna, chwilota, cryffa* (= *cryfhau*).

Although -*h*- has disappeared in writing in the above endings, its effect is seen and heard in the hardening of certain consonants, e.g. *bwyta* from *bwyd* + *ha*, *cryffa* from *cryf* + *ha*, *cardota* from *cardod* + *ha*.

NOTE. Like *byw* and *marw*, many of the verb-nouns listed above (xiii-xv) do not have corresponding conjugable verbs.

(xvi) Some endings have survived in only one example in each case: -YLL, *sefyll*; -AS, *lluddias* (= *lluddio*); -SACH, *llamsach* (= *llamu*). The verb-nouns of *bod* and its compounds, irregular verbs (§ 162) and a few others are anomalous: *aredig* 'to plough' (vb. *arddaf*); *chwerthin* 'to laugh' (vb. *chwarddaf*); *gweini* 'to serve' (vb. *gweinyddaf*, with mod. verb-noun *gweinyddu*).

§ 176. Some verb-nouns are accented in two ways, viz. (a) with no difference of meaning, *ymdrin* and *ymdrîn*, (b) with difference of meaning, *ymladd* 'to fight' and *ymlâdd* 'to tire oneself' (the verb *ymladdaf* means 'I fight' only); *ymddwyn* and *ymddŵyn* (xi) above, but *cydymddŵyn* 'to bear with'.

SYNTAX OF THE VERB-NOUN

§ 177. *As Noun:* (i) The article can precede the verb-noun like any common noun:

A ydych yn clywed *y canu?* Deffrowyd ef gan *y gweiddi.* Mae '*r dadlau* weithiau'n frwd.

Verb-nouns are masculine, except *cyfeddach* 'to carouse' (*y gyfeddach*) and *gafael* 'to grasp'. Today *cyfeddach* is generally considered to be a noun, 'carousal, feast'.

(ii) An adjective can qualify a verb-noun: *canu gwael*; *rhedeg cyflym*; *curo trwm*.

(iii) A verb-noun can be preceded by a pronoun:

Nid wyf yn deall *ei siarad* 'I do not understand his/her speaking'.
Y mae '*ch cerdded* wedi gwella 'Your walking has improved'.
Pa *floeddio* a glywaf? 'What shouting do I hear?'
Y mae *rhyw sisial* yma 'there's some whispering here'.

(iv) A verb-noun can be governed by a preposition: *wedi mynd*; *cyn dechrau*; *heb ddweud*; *gan ddymuno*; *i weld*; *wrth weithio*; *yng nghanu'r* oes hon.
(For mutations after prepositions see §§ 189, 195).

(v) It can be the subject or the object in a sentence:

Anodd yw *gweithio* heddiw 'working is difficult today'. Mae *cysgu* yn llesol 'sleeping is beneficial'. Hoffaf *glywed* yr adar 'I like hearing the birds'. A ellwch chwi *ateb?* 'are you able to answer?' A verb-noun can be the 'object' of another verb-noun: *hoffi darllen; dysgu cerdded* (§§ 123 (iv); 180 (i)). (*Bod* and *darfod* and some other verb-nouns can be objects of verbs and verb-nouns in noun-clauses, § 250).

(vi) A verb-noun can depend on a noun and serve as an adjective: esgidiau *dawnsio;* cae *chwarae;* ystafell *fwyta;* stôl *odro;* carreg *hogi;* padell *olchi.*

§ **178.** *As verb:* An adverb can modify a verb-noun: *gweithio'n galed; cysgu'n ysgafn; rhedeg yn gyflym.*

In a sentence like *Y mae gweithio'n galed yn angenrheidiol* the subject is *gweithio,* which is also a verb, modified by the adverb *(yn) galed.*

When an adjective is used adverbially before a verb-noun a compound is formed; i.e. *cyflym gerdded,* or *cwbl gredu,* is a compound verb-noun. A few compound verb-nouns can serve as adjectives: *plentyn newydd-eni; dyn newydd-ddyfod.* Like other verb-nouns such compounds can be used after *wedi* + pronoun in a passive sense: Yr oedd y bwrdd *wedi ei newydd-osod* (see § 182 (iv)).

(ii) The periphrastic construction on the following pattern is extensively used: one of the forms of *bod* + preposition (*yn, wedi* etc.) + verb-noun:

Y mae (ef) yn/wedi cerdded. Buom yn rhedeg. Yr wyf ar fynd. Yr oedd ef ar fedr cychwyn. Y maent heb weld.

(iii) The verb-noun is used with prepositions in a construction which is equivalent to the participle in other languages, i.e. in a sub-predicate:

Tynnodd ei het, *gan ddangos* y graith ar ei dalcen 'he took off his hat, showing the scar on his forehead'.

'chwithau, *yn gweled,* nid edifarhasoch' (Mt. xxi. 32).

Aeth hi allan o'r tŷ *dan chwerthin.* § (205 v).

There is a similar usage in 'absolute' expressions:

A'r dydd yn gwawrio, deffrodd y teithiwr.

'Hwn yn addo mawredd i'w gariad, *ac yntau ar werthu* ei dir' (B.Cw. 31) "This (fellow) promising his lover greatness, while on the verge of selling his land" (§ 252).

(iv) In abnormal sentences a verb-noun can be the object of the verb *gwneuthur* (§ 247):

Pan glywodd y sŵn, *ofni*'n fawr a *wnaeth.*

Credu a *wnâi,* mai hynny oedd yn iawn.

'Canys *ceisio* a *wna* Herod y mab bychan' (Mt. ii. 13).

[Note that the following sentence is not abnormal but a simple verbal sentence: 'Gwnaeth gofio ei ryfeddodau' (Ps. cxi. 4), 'He hath made his wonderful works to be remembered'.]

(v) In a series of co-ordinate statements the verb-noun can replace a finite verb if they have the same subject. Usually a previous verb, or the context, has indicated the tense and person concerned:

'Yna *rhedodd eu mam* â'r ddau fabi . . . a *rhoi*'r ddwy i eistedd . . . Yna eu *strapio*'n dynn rhag i'r babi syrthio, a *thynnu*'r oilcloth dros eu traed' (K.R.TMC 23).

Aeth y ffermwr at y drws a *churo* arno ac *aros* am dipyn heb gael ateb. A verb-noun often comes in a phrase following an adverbial clause:

Os awn at y tŷ a *gweiddi* efallai y clyw ni.

'Ac wedi iddo gymryd bara, a *rhoi* diolch, efe a'i torrodd' (Luke xxii. 19).

(vi) The verb-noun may convey the speaker's feeling (e.g., seriousness, compassion, sorrow, anger, bitterness) in speaking of an action, even without reference to the subject:

'*Rhoi* awdwr bywyd i farwolaeth,
    A *chladdu*'r Atgyfodiad mawr!' (A.G. 27)

('Putting to death the author of life, and burying the great Resurrection!').

'*Mynd* i'r ardd i dorri pwysi,
Pasio'r lafant, pasio'r lili,
Pasio'r pincs a'r rhosys cochion,
Torri pwysi o ddanadl poethion!' (HB 45)

('Going to the garden to cut a posy, passing the lavender and the lily, passing the pinks and red roses, cutting a posy of stinging nettles!')

§ 179. The DOER of the action of the verb-noun. The subject or doer of the verb-noun action is expressed in three ways:

(i) by putting it before the verb-noun governed by the preposition *i*:
'A bu wedi hynny *iddo fyned* trwy bob dinas' (Luke viii. 1) ('And it came to pass afterward, that he went through every city'). Wedi *iddi ddod* i mewn eisteddodd wrth y drws. Yr oedd Dafydd wedi codi cyn *i*'r *athro* ei *weld* ('Dafydd had arisen before the teacher had seen him'). Wedi *i Owen fynd* allan, aeth pawb allan.
Note the initial mutation of the verb-noun when it comes immediately after the subject or after a masculine infixed or prefixed pronoun, e.g., *cyn i'r athro 'i weld* or *cyn i'r athro ei weld*. (If the object were feminine, this would be *cyn i'r áthro ei gweld*).

(ii) by putting its subject after the verb-noun and governed by the preposition *o*:
'Pan glybu hwn *ddyfod o'r Iesu*' (John iv. 47) ('When he heard that Jesus had come')

'cyn *canu o'r ceiliog* ddwywaith' (Mk. xiv. 30) ('before the cock crow twice')

This construction is now archaic or poetical:

'A welsant hwy . . . Cyn *dod ohonynt?'* (Hedd Wyn 139).

(iii) by putting it after the verb-noun without a preposition if the verb-noun is intransitive:

Wedi *marw pawb o'i deulu,* aeth Dewi i'r Unol Daleithiau.

'Ac *wedi dyfod dydd* y Pentecost' (Acts ii. 1).

'cyn *dyfod y dyddiau* blin' (Ecc. xii. 1).

Note than when the verb-noun is intransitive the construction with the prep. *o* can also be used, as in (ii) above ('pan glybu hwn *ddyfod* o'r Iesu').

When the doer is expressed by a pronoun in this construction it is the prefixed or infixed that is used:

'Gwn *ei ddyfod,* fis y mêl' (Eifion Wyn, *Telynegion* 66) ('I know that it has come, the month of honey').

'Ac wedi *ei hwyrhau* hi' (Mt. viii. 16) ('When the even was come').

Credaf na fu neb ohonynt yma a'*u bod* yn dweud y gwir 'I believe that no one of them has been here and that they are telling the truth'.

The above constructions frequently occur in noun-clauses; §§ 248, 250.

§ 180. The OBJECT of the verb-noun. The dual function of the verb-noun is clearly seen in considering its relation to its object.

(i) Since a transitive verb may take an object, the corresponding verb-noun may also do so. In this respect such a verb-noun has a verbal function. But the object of a verb differs from that of a verb-noun:

(a) The object of a verb is in the *accusative* case, e.g., *Yfaf ddŵr.* The object of a verb-noun is in the *genitive* case, e.g., *Yfed dŵr,* lit. 'the drinking *of water',* i.e., 'drinking/to drink water'.

(b) The object of a verb has soft mut. (except impersonal forms), e.g., *Gwelais geffyl* (but *Gwelir ceffyl).* The object of a verb-noun, following immediately, does not mutate, e.g., *Gweld ceffyl* (§ 123 (iv)).

The object of a verb-noun depends on it exactly as one noun may depend on another. In *pen ceffyl* the noun *ceffyl* depends on *pen* and is in the *genitive* case. In the same way, in *gweld ceffyl,* the object *ceffyl* is in the genitive. Because it has a noun depending on it, the function of the verb-noun here is that of a noun.

(ii) When the object of a verb-noun is a noun or another verb-noun, it is always preceded by the verb-noun: *bwyta bara; glanhau tŷ; hoffi canu; dysgu nofio.*

When the object of a verb-noun is a pronoun (prefixed or infixed) it precedes the verb-noun:

Yr oedd yn *fy ngweld.* Y mae yn *dy dwyllo.* Daethant yma i *'n gweld.*
Cydiodd yn y ci a *'i daflu* allan. (§§ 70-73).

In expression such as *beichio crio* 'howling', *bregliach siarad* 'to jabber' (mostly picturesquely colloquial) the second verb-noun in each case is not the object of the first, the function of which is adverbial (see J. E. C. Williams, BBCS xxvi, 21-29).

(iii) In biblical language there is another construction if the doer of the verb-noun is denoted by *o* + noun/pronoun (§ 179 (ii)), namely verb-noun + *o* + doer + independent pronoun:

'Edrychwch rhag *twyllo o neb chwi*' (Mk. xiii. 5) ('Take heed lest any man deceive you'). 'Ond oherwydd *caru o'r Arglwydd chwi*' (Deut. vii. 8) ('But because the Lord loved you').

The regular construction, with the pronoun preceding the verb-noun also occurs:

'Megis pe ffoai gŵr . . . a'*i frathu o sarff*' (Am. v. 19) ('As if a man did flee . . . and a serpent bit him').

§ 181. The Verb-Noun and the Negative. The negatives (*ni, na* etc.) can not be placed before the verb-noun to make it negative, but a negative meaning can be conveyed in two ways:

(i) By using *peidio â/ag* before the verb-noun:
Bod neu *beidio â bod* 'to be or not to be'.
Dywedwch wrtho am *beidio â mynd* 'tell him not to go'.
Yr oedd hi'n siarad ac yn *peidio â gwrando.*
Peidiwch â siarad! 'Do not talk!'

Other verbs have a negative implication, such as *gwrthod, gomedd, methu, pallu, ofni,* although their main implication is affirmative. The action conveyd even by *peidio â* may be almost affirmative when it means *pallu* and *gwrthod* 'refuse', as in *Yr oedd ef yn peidio â gwrando* 'he was refusing to listen'. But in negative commands, whether direct or indirect, it is always negative, e.g., *Paid â mynd! Dywed wrtho am beidio â mynd!* When used elliptically, i.e., without a following verb-noun, *peidio* is virtually a negative verb-noun:

'Bûm yn hir yn sad gysidro / P'un oedd orau, mynd neu *beidio*' (Folk-song).

It is fully negative as an alternative to a noun or adjective:

Glaw neu beidio, rhaid i mi fynd allan 'Rain or no rain, I must go out'.

Dyna oedd ei stori ef—*gwir neu beidio* '. . . true or not'.

(ii) By putting *heb* before the verb-noun:

(a) In periphrastic sentences we have the verb *bod* + *heb* + verb-noun to denote the perfect or pluperfect tense:

Yr wyf heb ddarllen y llyfr 'I have not read the book'.

Y mae hi heb gyrraedd 'She has not arrived'.

Yr oeddwn heb ddarllen y llyfr 'I had not read the book'.

Yr oedd ef heb gysgu 'He had not slept'.

Action in the perfect tense is implied also in adjectival phrases:

Un heb ddysgu gwell 'One (who has) learned no better'.

Dyn heb weld eisiau 'A man (who has) not known want'.

Dynion heb ofni dim 'Men (who have) not feared anything'.

Plant heb eu magu 'Children (who have) not been reared'.

'*Heb ei fai, heb ei eni*' 'He who is faultless has not been born'.

(Note that *heb eu magu* and *heb ei eni* are passive voice; § 182 (iv)).

(b) The tense in the verb-noun phrase can also depend on the context:

Bydd yn anodd imi fyw *heb gael* llythyr oddi wrtho *(future)*.

Paid â sefyll yn y fan yna *heb ddweud* dim! *(present)*.

Daeth i mewn i'r ystafell *heb edrych* ar neb *(past)*.

'Pe llefarwn . . . ac *heb fod* gennyf gariad . . .' (1 Cor. xiii. 1) *(imperfect)*.

NOTE. Formerly a finite verb preceded by *na(d)* would often be substituted for a negative verb-noun:

'Canys ni allwn ni *na ddywedom* (= *beidio â dywedyd*) y pethau a welsom' (Acts. iv. 20) 'For we cannot but speak the things we have seen'.

'Mi a ddeuthum yn oleuni i'r byd, fel y bo i bob un a'r sydd yn credu ynof fi, *nad arhoso* (= *beidio ag aros*) yn y tywyllwch' (John xii. 46) ('I am come a light unto the world, that whosoever believeth on me should not abide in darkness').

§ 182. The VERB-NOUN and the PASSIVE VOICE. As shown above, § 121, the impersonal forms serve to express the passive voice. These forms belong to the finite verb, and so other means are required when the verb-noun is passive:

(i) The verb-noun may be the object of an impersonal form, or else antecedent of a relative clause containing an impersonal form:

Dylid ei gadw ef 'he should be kept'; *Gellir* ei *gwerthu* hi 'she can be sold'; *Gallesid dweud* hyn 'this could have been said'; *Llosgi*'r rheini a *wneir* (lit. 'it is burning those that will be done', i.e. 'those will be burned'); *Cosbi*'r troseddwyr a *wnaed* yn gyntaf 'first the transgressors were punished'; *Gorchmynnwyd chwifio* baneri 'flags were ordered to be flown'.

(ii) It may be the object of a personal verb or of another verb-noun: *Gorchmynnodd* ef *dynnu*'r tŷ i lawr 'he ordered the house to be pulled down'; *Gwelais ddinoethi*'r holl wlad 'I saw the whole land being denuded'; *Gwelodd* hi *gladdu*'i gŵr a'i phlant 'she saw her husband

and her children being buried'; 'Rwyf yn *cofio codi*'r pentref hwn 'I remember this village being built'; Byddem yn *gweld hela* llwynogod 'we used to see the hunting of foxes, i.e. foxes being hunted'.

Note that in the above examples the verb-noun has an object. If it can not take an object there can be no passive voice: Annymunol yw *bod* yn sâl 'it is unpleasant to be ill'. The verb-noun is, of course, active when the doer is mentioned as in § 179 (i) (ii): *Cofiaf imi weld neidr yno* 'I remember that I saw a snake there'; *Credaf gelu o'r tad y gwir* 'I believe that the father concealed the truth'.

(iii) The various forms of the verb *cael* are commonly used (especially in speaking) with the verb-noun to express the passive voice:

Cafodd ei *ladd* yn y chwarel 'he was killed in the quarry'; *Cawn* ein *curo* ganddo 'we shall be beaten by him'; Maent yn *cael* eu *dysgu* 'they are being taught'; A ydych yn *gofyn* am *gael* eich *rhyddhau* 'are you asking that you shall be released?'; Bydd y cyfarfod wedi *cael* ei *gynnal* 'the meeting will have been held'; Mae hi heb *gael* ei *thalu* 'she has not been paid'.

(iv) The prepositions *wedi* and *heb* are used with the verb-noun without *cael* to express the perfect, pluperfect or future-perfect tense: Y mae ef *wedi* ei *alw* 'he has been called' *(perfect);* Yr oedd hi *wedi* ei *chaethiwo* 'she had been restricted' *(pluperfect);* Byddant hwy *wedi* eu *syfrdanu* 'they will have been bewildered' *(future-perfect);* Y mae'r ci *heb* ei *glymu* 'the dog has not been tied' *(perfect);* Yr oeddynt *heb* eu *darganfod* 'they had not been discovered' (pluperfect); Dywedwyd bod y dyn *wedi* ei *ryddhau* 'it was said that the man had been released' *(perfect* or *pluperfect).*

Cf. also adjectival phrases, § 181 (ii) (a): *Plant heb eu magu.* In the following verse of Thomas Lewis's hymn the verb-nouns *daro, arwain* and *hoelio* 'being struck, being led, being nailed' are passive and are equivalent to *cael ei daro* etc.:

Wrth gofio'i riddfannau'n yr ardd,
　A'i chwys fel defnynnau o waed,
Aredig ar gefn oedd mor hardd,
　A'i daro â chleddyf ei Dad,
A'i arwain i Galfari fryn,
　A'i hoelio ar groesbren o'i fodd;
Pa dafod all dewi am hyn?
　Pa galon mor galed na thodd?

The use of *cael* with the verb-noun to express the passive is shunned by the best writers if possible. E.g., *Mae ef wedi ei alw* is preferred to *Mae ef wedi cael ei alw;* and the impersonal form in *Gwelwyd ef* is usually preferred to the less concise periphrastic statement *Cafodd ef ei weld.*

(v) There is another periphrastic construction used instead of impersonal forms to signify the passive, viz., an impersonal form of *bod* + a prep. (*yn, wedi heb, ar* etc.) + verb-noun + noun object. (If the object of the verb-noun is a pronoun it is prefixed or infixed, § 69).

Yr ydys yn codi neuadd 'a hall is being built'.

Yr ydys yn ei roddi 'it is being given'.

Yr ydys ar godi tref 'a town is about to be built'.

Yr ydys wedi talu'r arian 'the money has been paid'.

Yr oeddid yn gwerthu bwyd 'food was being sold'.

Yr oeddid heb ei gael 'it had not been obtained'.

Nid oeddid wedi'i weld 'it had not been seen'.

Buasid yn helaethu'r adeilad 'the building had been enlarged'.

Y mae'r tŷ hwn i'w werthu 'this house is to be sold'.

(In the last example the 3 pres. sing. of *bod* replaces the impers. form because a subject is named; an impersonal form has no subject).

VERBAL ADJECTIVES

§ 183. A verbal adjective may be formed by adding a suffix to the stem of the verb; also the stem itself may be used as an adjective.

(i) Adding a suffix:

-edig: *arferedig, planedig, cuddiedig, lladdedig, bendigedig, crogedig, toredig,* etc. (These have the force of a past participle passive).

caredig ('kind', formerly 'loved'), *crwydredig* ('wandering'), *troëdig* ('turning'). (These now have an active force).

gweledig ('seen', also 'visible' = *gweladwy).*

gwneuthuredig ('made, fashioned')—formed from the old form of the verb-noun, *gwneuthur = gwneud.*

trancedig ('deceased, dead, perishable')—formed from an old stem, *tranc-, trang-,* now *treng-.*

syrthiedig ('fallen'), *gwywedig* ('withered').

-adwy: *credadwy, gweladwy, taladwy, ofnadwy* ('to be feared, terrible'), *cyraeddadwy* ('attainable, accessible'), *symudadwy* ('movable'), *nofiadwy* ('dyfroedd *nofiadwy* Ezek. xlvii. 5, 'waters to swim in'), etc. (These again have a passive force, denoting an action that is possible or obligatory).

safadwy ('established, stable, steadfast, lasting'), *rhuadwy* ('roaring'), *tyfadwy* ('growing well'). (These last three examples are active in force).

-ol: *cadarnhaol* ('affirmative'), *nacaol* ('negative'), *arferol* ('usual, customary'), *gweithredol* ('active, executive'), *goddefol* ('passive, allowed, admissible'), *dewisol* ('chosen, choice'), *dymunol* ('desirable, pleasant'), *boddhaol* ('satisfactory'), *canlynol* ('following'), *derbyniol* ('accepatable'), *cysylltiol* ('connected, connecting'), etc.

-us: *gwybodus* ('knowledgeable, well-informed'), *adnabyddus* ('well-known'), *medrus* ('capable'), *brawychus* ('terrifying'), *cynhyrfus* ('exciting, agitated'), etc.

If the stem ends in a vowel there is contraction to form a diphthong, and the accent falls on the ultima: *parhaus* ('continuous'), *ymarhous* ('tarrying'), *chwareus* ('playful'), *cyffrous* ('exciting'), *boddhaus* ('pleased').

-ed, -ad: *agored* ('open'); *caead* ('closed'), *crwydrad* ('wandering').

-og: (added to the verb-noun) *rhedegog* ('running, flowing'), *galluog* ('able'), *hedegog* ('flying'), *chwerthinog* ('laughing'); (added to the stem) *brathog* ('biting'), *sefydlog* ('settled, established').

-aidd: (added to the verb-noun) *caruaidd* ('loving').

The endings *-edig* and *-adwy* are exchangable according to the meaning, e.g., *dealledig* ('understood'), *dealladwy* ('understandable'). In some adjectives various endings are added to the stem without difference of meaning, e.g., *crwydrol, crwydrad, crwydredig, crwydrus; parhaus, parhaol.*

In the following the meaning differs widely: *arferol* ('customary'), *arferedig* ('used'); *boddhaol* ('pleasing, satisfactory'), *boddhaus* ('pleased, satisfied').

(ii) The stem of the verb used as an adjective:

Verb	Adjective (stem)
berwaf	berw (*also* berwedig)
briwaf	briw (*also* briwedig)
cloaf	clo (*also* cloëdig) e.g. *drws clo, maen clo* ('keystone')
collaf	coll (*also* colledig)
crogaf	crog (*also* crogedig)
cuddiaf	cudd (*also* cuddiedig)
cysgaf	cwsg (*with vowel mutation in verb*).
chwalaf	chwâl, e.g., *pridd chwâl* ('scattered soil')
llosgaf	llosg, e.g., *mynydd llosg* ('volcano'), *aberth llosg* 'burnt sacrifice'); also *llosgedig*
malaf	mâl, e.g., *aur mâl* ('wrought gold')
naddaf	nadd, e.g. *cerrig nadd* ('hewn/carved stones')
plannaf	plan, e.g., *coed plan* ('planted trees'), also *planedig*
prynaf	prŷn, pryn, e.g., *bara prŷn* ('bought bread'), *dillad prŷn*
pobaf	pob, e.g., *caws pob* ('toasted cheese'), also *caws pobi*
rhostiaf	rhost, e.g., *cig rhost* ('roast meat')
toddaf	tawdd, e.g., *haearn tawdd* ('molten iron'); *duwiau tawdd; 'malwoden dawdd'* (Ps. lviii. 8) ('a snail which melteth'); also *toddedig* ('molten, soft, sensitive')

trof   tro, e.g., *pwll tro* ('whirlpool'), *llygad tro*
              ('squint-eye'), *cudyn tro* ('curly tuft'); also *troëdig,*
              troeog.

§ 184. Byw, Marw. These may be verb-nouns, abstract nouns and
adjectives:

Y mae ef yn *byw* yno *(verb-noun)*. Ni fûm yno yn fy *myw (noun)* .
Yr oedd hwn yn *fyw;* anifail *byw* oedd ef *(adj.)*. Bydd *fyw! (adj.)*.
Yr oedd hi wedi *marw (verb-noun)*. Ni chlywais am ei *farw ef (noun)*.
Gorweddai yno'n *farw (adj.)*. Bu hi *farw* ddoe *(adj.)*.

In the last examples *(Bydd fyw!* and *Bu hi farw ddoe)* note that *fyw*
and *farw* are predicative, but not preceded by *yn* (§§ 141 (i); 143 (iii)).
Because no terminations can be added to *byw* and *marw* they are used
predicatively thus with forms of *bod* in a periphrastic construction.
Either the radical *byw* or the lenited *fyw* is used in such a construction;
no definite rule can be applied, but a full discussion appears in TC
335-40.

It is the radical that is heard mostly in sentences such as the
following:

Y mae fy nhad *byw* o hyd. Ni fu ef *byw* yn hir wedyn. Mi af yno os
byddaf *byw*. Pe byddai hi *byw*, fe fyddai'n gant oed. Bydd byd da
i'r sawl a fydd *byw*. Holais a oedd ei frawd *byw*.

On the other hand, *fyw* is often heard after the past *bu:*

Bu *fyw* am flynyddoedd wedyn. Lladdwyd un o'r milwyr ond bu'r
llall *fyw*. Bu farw'n dawel, fel y bu *fyw*.

(Of course, when *byw* means 'dwell, reside' it is the construction
with *yn* that must be used: *Buont yn byw yn Abertawe)*.

In the case of *marw* in the predicate, it is the lenited form *farw* that
is now usual:

Bu ei gŵr hi *farw*. Byddwn oll *farw* o newyn. Mi fyddaf *farw* cyn y
gwnaf fi hynny.

Formerly the plural *meirw (feirw)* could be used after a plural part of
the verb *bod*, e.g., 'fel y byddom byw, ac na *byddom feirw*' (Gen.
xliii. 8).

COMPOUNDS

§ 185. One may have the following combinations in compounds: 1.
noun + noun; 2. adj. + noun; 3. adj. + adj.; 4. noun + adj.;
5. noun + verb; 6. adj. + verb; 7. prefix + noun/adj./verb.
Examples: 1. *gweithdy;* 2. *glasfryn;* 3. *dugoch;* 4. *troednoeth;* 5. *clustfeinio;*
6. *cyflym redeg; hiraros;* 7. *cyfran, addfwyn, ymladd.*

§ 186. *Proper and Improper Compounds.* (i) PROPER. In the
combinations listed above, if the first element qualifies the second, a

proper compound is formed, in which the compound itself is the same part of speech as the second element, e.g., *glasfryn* (glas + bryn) is a noun because the second element *bryn* is a noun; and *troednoeth* is an adj. because *noeth* is an adj.

The second element undergoes soft mut. *(gweithdy* from *gwaith* + *tŷ)*, except in some old combinations where *-ll-* remains after *n*, as in *gwinllan, henllan, perllan, cynllun, hirllaes, cenllif (cefnllif), penrhyn.* There is also provection (or hardening) when *-d d-*, or *-g g-*, or *-b b-* come together, or when *-h-* follows one of these consonants, e.g., *abaty* (abad + dy), *wynepryd* (wyneb + bryd); *costawci* (costawg + gi); *drycin* (dryg + hin).

At the beginning of the second element *t* is written instead of *d* after *ff, ll, s* in the few words where such consonants come together, e.g. *beiston, maestref, maestir, llystad, calltrefn, alltud, hoffter.* Also, *f-ff* becomes *ff*, as in *priffordd* (prif + ffordd), and *th-dd* becomes *th*, as in *gwrthrych* (gwrth + ddrych). In this kind of compound the second element is unaccented, and it therefore loses an initial *h-* as in *moresg* (mor + hesg); *Hafesb* (Haf + hesb) and *Haffes.*

There is provection in strict compounds in the following combinations (mostly in the first consonant only): *pt, tb, tg, ct, cb, cll, tch, cff*, e.g., *popty* (pob + ty); *ytbys* (yd + pys); *gwritgoch* (gwrid + coch); *llygatgraff* (llygad + craff); *bracty* (brag + ty); *crocbren* (crog + pren); *crocbris* (crog + pris); *ffacbys* (ffag + pys); *dicllon* (dig + llawn); *lletchwith* (lled + chwith); *picfforch* (pig + fforch); *picffon* (pig + ffon).

A *strict* compound is one sounded as one word accented regularly on the penult, e.g., *pénrhyn, fférmdy, canhŵyllbren.* Many proper compounds have both elements accented. These are called *loose* compounds and are written in three ways:

(a) as two separate words, the first being an adj.: *hen ddyn; dedwydd awr; hoff gân; gwyn fyd; tyner fam*, etc. Some adjectives are almost invariably placed before the noun, thus forming loose compounds, e.g., *prif beth; hen ŵr; gwir Gristion* ('real Christian'; ctr. *stori wir* 'a story that is (factually) true'); *gau broffwyd* ('false prophet'); *yr unig ddyn* ('the only man'; ctr. *dyn unig* 'a lonely man'); *cryn amser* ('quite a time'); *cryn ddwsin* ('a full dozen'); *ail waith,* §§ 53 (iv); 59. The second element may be a verb-noun or a verb: *cyflym redeg; llwyr ddeall; uchel waeddodd ef* ('he shouted loudly').

(b) as two hyphenated words: *ôl-redeg* ('running backwards'); *ôl-ysgrif* ('postscript'); *amcan-gyfrif* ('to estimate'); *wyneb-ddalen* ('title-page'); *disgybl-athro* ('pupil-teacher'); *môr-forwyn* ('mermaid'), etc. Sometimes two adajectives are thus joined: *llwyd-olau* ('greyish-light'); *chwerw-felys* ('bitter-sweet'); *marw-anedig* ('still-born'), etc. (Exceptions: *drwgdybus* ('suspicious'); *uniongyrchol* ('direct')). The hyphen is used if the second element is an accented monosyllable: *cam-drin* ('to ill-treat'); *ail-ddweud* ('to repeat'); *cam-gred* ('false belief').

(c) as one word, but with a secondary accent on the first element: *camddefnydd* ('misuse'); *camgymeriad* ('mistake'); *prifathro* ('head-teacher, principal'); *prifddinas* ('capital'); *prifysgol* ('university'); *ysgolfeistr* ('schoolmaster'); *aralleiriad* ('paraphrase'); *ailadrodd* ('to repeat'), etc. A loose compound composed of a noun and a verb or verb-noun is written as one word: *llygadrythu* ('to stare'); *torheulo* ('to sun-bathe'); *croeshoelio* ('to crucify'); *blaendarddu* ('to sprout'); *llofnodaf* ('I sign'); *mingamodd* ('he grimaced'), etc.

(ii) IMPROPER COMPOUNDS. Expressions such as *gŵr da, dau bwys, pen tân* are *not* compounds because they contain words in their ordinary and natural order. But if they are joined and accented as one word they form improper compounds: *gwrda, deubwys, pentan, hindda, Llanfair, heulwen, tridarn, gwreigdda, coelcerth, canpunt*, etc.

Many adverbs are improper compounds, e.g., *yr awron* (= yr awr hon); *weithion, weithian* (= y waith hon); *unwaith, rhywdro, rhywbryd.* So also compound prepositions, *tua, gyda, imi, iti, inni, ichwi.*

Place-names containing a noun + adj. or a noun + dependent noun are accented on the penult and thereby become improper compounds, e.g., *Nanmor* (Nant + mawr), *Bryngwyn* (Bryn + gwyn); *Llanfor, Penmon, Minffordd.* In some places *Penrhos* is pronounced as an improper compound, but in others as proper: *Pen-rhos.*

A few improper compounds are accented on the ultima, e.g., *prynhawn, heblaw, drachefn, ymlaen, gerllaw, gerbron.*

NOTE: In proper compounds, both strict and loose, there is initial lenition in the seond element (with a few exceptions mentioned in (i) above). In improper compounds there is no initial mutation of the second element unless the first element (as a separate word) is regularly followed by mutation; e.g., adjectives after sing. fem. nouns, *hin dda (hindda), Llan Fair (Llanfair), gwraig dda (gwreigdda), haul wen (haul* being formerly fem.) *(heulwen);* nouns following certain numerals (§§ 62, 63), *dau bwys (deubwys), dwy foch (dwyfoch), ail ddydd (eilddydd).*

Because the spirant mut. follows *tri (tri phwys)* and *chwe (chwe chant)* we have as improper compounds *triphwys* and *chwechant.* And because *yn* takes the nasal, *ym mlaen, yng nghlwm* we have *ymlaen, ynghlwm* (§ 213, Note (a); Appendix A (iii) (b)). On the other hand *tri darn, can punt* are written *tridarn, canpunt* as improper compounds. There is natural hardening or provection in *popeth (pob peth)* and *pompren (pont bren).*

§ 187. *Prefixes*. Prefixes occur frequently as the first element of both strict and loose compounds. They are classified below according to the mutations which follow them:

(i) Soft:

ad-, at-: 'second, re-, very, hateful'; strict, *adladd, adlais, atal, atgof, atgas, adfyd, adflas;* loose, *adennill, adolygu, ad-dalu, atgyfodi.*

add-: 'very'; strict, *addfwyn, addoer, addolaf.*

af-: negative; strict, *aflan, afraid;* loose, *afresymol, aflafar.*

all-: 'other'; strict, *alltud,* § 186, *allfro, allblyg* ('introvert').

am-, ym-: 'around'; strict, *amdo, amgylch, amgorn, amwisg, amgyffred, amgeledd, ymgeledd;*
mutual; strict, *ymladd, ymdrechu, ymweled (ymwéld)*—verbs followed by prep. â; *ymgais, ymdrech.*
reflexive; strict, *ymolchi, ymburo, ymddwyn, ymlâdd,* § 176.
'various'; strict, *amryw, amliwiog, amyd.*
'very'; strict, *amdlawd, amdrwm.*

ar-: 'on, near'; strict, *arddwrn, arfordir, Arfon, argae.*

can-, cyn-: 'with'; strict, *canlynaf, canmol, cynhebrwng, canllaw* (§ 186 (i)).

cyd-: 'together, common'; strict, *cydradd, cydfod, cytbwys, cydnabod, cytsain, cydymaith, cydwybod, cydnerth;* loose, *cyd-addolwyr; cydeistedd, cydfwyta, cyd-fyw, cydgyfarfod.*

cyfr-: intensive; strict, *cyfrgoll;* loose, *cyfrgolledig(aeth).*

cyf-, cy-: 'equal'; strict, *cyfwerth, cyfurdd, cyfliw, cyfran, cyfun;* intensive; strict, *cyflym, cyflawn, cywir.*

cynt-, cyn(h)-: 'former, preceding'; strict, *cynsail, cynddydd, cynllun* (§ 186), *cynhaeaf, cynddail, cyntaid, Cynfeirdd, cynfyd;* loose, *cyn-faer, cyn-gadeirydd.*

di-: 'extreme'; strict, *dinoethi, diddanu, diben;* 'without', negative with adjectives; strict, *diflas, diwylliedig, diwerth, diboen;* loose, *diflas, di-boen, di-dduw, disynnwyr, dihalog, di-enw, didrafferth;* verbs, *diddilladu, di-arddel, digroeni.*

dis-: intensive; strict, *distaw;* negative; strict, *disgloff.*

dir-: intensive; strict, *dirfawr, dirboen, dirgel, dirgrynu.*

dy-: 'to, together'; strict, *dyfynnu, dygyfor, dygynnull, dyhuddo.*

dy-: 'bad'; strict, *dybryd.*

dad-, dat-: 'un-'; strict, *datod* 'undo'; *dadmer, dadlaith, datguddio;* loose; *dad-wneud, dadlwytho, datgysylltiad;* intensive; strict, *datgan.*

dar-: intensive; strict, *darostwng, darbwyllo, darogan;* with radical, *darpar.*

e- (eh-), ech-: 'before'; strict, *echnos, echdoe;* negative; strict, *eofn, eang, ehangder.*

go- (gwo-), gwa-: 'sub-, rather, fairly'; strict, *gogan, gobennydd, goben, godywyll, golosg, gwared;* (with adjs.) loose, *go dda, go fawr.*

gor-: intensive; strict. *gorfoledd, goresgyn, gorfod, gorúwch, goris;* 'too, over'; loose, *gorofalus, gor-ddweud, gorgynnil.*

gwrth-: 'contra-, back'; strict, *gwrthglawdd, gwrthwyneb, gwrthrych (= gwrth + ddrych), gwrthgilio, gwrthblaid, gwrthsefyll;* loose, *gwrthwynebu, gwrthgyferbynnu.*

hy: 'easy, good'; strict (obscure *y*); *hyglyw, hygar, hyfrýd, hygoelus, hynaws.*

rhag-: 'fore-, pre-'; strict, *rhagfarn, rhaglaw, rhagrith, rhagfur, rhagluniaeth, rhaglen, rhagdraeth;* loose, *rhagbaratoi, rhagfynegi, rhag-weld, rhagymadrodd, rhagredegydd.*

rhy-: 'too, very'; (with obscure *y*) strict, *rhyfedd, rhywyr, rhydyllu;* In loose compounds with adjs. *rhy* is written separately (pronounced with clear *y*) and serves as an adverb, *rhy fawr, rhy gynnes.*

rhyng-: 'inter-'; loose, *rhyngwladol, rhyng-genedlaethol, rhyng-golegol.*

tan-: 'under'; loose, *tanseilio, tanlinellu, tanddaearol, tanysgrifiad.*

traf-: intensive; strict, *traflyncu.*

traws-, tros-: 'trans-'; strict, *trosglwyddo;* loose, *trawsfeddiannu, trawsfudo, trawsgyweiriad, trawsblannu.*

try-: 'through, thorough'; strict, *tryloyw, tryfrith, trydan, trywanu.*

ym-: reflexive; strict, *ymatal, ymborthi, ymddangos, ymddwyn, ymdroi;* 'mutual'; *ymgaru, ymladd, ymgecru, ymgodymu;* followed by prep. *â, ymadael â, ymwrthod â, ymweld â;* followed by other prepositions, *ymafael yn, ymhyfrydu yn, ymdrechu i;* see **am-**.

(ii) Spirant:

a-: intensive; strict, *athrist, achul, gwachul (= go achul).*

dy-: intensive; strict, *dychryn;* pejorative; strict, *dychan, dychanu. (dy + a-* has given *da-* in **dam-, dad-, dat-, dar-** above; and *dy + os-* has given **dos-**).

go-: strict, *gochel, gochelgar, gochelyd.*

gor-, gwar-: strict, *gorffen (gor + pen), gorchudd, gorthrwm, gorthrymder, gwarchod* (formerly *gwarchadw*), *gwarchae.*

tra-, dra-: strict, *drachéfn, draphlith (blith draphlith); tradwy* and *tramor* (radical); *trachul.* Like *rhy,* in loose compounds with adjs. *tra/dra-* is written separately as an adverb; *tra chryf, tra phwysig, tra thrwm.*

(iii) Nasal:

an-, a(m)-, a(ng)-: negative; loose, *annheilwng, annedwydd, amhriodol, amherffaith, annheg, amhur, angharedig, anghywir;* strict, *amrwd, amarch, angof, annoeth, anghrist.*

cym-, cyn-, cy(ng)-: strict, *cymod, cynnwrf, cynnal cynghanedd.*

PREPOSITIONS

§ 188. Welsh prepositions may be classified in more than one way. The simplest is the following:

(i) Conjugated prepositions, i.e., those that have personal forms.

(ii) Uninflected prepositions.

§ 189. Conjugated prepositions. (i) These have a simple form, which is used when the object governed by the preposition is a noun or verb-noun: *dan bont; ar ddyn; o dŷ; i ganu; rhag cwympo*. The soft mutation follows all prepositions except *er, rhag* and *rhwng*, which take the radical, and *yn* which can take the soft mut., the nasal or the radical according to its function (§§ 141 (i); 213).

(ii) They also have personal forms in the manner of verbs, except that the 3 pers. sing. has separate forms for masc. and fem. Some prepositions also have adverbial forms.

Auxiliary pronouns are often added to prepositions, viz. *fi/i, ti, ef*, etc. (§§ 69 (c); 74). They are sometimes added for emphasis, as with verbs, and the conjunctive auxiliary pronouns are specially emphatic: *arnom ninnau; wrthych chwithau* (§ 67 (c)).

§ 190. Conjugations of Prepositions. There are three conjugations classified according to the terminations. The 1 sing. of the first is *-af*, that of the second is *-of*, and that of the third is *-yf*.

§ 191. *First Conjugation.* To this belong *ar* 'on' (with stem *arn-*), *at* 'to', *o* 'from', (with stem *ohon-*); but the terminations *-af, -at*, 1 and 2 sing. of *o* have become *-of, -ot*.

ar

Sing.	Plur.
1. arnaf (fi)	1. arnom (ni)
2. arnat (ti)	2. arnoch (chwi)
2. *masc.* arno (ef)	3. arnynt (hwy)
fem. arni (hi)	

Adverbial form arnodd 'above' *(oddi arnodd* 'from above', Job xviii. 16).

at: ataf, atat, ato, ati, etc.

dan (tan) under: danaf (tanaf), danat, dano, dani, etc.; *o dan: odanaf,* etc. *Adverbial form* danodd 'below, underneath'.

am: (stem *amdan-*) amdanaf, etc.

o: ohonof, ohonot, ohono, ohoni; ohonom, ohonoch, ohonynt.

oddi ar (lit. 'from on') 'from, off': oddi arnaf, etc.

hyd at 'up to': hyd ataf, etc.

tuag at 'towards': tuag ataf, etc.

§ 192. *Second Conjugation.* To this belong *er* 'for'; *heb* 'without'; *rhag* 'before, against'; *trwy/drwy* 'through'; *tros/dros* 'over'; *rhwng* 'between' (stem *rhyng-*); *yn* 'in' (**§ 213**).

tros/dros

Sing.	*Plur.*
1. trosof	1. trosom
2. trosot	2. trosoch
3. trosto (ef)	3. trostynt
trosti (hi)	

Adverbial form trosodd

trwy/drwy

Sing.	*Plur.*
1. trwof	1. trwom
2. trwot	2. trwoch
3. trwyddo (ef)	3. trwyddynt
trwyddi (hi)	

Adverbial form trwodd

er

Sing.	*Plur.*
1. erof	1. erom
2. erot	2. eroch
3. erddo (ef)	3. erddynt
erddi (hi)	

rhag: rhagof, rhagot, rhagddo, rhagddi; rhagom, rhagoch, rhagddynt.

rhwng: rhyngof, rhyngot, rhyngddo, rhyngddi; rhyngom, rhyngoch, rhyngddynt.

yn: ynof, ynot, ynddo, ynddi; ynom, ynoch, ynddynt.

heb: hebof, hebot, hebddo, hebddi; hebom, heboch, hebddynt; *adv. f.* heibio.

§ 193. *Third Conjugation.* To this belong *gan* 'with' and *wrth* 'by'. They have no adverbial form.

gan

Sing.	*Plur.*
1. gennyf	1. gennym
2. gennyt	2. gennych
3. ganddo (ef)	3. ganddynt
ganddi (hi)	

wrth: wrthyf, wrthyt, wrtho, wrthi; wrthym, wrthych, wrthynt.

oddi wrth 'from': oddi wrthyf, oddi wrthyt, etc.

§ 194. *Conjugation of the Preposition* **i.** This conjugation is irregular:

Sing.	*Plur.*
1. im, imi	1. in, inni
2. it, iti	2. ichwi (iwch)
3. iddo (ef)	3. iddynt
iddi (hi)	

The auxiliary pronoun is often emphasised and the forms of the first and second persons are then written: *i mi; i ti; i ni; i chwi.* In speaking *i fi* often takes the place of *i mi.* The second plural form *iwch* is found only in old or poetical language, but it is heard in a contracted form in *nos dawch (= nos da iwch)* and, more rarely, in *dydd dawch.*

Note the difference between the two pronouns *im* and *in* on the one hand, and the preposition + infixed pronoun in *i'm* 'to my' (with nouns and verb-nouns) and *i'n* 'to our', on the other (§§ 69; 72).

§ 195. Uninflected Prepositions. These have no personal terminations, but some can be followed by independent pronouns (§§ 67; 68 (vii)), and compounds can have prefixed or infixed pronouns inserted between the two elements, see **§ 196.** Nouns governed by these uninflected prepositions are not mutated, except *â* and prepositions compounded with *â,* which take the spirant mutation and *hyd* (soft).

â, ag (before vowels); *gyda(g)* 'with'; *ynghyda(g), ynghyd â (ag)* 'together with',; *gyferbyn â* 'opposite'; *gogyfer â* 'opposite'; *gyfarwyneb â* 'facing'; *parth â* 'towards'; *tua* (but *tuag at* is conjugated, **§ 191).**

achos: = o achos (below).

am ben 'in addition to'.

ar ben 'on top of'; *ar bwys* 'near'; *ar draws* 'across'; *ar gyfer* 'for, opposite'; *ar gyfyl* 'near'; *ar hyd* 'along'; *ar ôl* 'after'; *ar uchaf* 'upon'; *ar warthaf* 'upon'; *ar gefn* 'on back of'; *ar fedr* 'on point of'; *ar fin* 'on edge of'; *ar ochr* 'on side of'; *ar ymyl* 'on edge of'; *ar flaen* 'in front of'.

efo (= efô + â) 'with', see *gyda.*

er mwyn 'for the sake of'; *er gwaethaf* 'in spite of'.

ers 'for', used before a noun denoting a period of time past, e.g. *ers mis; ers blwyddyn.* (Often confused with *er* 'since': *er y Pasg* 'since Easter'; *er pan ddaeth* 'since he came').

erbyn; yn erbyn 'by, against'.

fel 'like'; *(fel fi; fel ti; fel dyn).*

ger; gerbron; gerllaw; 'near' (with prefixed object: *ger fy mron,* etc.).

gerfydd 'by' *(ei arwain gerfydd ei law* 'leading him by the hand').

heblaw 'besides'.

herwydd 'according to'; *oherwydd; yn herwydd* 'because of'.

hyd 'as far as, along' (soft mut.); *ar hyd* 'along' (radical). (Late personal forms used: *ar hyd-ddo, ar hyd-ddi, ar hyd-ddynt*).

islaw 'below, beneath'; *is* 'beneath, below'.

llwrw 'in the direction of'; now obsolete except in expressions like *lwrw fy mhen* 'head foremost'; *lwrw'i gefn* 'backwards'.

megis 'like, such as'; *(megis anifail; megis hi; megis hwy)*.

mewn 'in' (used before an indefinite noun, *mewn tref*); *o fewn* 'within'; *(i mewn i, tu mewn i, tu fewn i, o fewn i* are all conjugated like *i*).

nes 'until': (before verb-nouns in adverbial clauses) *nes gweld, nes mynd (nes i* is conjugated like *i mewn i; nes imi weld; nes iddo fynd;* with the same meaning, *hyd nes* and *hyd nes i*).

o achos, oblegid 'because of'; *o ethryb* 'because of' (rare); *o ran* 'as regards, because'; *o flaen* 'before'; *o gylch* 'around'; *o amgylch* 'around'; *o gwmpas* 'about, around'. The object in these compounds can be an infixed pronoun after *o*: *o'm hachos (i); o'i blegid (ef); o'm rhan i* 'for my part'; *o'th flaen; o'n cylch,* etc.

rhag bron 'in front of' *(rhag fy mron,* etc.)

tros/dros ben 'over (the top of)' *(dros ben y wal; dros fy mhen i).*

uwchben; uwchlaw; uwch; 'above' *(uwch ein pennau; uwch dy ben).*

wedi 'after'; followed by a demonstr. pron., *wedi hyn, wedi hynny,* or by numeral, *wedi tri (o'r gloch),* or by verb-noun in periphrastic constr. *wedi mynd,* or to form the equivalent of a perfect participle, *coeden wedi syrthio, wedi iddo ddyfod.*

yn is compounded with several nouns, *ynghylch, ymhlith, ymhen, yn ôl, yn ŵysg* 'in the direction of', and with a preposition, *yn anad* 'more than, above'.

Many of the compound prepositions listed above have the noun-element used metaphorically, e.g., *ar ben* popeth, *ar fin* cysgu, *o gylch* y tân; *gerllaw'r* afon. When the noun is used in its literal meaning, it is considered to be an ordinary noun governed by a simple preposition, e.g., *ar ben* y plentyn; *ar fin* y ffordd; neidiodd *o gylch* y tylwyth teg.

§196. As indicated above, independent pronouns can be objects of *â, gyda,* etc. (except *tua),* and of *fel, megis, heblaw:* e.g., *fel fi, megis ti, ynghyd â thi, heblaw ni.* Prefixed pronouns can follow the first element, e.g., *ar fy mhen; ar ei gyfer; ar ein hôl; rhag eich bron; ger ei bron;* but when the first element is *o,* it is the infixed pronoun that is used, *o'm hamgylch; o'n plegid; o'u rhan hwy.* Auxiliary pronouns can follow, as after conjugated prepositions; *o'm cwmpas i; yn eu plith hwy; o'i blaen hithau; yn f'erbyn i; yn ei erbyn ef.*

§ 197. Many prepositions are used in special constructions and idiomatic expressions. In the lists given below the ordinary simple meanings of the prepositions are not noted.

§ 198. â, ag: (i) After verbs with the following prefixes: *ym-*, *cyf-(cyff-), cyd- (cyt-);* see § 187; e.g., *ymweld â; ymladd â; ymwybod â* ('to be conscious of'); *cyfarfod â; cyffwrdd â; cyfamodi â* ('to make covenant or peace with'); *cytuno â; cyd-weld â; cydymffurfio â.*

(ii) after a few other verbs: *peidio â; tewi â; methu â, arfer â* (but also *methu, arfer* without *â). Mynd* and *dyfod* when followed by *â* can take an object: *mynd â* (take'); *dyfod â* (bring').

(iii) With adverbs to denote movement:
I ffwrdd *â* hi, fel y gwynt 'Away she went, like the wind'.
Yn ôl *ag* ef i'r tŷ 'Back he went to the house'. Ymaith *ag* ef! 'Away with him!'

§ 199. am: (i) 'for, in exchange for':
prynu llyfr *am* bunt; 'llygad *am* lygad a dant am ddant'; canu *am* wobr; rhedodd *am* ei fywyd.

(ii) in the compound conjunction *am y,* in a conditional clause, 'provided that'; see §§ 118 (ii) (b); 236 (iii) (d).

(iii) 'because of', with noun or pronoun:
'y maent hwy yn tybied y cânt eu gwrando *am* eu haml eiriau' (Mt. vi. 7); *am hyn; am hynny;*
with a verb-noun:
am fod hyn yn wir 'because this is true; *am* ei *fod* yn dda 'because he is good'; *am* iddi hi *ddyfod* 'because she came (has come)'; *am wneuthur* ohonot hyn 'because thou hast done this;
with a negative clause:
'*Am nad oedd* gwyrthiau'r Arglwydd/Ar lannau Menai dlawd' (W.J.G. *Ynys yr Hud*, 9) 'Because the Lord's miracles were not (to be found) on the banks of poor Menai'.

(iv) 'corresponding to':
Yr oedd dau afal drwg *am* bob afal iach; gellid rhannu'r llyfrau yn ôl un *am* bob tri o'r plant.

(v) to express a desire, with a verb-noun:
'Mae fy nghalon *am* ymadael/â phob rhyw eilunod mwy' (A.G. 31), 'My heart desires to leave all images henceforth'.
A strong desire is expressed by *O! am* with verb-noun:
'*O! am* aros/yn Ei gariad ddyddiau f'oes!' (A.G. 58) 'O that I could remain in His Love all the days of my life!'

(vi) with a superlative adj.:
Rhedwch *am y cyntaf!* 'Run to be first!'; canu *am y gorau* 'singing to be best'; § 52 (iv).

(vii) after some nouns and verbs:
pryder am; gofal am; awydd am 'desire for'; *dweud am (dywedodd wrthym am yr anifail* 'he told us about the animal'); *sôn/siarad am*

(bydd hi'n sôn/siarad am yr India 'she will be talking about India'); §
156 (a), *darfod am* 'perish'.

(viii) 'towards, for', with verbs denoting movement:
rhedeg am y drws; mynd am y plentyn; rhuthro am y bêl. (When the
meaning is simply 'towards' *at* is used: *rhedeg at y drws; cyrchu at y
nod* 'to press towards the mark').

(ix) *am . . . â,* 'on the other side of . . . from':
Eisteddai hi *am y tân ag ef* 'She sat on the other side of the fire from
him'; Safai *am y wal â mi* 'He was standing on the other side of the
wall from me'.

(x) with verbs in a noun-clause after *dweud* 'tell, command':
Dywedodd wrth y bachgen *am fynd* 'He told the boy to go'.

(xi) Expressions such as *Mae hi am law* 'It is going to rain' and *Am
le!* 'What a place!' are restricted to NW dialects.

§ 200. ar: (i) with verbs, 'about to, on the point of'; *ar, ar fin, ar fedr,*
§ 178 (ii):
Yr wyf *ar fynd;* Yr oedd hi *ar fin ymadael;* 'canys hwn oedd *ar fedr* ei
fradychu ef' (John vi. 71).

(ii) in prepositional adverbial phrases: *ar agor* 'open' (= *yn agored); ar
ddamwain* 'accidentally'; *ar ddisberod* 'astray, wandering'; *ar fai* 'at
fault'; *ar gof/ar gof a chadw* 'remembered, recorded'; *ar goll* 'lost'; *ar
drai* 'ebbing, declining'; *ar chwâl* 'dispersed, scattered'; *ar wasgar*
'dispersed'; *ar gyfeiliorn* 'erring, astray'; *ar unwaith* 'at once'; *ar dro*
'once upon a time, by chance'; *ar brydiau* 'occasionally, sometimes';
ar gerdded 'a-journeying, away'.

(iii) after an adj. denoting condition:
Mae hi'n *dda arno ef* 'He is well off'; Yr oedd yn *esmwyth arnynt*
'They were in easy circumstances'; Bydd hi'n *ddrwg arnat* 'You
will be in a bad way'; Mae hi'n *galed arnaf* 'I am in distress';
with adjectives denoting attitude:
Paid â gadael iddo fynd yn *hy arnat* 'Don't let him become
presumptuous with you'; Mae ef yn rhy *eofn ar* ei feistr 'He is too
bold towards his master'; Peidiwch â bod yn *galed arno* 'Don't be
hard on him'.

(iv) after nouns such as *eisiau, ofn, angen, dyled, arswyd, cywilydd,
chwant:*
'Ni bydd *eisiau arnaf*' 'I shall lack nothing'; Nid oedd *ofn marw arno*
'He did not fear death'; Mae *angen bwyd ar y plant* 'The children
need food'; Mae dyled *arnom iddynt* 'We owe them a debt'; *Faint*
sydd *arnaf* i ti? 'How much do I owe you'; Gyrrodd hynny *arswyd
arni* 'That struck terror into her'; Mae *chwant* bwyd *arnaf* 'I desire
food'; Bu *cywilydd arnaf* 'I felt ashamed'; *Beth* sydd *arnat?* 'What is
the matter with you?'

after names of diseases:

Mae annwyd arnaf 'I have a cold'; *Yr oedd y pas arno* 'He had whooping-cough'; *Mae'r ddannoedd arni* 'She has toothache'; *Yr oedd y frech goch ar y plentyn* 'The child had measles'.

(v) after many verbs, e.g., *achwyn ar, aflonyddu ar, beio ar, cefnu ar, cwyno, crefu, deisyf, dymuno, dotio, ffoli, gweddïo, gwrando, galw, gweiddi, mennu (menu, mannu), myfyrio, sylwi, ymosod.*

Yr oedd y wraig yn *achwyn ar* ei gŵr 'The wife was complaining against her husband'; Mae dy dad yn brysur; paid ag *aflonyddu arno* 'Your father is busy; don't disturb him'; Nid yw hynny'n *effeithio arnaf* 'That does not affect me'; A ydyw'r sŵn yn *mennu arnoch?* 'Does the noise affect you?'

In idioms:

Yr oedd yn *cymryd arno* ei fod yn cysgu 'He pretended that he was sleeping'. Byddai ef yn aml yn *lladd ar* y masnachwyr 'He would often denounce the merchants'. Byddai Dewi bob amser yn *dal sylw ar* yr hyn a ddywedai ei fam 'Dewi always paid attention to what his mother was saying', § 250 (v). See also *ar i*, § 207 (ii).

§ 201. **at**: 'to'; (i) after verbs, e.g., *agosáu at, anelu at* 'aiming at'; *anfon at, cyrchu, chwanegu, dwyn, dotio, mynd, nesu, nesáu, gogwyddo, rhedeg, tueddu, troi.*

(ii) after a few nouns and adjs., e.g., *annerch at, apêl at, serch at, archwaeth at, cariad at, agos at, nes at, llythyr at.*

(iii) in some compound prepositions: *tuag at* 'towards'; *hyd at* 'as far as'.

(iv) some idioms: *at ei gilydd* 'on the whole'; *at hynny* 'in addition to that'.

(v) 'for use, for': *dillad at waith* 'clothes for working'; *esgidiau at chwarae* 'boots for playing'; *moddion (ffisig) at beswch* 'medicine for a cough, cough medicine'; *padell at olchi* 'a bowl for washing'.

§ 202. **dros/tros**: 'on behalf of, for'; after verbs, e.g., *ateb dros, eiriol dros* 'to intercede on behalf of'; *erfyn dros* 'to plead on behalf of'; *dadlau dros* 'to argue on behalf of'; *gweddïo dros* 'to pray for'; *gwylio dros* 'to watch over'; *wylo dros* 'to weep for'; after a few nouns; *amddiffyniad dros* 'defence for'; *esgus dros* 'excuse for'; *iawn dros* 'redress, compensation, atonement for'; *meichiau dros* 'surety, bail for'; *cysgod dros* 'shadow over, protection for'; *rheswm dros* 'reason for'.

In an idiom: Ni wnâi ef hynny *dros ei grogi* 'He would not do that in exchange for being hanged, i.e., to save his skin'.

§ 203. er: (i) 'in order to, for the sake of':

dringo'r mynydd *er* mwyn gweld y wlad 'climbing the mountain (in order) to see the land'; gwario punt *er* arbed ceiniog 'spending a pound to save a penny'; *er mwyn* ei wlad 'for his country's sake'; gwnaeth hynny *erom ni* 'he did so for our sake'; *er cof am* 'in memory of'; *er clod* 'in honour'; *er anrhydedd* 'honoris causa'; *er lles* 'for the good of'; *er drwg* 'for ill'.

(ii) 'for, in exchange for':

'onid *er* ceiniog y cytunaist â mi?' 'didst thou not agree with me *for* a penny?' (Mt. xx. 13); 'Canys fe allesid gwerthu'r ennaint hwn *er llawer*' 'For this ointment might have been sold *for much*' (Mt. xxvi. 9).

(iii) 'despite, however, though': (a) with an equative adj.; *er cymaint* 'however much'; *er teced* 'though so fair'; *er mor fawr* 'despite the greatness'; see § 50 (ii).

(b) with a noun:

'*Er ofnau* di-ri/Ni cheisiaf ond Ti' (Elfed CAN 610) 'Despite countless fears, I seek no one but Thee'. '*Er grym* y stormydd sydd/Yn curo f'enaid gwan' (T.R. CAN 234) 'Despite the strength of the storms that strike my weak soul'. *Serch* 'though' is often used instead of *er*, e.g. *serch hynny* 'in spite of that'.

(c) *er* + *yn* + positive adj.:

'*Er yn euog, er yn ofnus* . . . Cefais ganddo fodd i ganu' (J.P.R. ETM 568) 'Though guilty, though timid . . . he gave me the means to sing'.

(d) with a verb-noun:

'*Er chwilio*'r holl fyd/A'i fwyniant i gyd,/Nid ynddo mae'r balm' (T. Jones, Rhydwilym, CAN 696) 'Though I have searched the whole world and all its pleasure, the balm is not therein'. *Er fy mod* i'n clywed, nid wyf yn deall 'Though I can hear, I do not understand'. *Er bod* y tywydd yn ddrwg, mynnodd ef fynd allan 'Though the weather was bad he insisted on going out'.

(e) *er na, serch na* + verb:

'*Er nad yw* 'nghnawd ond gwellt/Na'm hesgyrn ddim ond clai' (Ehedydd Iâl, FG 95) 'Though my flesh is nought but grass, and my bones nought but clay'. Yr oedd ef yno *serch na* welais i ef '. . . though I did not see him'.

(iv) 'since', before a word or phrase denoting a point in time in the past:

Yr wyf wedi bod yma *er nos Sadwrn* 'I have been here *since Saturday night*'; *er y llynedd* 'since last year'. Ni welais ef *er pan ddaeth* adref 'I have not seen him *since* he came home'. 'A gofynnodd yr Iesu i'w dad ef, Beth sydd o amser *er pan ddarfu* hyn iddo? Yntau a ddywedodd, *Er yn fachgen*' (Mk. ix. 21) 'And he asked his father, How long is it *since* this came unto him? And he said, Of a child'.

NOTE: Ni fûm allan *er y Nadolig* 'I have not been out *since* Christmas'. Ni fûm allan *ers* deuddydd 'I have not been out *for* two days'. § 195.

§ 204. erbyn: (i) 'by' with a word denoting a point in time or the time of an action:

erbyn heddiw 'by today'; *erbyn diwedd yr wythnos* 'by the end of the week'; *erbyn hyn o amser* 'by this time';

'by the time, after' with verbs:

Erbyn cyrraedd pen y bryn ni welent ddim 'by the time they reached the hilltop they could see nothing'; *Erbyn inni fynd* yno yr oedd y lle'n wag 'by the time we went there the place was empty'; *Erbyn meddwl* am y peth gwelaf ei fod yn wir '*after* thinking about the matter I see that it is true'.

(ii) *yn erbyn,* 'against'; literally, *Safai yn erbyn y drws* 'he was standing *against* the door'; *Yr oedd craig fawr yn ein herbyn* 'there was a huge rock against us'.

metaphorically, *Yr oedd ef yn erbyn pob newid* 'he was against all change'.

(iii) *i* + infixed pronoun + *erbyn:*

i'th erbyn 'against thee'; *i'm herbyn* 'against me'; *i'w herbyn hi* 'against her'.

i'w erbyn e' is used colloquially meaning 'to meet him'; and *erbyn* is still heard for *derbyn* 'to receive'.

§205. gan: (i) 'by', before a noun, or an inflected form of a prep., to denote the doer of an action:

Rhoddwyd anrheg i'r bachgen gan yr athro 'a gift was given to the boy *by* the teacher'; *Canwyd y gân gennym* 'the song was sung *by* us'; *Paid â chymryd dy sarháu ganddo* 'do not take being insulted *by* him'.

(ii) 'from':

Prynwch rywbeth gan y truan! 'Buy something *from* the poor fellow'; *Dysgwch ganddi!* 'learn from her!'; *Nid wyf yn ceisio dim ganddynt* 'I do not seek anything *from* them'.

(iii) with the forms of *bod* to denote possession:

Mae gan y gŵr hwn ddau fab 'This man *has* two sons'; *Aur ac arian nid oes gennyf* 'gold and silver *I have none*'; *Rhoddodd ef y cwbl a oedd ganddo* i'r tlodion 'he gave all that he *had* to the poor'.

After the conj. *a* 'and', but without the verb, a phrase equivalent to a present participle is formed. Instead of initial *g-* in *gan* an old spirant mutation is preserved in *a chan,* from the medieval form *can* of the preposition:

Dyn *a chanddo* law wedi gwywo oedd ef 'he was a man *having* a withered hand'; A oes rhywun, *a chanddo* lygaid, na all weld hyn? 'Is there anyone having eyes who can not see this?'

(iv) with an adj. to denote feeling or opinion:

Hoff gan bob aderyn ei lais 'Every bird is fond of its voice'; Mae'n *dda gennyf* eich gweld 'I *am glad* to see you'; Yr oedd yn *edifar* ganddo 'he felt regret'; Mae'n *sicr gennyf* 'I feel sure'; also, *diau gan, gwiw gan, rhyfedd gan, blin gan,* etc.

(v) with a verb noun in a sub-predicate, i.e., in the equivalent of a participial phrase (see § 178 (iii)):

'ac a'u dysgodd hwynt, *gan ddywedyd* . . .' (Mt. v. 2); 'I'r rhai hefyd yr ymddangosodd efe yn fyw . . . *gan fod* yn weledig iddynt' (Acts i. 3); '*gan anghofio* y pethau sydd o'r tu cefn, ac *ymestyn* (= *a chan ymestyn*) at y pethau o'r tu blaen, Yr ydwyf yn cyrchu at y nod' (Phil. iii. 13).

NOTE: The action of the verb-noun in *gan bregethu* is not strictly part of the action of the preceding main verb *daeth* in the following sentence: 'Ac yn y dyddiau hynny y *daeth* Ioan Fedyddiwr, *gan bregethu*' (Mt. iii. 1). There is a similar construction with *dan* instead of *gan,* but in that case the action of the verb-noun is not part of the action of the main verb, e.g., *Aeth* allan o'r tŷ *dan chwerthin* 'he went out of the house laughing'; Cododd ar ei draed *dan ŵylo* 'he got up on his feet weeping'.

(vi) In the Bible there is an exceptional construction with *gan,* in which the action of the main verb is emphasized:

'*Gan amlhau* yr *amlheaf* dy boenau di' (Gen. iii. 16) 'I will *greatly multiply* thy sorrow'; '*gan farw y byddi farw*' (Gen. ii. 17) 'thou shalt *surely* die'.

(It has been maintained that this is a borrowed construction).

(vii) 'because'; *gan* + verb-noun:

Cerddodd yr hen wraig yn ofalus *gan fod* rhew ar yr heol '. . . because there was ice on the road'; 'Nid oes mwy hynawsedd . . . *Gan roi*'r un garuedd a llariedd i'r llwch' (E.R. FG 68) 'There is no longer any gentility . . . *because* the loving and gentle one *has been laid* in the dust'.

In a negative clause a verb replaces the verb-noun:

Ni allaf dalu *gan nad oes* gennyf arian 'I can not pay because I have no money'; Yr oedd yn oer yn yr ystafell *gan nad oedd* y tân wedi ei gynnau 'it was cold in the room as the fire had not been lit'.

(viii) adverb; *gan mwyaf:*

Merched sy'n gweithio yno *gan mwyaf* 'it is girls who work there mostly'.

'most often'; *gan amlaf:*

Y forwyn fydd yn godro *gan amlaf* 'it is the maid who does the milking most often'.

§ 206. heb 'without': (i) to make a verb-noun negative; see §§ 181 (ii); 177 (iv).

(ii) *heibio i; heibio* 'past' is the adverbial form of the prep.; *mynd heibio* 'to go past'; yr oedd angladd yn mynd *heibio.*

heibio i is a compound preposition, and governs an object: Aethant *heibio i*'r dref; *heibio i*'r car; *heibio iddynt.*

§ 207. i 'to': (i) following various verbs to fulfil the meaning: *llwyddo i* 'to succeed in'; *ymddarostwng i; cyffelybu i; ufuddhau i; tystiolaethu i; ymroddi i* 'to devote oneself to'.

(ii) marking the indirect object of verbs such as *rhoddi, caniatáu, dysgu, gadael, gwarafun, rhwystro, gofyn, gorchymyn, erchi:*

Rhoddais ddillad *i* gardotyn; Dysgodd hi gân *i mi;* Gadewch *iddi* fwyd a diod! 'leave food and drink for her'.

The object of the verb may be a verb-noun:

Caniatewch *i'r bobl fynd* i mewn! 'Allow the people to go in!'; Dysgodd *inni ddawnsio;* Mae ef yn gwarafun *i ni gerdded* ar ei dir 'he forbids us to walk on his land'.

With *gadael, dysgu, rhwystro* another construction is possible, viz. putting *i* immediately before the verb-noun, thus making it to be governed by the prep. *i:*

Gadawodd y plant *i redeg* allan; Mae ef yn eu rhwystro *i ddyfod;* Dysgodd y tad y plant *i nofio.*

(This last construction has during the present century been condemned as a borrowing from the English construction, but is found in Welsh as early as the fifteenth century).

In commands or requests *ar i* is used instead of *i* sometimes:

Mae cais *ar i chwi* gau'r drysau; Dyma'r gorchymyn, *ar i ni* fynd allan yn dawel.

(iii) *i* is used in constructions with the subject of a verb-noun:

(a) in a noun-clause which is the subject in a noun-predicate sentence:

Gresyn *i'r gŵr* adael ei gartref 'that the man left his home (is) a pity' (the predicate is *gresyn,* and the remainder of the sentence is the subject); Diau *i'r trên* gychwyn yn brydlon ddoe 'it is doubtless that the train started punctually yesterday'.

See §§ 248; 250 (i); 179.

(b) in noun-clauses after verbs of 'saying, believing, knowing' such as *dywedaf, credaf, gwn:*

Dywedais *imi brynu*'r ffon; Gwn *i'r ferch* gael ei thalu; Credaf *iddo ddweud* hynny; Tyngodd y forwyn *i'r gath* dorri'r ddysgl.

(The tense implied by the verb-noun in the above examples is past. Formerly it could sometimes be future or present).

(c) in adverbial clauses (§ 251) after the prepositions *am, gan, o achos, oherwydd, oblegid,* with the action of the verb-noun in the past:

am i mi ddweud 'because I said'; *gan i'r dyn* aros yno 'because the man remained there'; *oherwydd iddynt* gredu hynny; *oblegid i mi* agor y ffenestr; *o achos* i'r plentyn grio;

after the prepositions *er, wedi, cyn, ar ôl, gyda, erbyn, wrth, nes, er mwyn, rhag, oddieithr,* with the tense of the verb-noun action varying according to the context:

Er ichwi fynd ato *yfory,* ni chewch ddim ganddo 'though you may go to him *tomorrow,* you will get nothing from him'; *Wedi i'r* gelyn adael y wlad 'after the enemy leaves/left/had left the country'; Ni welsom neb *nes i'r llanc* redeg o'r beudy 'we saw no one until the lad ran from the cowshed'; Postiais y llythyr yn gynnar *er mwyn iddo* gyrraedd yfory 'I posted the letter early in order that it will arrive tomorrow'; Ni chawn wybod pwy yw'r lleidr *oddieithr inni* ei ddal 'we shall not know who the thief is *unless* we catch him'; Arhoswch yma *rhag ichwi* rwystro'r dynion 'stay here lest you should hinder the men'.

(iv) with nouns and pronouns to denote ownership or possession (like *gan):*

Yr oedd *i'r wraig* hon dri o blant; Gwelsom ddinas fawr *ac iddi* fur uchel; Mab *i bwy* yw hwn?

(v) with verb-nouns to denote purpose:

Aeth y ffermwr i'r cae *i hau;* Dewch â dŵr *i'w roi* yn y badell!; Prynodd gar *i fynd* i'w waith.

§ 208. o: (i) *o* is used with a noun or pronoun to denote the doer of the action of a verb-noun; see § 179 (ii).

(ii) 'because of, with, out of'; with abstract nouns:

'ni fedrais inneu nad wylais beth *o dosturi* (B.Cw. 28) 'nor could I refrain from weeping a little out of compassion'; neidio *o lawenydd* 'leaping with joy'; Gwnaeth hynny *o genfigen* 'he did so because of jealousy'

'by, through, from'; with verb-nouns and nouns:

'Ond *o hir graffu,* mi a'u gwelwn hwy'n well' (B, Cw, 6); 'But by gazing long and intently, I could see them better'; Yr oedd ef yn glaf *o gariad* 'he was sick from love'; Bu hi farw *o yfed* dŵr gwenwynig 'she died from drinking poisonous water'; Aeth ef yn eofn *o nerth* 'he became bold through strength'.

(iii) It occurs between two nouns, the second of which describes the first:

'Nol hedeg a gadael fy nyth,/A chuddio fy mhabell *o glai*'
(T.W. 48) 'after fleeing and leaving my nest, and after my abode
of clay has been buried'; Tŷ *o gerrig;* Cadwyn *o aur;* Bachgen *o
Gymro;* Mae ganddi fab *o bregethwr;* Llanc *o fugail;* Dyn *o awdurdod;*
Rhywun *o bwys.*

(iv) It is also inserted between a word denoting number, size or
quality and a noun:

> *tri o blant; chwech o ferched; llawer o ddynion; bagad o bethau; torf o
> filwyr; digon o fwyd; tipyn o fara; gwydraid o laeth; dull o siarad; llai o
> sŵn; rhagor o arian.*

The noun following *o* may be definite: *llawer o'r bobl; ychydig o'r gwin;
pedwar o'r plant.*

After *rhai, pawb, neb, dim, cwbl, peth* it is always definite:

> *rhai o'r plant; pawb o'r disgyblion; neb o'r trigolion; peth o'r bara; y cwbl
> o'r llyfrau.* See §§ 104; 106-111.

With inflected forms of *o: pawb ohonom; neb ohonynt; rhai ohonoch.*

(v) The descriptive element may come first:

> *cywilydd o beth* 'a shameful thing'; *mawr o beth; gwyrth o ddigwyddiad;
> ynfyd o ŵr; truan ohono; tipyn o fardd; hyn o ysgrif; pwt o lythyr;* mae ef
> yn *fwy o ddyn* na'i frawd.

(vi) It occurs in adverbial phrases before a word denoting measure:

> *mwy o lawer; gwell o ddigon; rhy fach o'r hanner* 'too little by a half';
> *gormod o ddau* 'too many by two'; *rhy lydan o droedfedd* 'too wide by a
> foot'. See § 217 (iii).

(vii) It is used after several verbs and adjectives to fulfil the meaning,
e.g.,

> *argyhoeddi o bechod; amddifadwyd ef o'i rieni* 'he was deprived of his
> parents'; *cyhuddid hi o ladrad* 'she was being accused of theft';
> *cyfranogasant o'r bara* 'they partook of the bread'; *yr wyf yn falch o
> hynny* 'I am glad of that'; *mae hi'n hoff o'i brawd* 'she is fond of her
> brother'; *yr wyf yn sicr o hyn.*

Also after a few nouns such as *gwybodaeth o, hysbysrwydd o, adnabyddiaeth
o, arwydd o, rhybudd o.*

(viii) To denote 'partition':

> y cyntaf o'r mis; y trydydd (dydd) o Fawrth; y pedwerydd dydd
> o'r gwyliau; y rhan olaf o'r llyfr; y gweddill o'r briwsion; y cwbl
> o'r gwir; y bedwaredd adnod o'r drydedd bennod; y pennill cyntaf
> o'r gân; yr ardal dlysaf o'r wlad; y rhan bwysicaf ohonynt; aelod
> o'r corff; aelod o'r côr.

(ix) Between a definite abstract noun and a verb-noun in apposition:

> y fraint o lywyddu 'the privilege of presiding'; yr anrhydedd o
> weld; y weithred o gredu; yr act o fwyta; y pechod o ladrata; yr
> arfer o weddïo; y gelfyddyd o fyw.

In the same way *o* can come between two abstrct nouns in apposition:
y fendith o gwsg; y rhinwedd o eirwiredd 'the virtue of
truthfulness'; yr ordinhad o fedydd.

NOTE: In south-eastern dialects *o* is often used instead of *â* to imply an
'instrumental' meaning to a following noun: *cwnnu pridd o raw* 'to lift
soil *with* a shovel'; *torri glo o fwrthwl;* see Morgan, TC 349-51.

§ 209. **tan, dan:** In a sub-predicate with a verb-noun; see § 205 (v).
Also 'until', *tan yfory* 'until tomorrow'.

§ 210. **rhag:** 'from'; (i) after verbs such as *amddiffyn, achub, arswydo,
atal, cadw, cysgodi, dianc, diogelu, gwared, ymguddio: cysgodi rhag y glaw;
'gwared ni rhag drwg'.*

(ii) in negative purpose clauses:
'Chwerddais *rhag gorfod* wylo' (T.G.J. *Caniadau* 186) 'I laughed lest
I should be obliged to weep';
Paid â rhedeg *rhag* iti *gwympo/rhag cwympo. (Rhag cywilydd!* 'For
shame', has become an interjection.)

(iii) 'because'; before an equative adj.:
Rhag mwyned oedd y tywydd aethom am dro; *rhag nesed* yw'r eglwys
rhaid i chwi fynd i'w gweld. (§ 50 (ii)).

§ 211. **wrth:** 'to'; (i) after verbs such as *addef, dweud, cenfigennu,
cyffesu, disgwyl, llidio, sorri, trugarhau, ystyried:*
Addefodd ef y gwir *wrth* ei dad; *dywedwch* y gwir *wrtho;* peidiwch â
chenfigennu wrthynt; nid wyf wedi *digio wrthi; Trugarha wrthym!;*
'Gwyn ei fyd a *ystyria wrth* y tlawd' (Ps. xli. 1) 'Blessed is he that
considereth the poor'; yr ydym yn *disgwyl wrthyt* am gymorth 'we
look towards you for help; y mae wedi *sorri wrth* ei brawd 'she has
sulked towards her brother'.

(ii) 'towards': after adjectives such as *caredig, cas, tyner, tirion, mwyn,
dig:* Bu'n *garedig wrthyf;* byddwch yn *dirion wrthi;* buoch yn *gas wrth* y
truan.

(iii) to denote the subject of *rhaid* (i.e. *object* in English):
Mae'n *rhaid* i mi *wrth help;* mae'r lle'n dywyll, a *rhaid* i'r gweithiwr
wrth gannwyll 'the place is dark, and the workman must have a
candle'.

(iv) 'compared with':
'tan synfyfyrio deced a hawddgared, *wrth* fy ngwlad fy hun, oedd y
gwledydd pell . . . a dedwydded y rhai a welsent gwrs y byd *wrthyf*
fi a'm bath' (B.Cw.5); Nid yw'r mynyddoedd hyn yn ddim *wrth* yr
Alpau'.

(v) Activity or industriousness can be conveyed by *bod* + *wrth:*
Mae fy mam *wrthi'n golchi* 'my mother is busy at the washing'; *yr*

oedd ef yn ddiwyd wrthi er y bore 'he was busy at (the task) since morning'; ni fûm i *wrth* y gwaith hwnnw 'I have not been engaged in that work'.

(vi) 'while'; in adverbial clauses:

'*Wrth* ddychwel tuag adref/Mi glywais gwcw lon' (Ceiriog) 'while returning home I heard a merry cuckoo'.

'*Wrth* iddynt sôn am weddi, mi a riddfenais' (B.Cw. 8) 'while they were talking about prayer, I groaned'. (§ 207 (iii) (c)).

(vii) *wrth* + *hun(an)* 'alone, by (one)self':

wrthyf fy hun(an) 'by myself'; *wrthyt dy hun; wrtho ei hun, wrthi ei hun, wrthym ein hunain; wrthych eich hunain; wrthynt eu hunain.*

§ 212. wedi: (i) It is used before demonstrative pronouns, numerals, and nouns denoting time or happenings:

wedi hynny; wedi hyn; wedyn; wedi'r Nadolig; wedi mis Mai; wedi deg o'r gloch; wedi'r deuddegfed o Fawrth; wedi'r ddamwain; wedi'r rhyfel.

(To some extent *ar ôl* is used in such expressions instead of *wedi*).

(ii) In periphrastic expressions *bod* + *wedi* + verb-nouns form the equivalent of past tenses verbal forms:

yr wyf wedi gweld (= *gwelais); yr oedd wedi gweld* (= *gwelsai);* § 178 (ii).

(iii) before verb-nouns in an adverbial phrase, in adjectival expressions, and in absolute phrases:

Wedi iddo fynd ymaith; wedi edrych o gwmpas, dechreuodd hi siarad; *llaw wedi gwywo; pren wedi cwympo;* Dywedodd na fuasai yn y siop, a minnau *wedi* ei *weld* yno!

§ 213. yn: 'in'; (i) The noun governed by *yn* 'in' is definite:

yn y cae; yn yr afon; yn nhŷ fy mrawd; yn Abertawe; yn y Bala; ym Mangor; yng ngwaelod y sach; Appendix A (iii) (b).

Before an indefinite noun *mewn* takes the place of *yn:*

mewn cae; mewn munud; mewn tref (o'r enw Llanfair) 'in a town (called Llanfair)'; mewn carchar 'in a prison'.

A noun followed by a genitive is usually definite:

trefi Cymru 'the towns of Wales'; *gwlad fy nhadau; ysgol y bechgyn;* we therefore have *yn nhrefi Cymru; yng ngwlad fy nhadau; yn ysgol y bechgyn.*

But the genitive noun is sometimes adjectival, i.e. it expresses quality rather than relationship, and so the expression of noun + genitive is regarded in such a case as a compound indefinite noun, which is preceded by *mewn:*

mewn tŷ cerrig; mewn tŷ cyngor; mewn ystafell wely; mewn dillad gwaith (see § 43 and Morgan, TC 68).

Words like *angau, paradwys, uffern, tragwyddoldeb, pawb, neb*
(sometimes) are considered to be definite, and so they are preceded
by *yn* (but *dim* is indefinite in *mewn dim* 'in anything', and definite in
ym mhob dim 'in everything' and *yn y dim lleiaf* 'in the least thing').

Formerly one would have *yn* with an indefinite noun, e.g.,

'Ni chysgaf, nid af o dŷ/*Ym mhoen* ydd wyf am hynny' (DGG 67);

'Mwyaf hiraeth *ym mywyd*/Am ŵr byw yw'r mau o'r byd'
(Maredudd ap Rhys).

Distinction is still made between *yng ngharchar* 'in jail' and *mewn
carchar* 'in a jail', and the article *y* is elided in such phrases as *yn tân*
(for *yn y tân*), *yn tŷ* (for *yn y tŷ*), *yn Gymraeg* (for *yn y Gymraeg*). (When
Cymraeg means 'an example or kind of Welsh' it is regarded as
indefinite, and therefore preceded by *mewn: Mae ef yn ysgrifennu mewn
Cymraeg da* 'he writes in good Welsh'; *Mae'r stori gyntaf, mewn
Cymraeg* graenus, yn un dda 'the first story, in polished Welsh, is a
good one').

The pronominalia *un, unrhyw, rhyw, rhai* are sometimes definite and
sometimes indefinite, so that the use of *yn* or *mewn* depends on the
exact meaning:

Ni allaf wneud hynny *mewn un* modd *(mewn unrhyw* fodd) 'I can not
do that in any way'; Yr oedd arian *yn un* o'r blychau 'there was
money in a certain one of the boxes'; Mae ef yn y tŷ *yn rhywle* 'it is
in the house in some place'; Dodwch ef *mewn rhyw le* diogel 'Put it
in a safe place'; Mae *rhai mannau* yn y cwm yn hardd 'some places
in the valley are beautiful'; Mae coed ceirios *yn rhai* o'r gerddi yno
'there are cherry-trees in certain gardens there'; Byddai'n eistedd
yn yr un man bob amser 'he would always sit in the same place';
Hoffai gysgu *mewn un* gwely arbennig yn unig 'he liked to sleep in
one particular bed only'; Nid oedd i'w weld *yn un man (unman)* 'he
could not be seen anywhere'.

Pa and *pwy* are definite, and therefore *yn* is used with them:

Ym mha le y mae?; Ym mhwy yr wyt ti'n ymddiried?

(ii) As shown above, §§ 114; 178 (ii), *yn* is a particle in periphrastic
constructions and absolute phrases:

Mae ef *yn cysgu;* Aeth allan i'r stryd, a'i fam *yn galw* arno.

(iii) It is also a predicative particle with nouns and adjectives:

Mae ef *yn ganwr;* mae hi *'n brydferth;* nid yw hyn *yn iawn;* daeth yma
yn fachgen ifanc; § 141 (i).

(iv) With an adj. it can form an adverbial phrase:

Canodd *yn uchel;* cerdded *yn gyflym;* § 178 (i).

(v) It is used before a definite noun after various verbs such as *credu,
cydio, gafael, glynu (yn/wrth), gorfoleddu, llawenychu, ymffrostio, ymserchu,
ymaflyd, ymhyfrydu, ymddiried (yn/i):*

credu yn Nuw; mae ef yn gafael ynof; mae hi wedi ymserchu yn y
llanc.

NOTE: *Mutation and Non-mutation* after **yn**:

(a) *yn* 'in': nasal mutation in nouns (including compound nouns, §
186) and verb-nouns: *yng ngwaith y bardd; ym Methel; yng nghochliw'r
machlud; yn nheg dywydd Mehefin; yng nghanu'r adar.* Also *yn* becomes *ym*
before a radical *m; ym Môn;* see Appendix A (iii).

(b) predicative *yn;* soft mutation in nouns and adjectives: *Mae ef yn
feddyg/yn dda; cysgodd yn drwm; canu'n glir.* Note that *ll-*, *rh-*, do not
muitate after *yn: yn llanc, yn llon, yn rhyfelwr; yn rhydd* (cf. *y, mor, cyn;* §§
8 (i); 48; 50 (i)). Exception: Mae hi*'n braf* yma.

(c) *yn* with verb-nouns in periphrastic conjugation (including
compound verb-nouns; § 178 (i)): mae ef *yn teithio; yn cyflym redeg.*

(d) as well as the soft mut. in an adj. after predicative *yn*, ((b) above),
we have the nasal mut. when *yn* is compounded with the adj.: *yn bell,
ymhell; yn gynt, ynghynt; yn gyntaf, ynghyntaf; yn gam, yngham; yn gudd,
ynghudd; yn gau* 'hollow', *ynghau* 'shut'; *ynghrog* (but *yn grogedig); ynghyn*
'lit'; *ynghlwm* 'tied' (but *Mae hwn yn glwm da* 'this is a good knot').

ADVERBS

§ 214. The following are now simple adverbs, although they are not
all so by derivation:

(i) Adverbs of time: *beunos* 'every night'; *beunydd* 'every day'; *byth,
fyth* 'ever'; *doe (ddoe)* 'yesterday; *heddiw* 'today'; *heno* 'tonight'; *yfory*
'tomorrow'; *echdoe* 'the day before yesterday'; *echnos* 'the night before
last'; *trennydd* 'the day after tomorrow'; *trannoeth* 'the following day';
eleni 'this year'; *y llynedd* 'last year'; *eto* 'again'; *tradwy* 'two days
hence'; *gynt* 'formerly'; *cynt (= cyn hynny)* 'previously'; *yn awr* 'now';
yr awron (coll. *rŵan*) 'now'; *wedyn* 'afterwards'; *weithiau* 'sometimes';
weithian/weithion 'now'; *yrhawg* 'for a long time to come'; *yna* 'then';
mwyach, bellach 'any longer'; *mwy* 'any more'.

(ii) Adverbs of place, manner and measure: *acw* 'yonder'; *adref, tua
thref,* 'homewards'; *allan* 'out'; *gartref* 'at home'; *draw* 'yonder'; *ddim*
'at all'; *hefyd* 'also'; *hwnt* 'yonder'; (*yn*) *hytrach* 'rather'; *lled* 'fairly';
oll 'altogether'; *prin* 'hardly'; *ynteu* 'then, or else'; *uchod* 'above'; *isod*
'below'; *ymaith* 'away'; *ymlaen* 'forward, on'; *ysywaeth* 'more the
pity'; *modd bynnag/(pa) fodd bynnag* 'however'; *(pa) beth bynnag* 'whatever,
however'; *efallai, nid hwyrach* 'perhaps'; *dyma, dyna* 'here/there'.

Adverbial forms of prepositions: *arnodd* 'above'; *oddi arnodd* 'from
above'; *danodd* 'underneath, below'; *trwodd/drwodd* 'through';
trosodd/drosodd 'over'; *heibio* 'past'; §§ 191-2;

(N. Wales *acw* and S. Wales *yco* 'yonder' are derived from Middle
Welsh *racco, raccw,* adverbial forms of *rhag* 'before, from').

See §§ 51 (v); 100 (v); 101 (v); 103 (ii); 106 (v); 107 (iii); 108 (iii);
109 (ii); 110 (iv).

§ 215. (i) Many adverbial phrases consist of a preposition + noun, e.g., *ar ôl; ar led; gerllaw; rhag llaw; rhag blaen* 'at once'; *i fyny/i fynydd; i maes; i ffwrdd; i waered; yn ôl; o gwbl; yn gwbl* (§ 104); *i mewn* (prep. + prep.). Some have the article preceding the noun: *o'r neilltu; ar y neilltu; o'r herwydd; o'r bron* 'completely'; *i'r lan*, etc. In speaking *i* is often elided in *maes (mas); lan; mewn*.

On adverbs formed from prepositions + demonstratives see § 91.

(ii) A preposition + adjective may form an adverb: *ar fyr, trwy deg, trwy iawn:* yn + adjectives: *ymladd yn ddewr; canu'n llon;* § 213 (iv); *rhedodd ynghynt; aeth ymhell;* § 213, NOTE (d).

(iii) A prep. + article + superlat. adj.: *ar y cyntaf; i'r eithaf* 'to the extreme'; *o'r gorau (mi wnaf hynny o'r gorau* 'I will do so quite well'); *o'r rhwyddaf* 'very easily'; *ar y mwyaf (yr oedd hi'n canmol ar y mwyaf* 'she was praising rather too much').

(iv) A superlat. adj. without *yn: Dos adref gyntaf y medri!* 'go home as fast as you can!'; § 52 (v).

(v) A prep. + pron. + superlat. adj.: *ar ei orau; ar/er ei waethaf;* § 52 (iv).

§ 216. Nouns denoting time or measure are commonly used adverbially: *diwrnod, dydd, ennyd, encyd, bore, nos, prynhawn, wythnos, modfedd, troedfedd, llath(en), milltir,* etc.

When these adverbial nouns express measure or *length* of time there is soft mutation:

Arhosodd yno *fis* 'he stayed there a month'; Bu i ffwrdd *ddiwrnod* cyfan 'he was away for a whole day'; Cerddodd *filltiroedd* lawer 'he walked for many miles'; *Oedodd dridiau cyn dychwelyd* 'he tarried for three days before returning'.

In denoting the time of an event or action with *dydd, prynhawn, bore* there is usually soft mutation in N. Wales but not in S. Wales:

Af yno *ddydd* Llun (N.W.). Af yno *dydd* Llun (S.W.).

In announcements of events, etc. the mutation is very often ignored:

'Bydd Eisteddfod . . . *Dydd* Sadwrn . . .'

(On these inconsistencies see TC 255-266).

The adverbs *rhywbryd, rhyw ddiwrnod, llawer gwaith,* § 101 (v); *rhai troeon,* etc. are mutated except when they come first in a sentence:

Dof i'ch gweld *rywbryd/ryw ddiwrnod* 'I shall come to see you sometime/ some day'; Bûm yno *lawer gwaith* 'I have been there many times'; *Rhyw brynhawn* gwelais ddieithryn yn yr ardd 'One afternoon I saw a stranger in the garden'; Daeth yn ôl *rai dyddiau* wedyn 'he returned some days afterwards'; *Rhyw noson* yr oeddwn yn darllen wrth y tân 'one evening I was reading by the fire';

§ 217. (i) The adjectives *iawn, odiaeth, aruthr, ofnadwy, rhyfeddol, digon,* etc. are used adverbially with another adjective: *mawr iawn;*

da odiaeth 'exceedingly good'; *gwych ryfeddol; cywir ddigon; drwg ofnadwy*. (The initial cons. of the adverbial adj. is mutated here).

(ii) In periphrastic usage *mor, mwy, wyaf* (§ 48) are adverbs; so also are *llai, lleiaf, eithaf, digon* before a positive adj.: *mwy cryf; llai cywir; eithaf da; digon trwm*.

(iii) The prefixes *go-, rhy-, tra-* (§ 187 (i) (ii)) are independent adverbs before adjectives: *go gadarn* 'fairly firm'; *rhy fawr* 'too big'; *tra* chryf 'very strong'. In other loose compounds an adj. is used adverbially before anothr adj., verb-noun or verb: *gwir fawr; pur gyflym; rhyfeddol dda; prysur weithio; cyflym redodd* (§ 185).

There is another construction in which the prep. *o* is placed between an adverbial adj. and another adj.: *yn hynod o gryf; yn rhyfeddol o fach; yn od o dda; yn boenus o faith; yn warthus o ddrud*.

(iv) Adverbial phrases can be formed by *mwy/fwy na:*
Nid wyf fi ar fai *mwy na thi* 'I am not to blame any more than you'; Er imi weiddi, ni'm clywai *mwy na chynt* 'though I shouted, he could not hear me more than before'; "Roedd yno gordial at bob clwy/Mewn unigeddau *fwy na mwy*" (R.W.P. 40) 'There was there in excess a cordial for every affliction in solitary places'; "Nid oes yn fy nghorff un galon/*Mwy na*'r gleisiad sy'n yr afon" (HB 103) 'there is no heart in my body any more than the young salmon which is in the river'.

(v) The conj. *ond/onid* and the negative *nid* occur in adverbial phrases: *ond odid* 'perhaps'; *ond antur* 'probably, perhaps'; *onid e* 'otherwise'; *ond hynny (ni fûm yno ond hynny* 'I have not been there except that once'); *nid hwyrach* 'perhaps' (colloquially contracted to *hwyrach); "*Angylion gwynion, *nid gwaeth,*/Sy o'r nef yn saernïaeth" (DGG 68) 'It is white angels, no less, who are fashioning from heaven'.

(vi) The following are interrogative adverbs: *pa le? (ple? ble?); pa fodd?; paham? (pam?); pa sut? (sut?); pa ddull?; pa ddelw?; pa wedd?; pa ffordd?; pa sawl gwaith?; pa mor aml?; pa mor fynych?* etc. § 88 (iv).

(vii) An adj. before a particle at the beginning of a mixed sentence has an adverbial function; § 246:
Da y dywedaist; *Hawdd y* gelli ddweud hynny; *Hyfryd y* canai hi.
In poetical language the equative adj. is used adverbially thus:
"*uched* y cwynaf!" (Gruffudd ab yr Ynad Coch GG 43); *Gyflymed* y rhedai'r ceffyl!
With *mor* + adj. we have: *Mor deg y* gwenai hi! *Mor fwyn y* siaradai!

There is a similar construction with *braidd y/na; odid y/na; prin y/na:*
"*braidd yr* ataliasant y bobl" (Acts xiv. 18) 'scarce restrained they the people'; *Braidd* na lithrodd ar y llwybr 'he almost slipped on the path'; *Odid y daw* ef drwy'r glaw 'it will be strange if (i.e. he will

probably not) come through the rain'; *Odid na ddaw* ef gan fod y
tywydd yn sych 'it will be strange if he will not come as the weather
is dry'; *"Siawns na* byddwn yn gyfeillion yrhawg" (T.H.P.-W.,
Ysgrifau 7) 'It is probable that we shall be friends for a long time';
Siawns y gwelwn ef byth eto 'it is improbable that we shall ever see
him again'.

Sometimes *ond odid* and *odid na* are combined:
    "ond odid nad dyma'r rheswm"; (T.H.P.-W. *Ysgrifau* 7) 'this is
very likely the reason'.

(viii) Some short expressions serve as adverbs, e.g., *mae'n debyg* 'it is
likely'; *debyg iawn* 'probably, of course'; *ysywaeth* 'alas, more the
pity'. (An old form in a past tense of the latter is still heard in
Glamorgan: *sgwaethérodd, sgwaethirodd* from *ys gwaeth yr oedd*).

PRE-VERBAL PARTICLES

POSITIVE

§ 218. Y(r). *Yr* is the form before a vowel and *y* before a consonant:
they occur: (i) before forms of the verb *bod* in the indicative present
and imperfect: *yr wyf; y mae; yr oeddwn*, etc. They are used only in
affirmative simple statements. They are not used in replies, nor after
other particles or conjunctions. *Y mae, y maent* become *mae, maent* in
speaking and often in writing. §§ 141 (i); 142 (ii) (iii); 148.

(ii) in noun clauses:
    Gwn *y daw;* Dywedodd ef *y byddai*'n mynd; Ni chredai hi *yr âi* yno.
(§ 249).

(iii) in oblique relative clauses:
    Dyma'r dref *y* chwalwyd ei thai; Hwn yw'r tŷ *y* buom yn byw
ynddo; Ni welais ef er y dydd *yr* aeth i ffwrdd; Pwy yw'r dyn *y*
buoch yn ei gwmni?; Beth *yr* ydych yn ei geisio? See §§ 79-82;
230 (i) (a).

(iv) after an adverb or adverbial phrase in a mixed sentence or in an
abnormal sentence:
    Yma y gwelsom ef; *Nid arno ef yr* oedd y bai; *Wedi hynny yr* anfonwyd
y llythyr; *"Ac ar y seithfed dydd y* gorffennodd Duw ei waith" (Gen.
ii. 2); *Felly y* cosbwyd hwy; *Megis wrth blant y* siaradodd â ni. See §§
246-247.

(v) in adverbial clauses after *am, fel, megis, pryd, lle, hyd,* etc. See §§
233-234.

§ 219. a: The particle *a* occurs before a verb in an abnormal
sentence; § 247:

"A Duw *a* ddywedodd, Bydded goleuni, a goleuni *a* fu" (Gen.
i. 3); "A'r ysgrythur *a* gyflawnwyd" (Mk. xv. 28).
(In a mixed sentence, in which the subject or the object is emphasised, *a* is a relative pronoun; §§ 76; 246-247).

§ 220. The simple personal pronouns *(mi, ti, ef,* etc.) are used as pre-verbal particles; see § 68 (iv). The form most commonly used is *fe,*
not only with personal but also with impersonal forms of the verb: *Fe
ddônt adref; Fe roddwyd* bwyd iddynt; *Fe'i gwelir.*

Note that these particles can not take the place of *yr, y* before *wyf, mae,*
etc. (§ 218 (i)), nor can they be put before *yr ('r).* Such expressions as
fe'r oedd, mi'r ydwyf are recent solecisms which are not found in
standard writing or speech.

Instead of the simple forms *mi, ti, ef,* etc., *mi a, ti a, ef a* are
extensively used in biblical language:
"Mi a godaf, ac a af at fy nhad"; *"Ac efe a aeth"* (Luke xv. 18, 15);
"Ti a arlwyi ford ger fy mron" (Ps. xxiii. 5).

NEGATIVE

§ 221. ni(d), na(d). For the mutations see § 77. *Ni* and *na* are used
before an initial consonant of a verb, and *nid* and *nad* before an initial
vowel.* Before other parts of speech *nid* and *nad* are the invariable
forms. The choice between *ni(d)* and *na(d)* depends on the kind of
sentence that follows.

(i) In a main clause a verb is preceded by *ni(d),* and other parts of
speech by *nid* (whether a vowel or consonant follows):
Ni ddywedais ddim; *Nid* agorodd ei enau; Yno *nid* oes dim;
Heddiw *ni* ddaeth neb; *Nid* plentyn yw ef; *Nid* gwyn yw hwn;
Felly *nid* arnaf fi mae'r bai; *Nid* aur popeth melyn.
In a few cases both *nid* and *ni* are admissible: *nid rhaid/ni raid; nid
gwiw/ni wiw; nid gwaeth/ni waeth.*

(ii) In a noun clause *na(d)* is always used:
Credaf *na* ddaw glaw; Nid wyf yn amau *nad* yw hyn yn wir;
Gofalwch *nad* ewch drwy'r dŵr. § 249.

(iii) In a relative clause either *na(d)* or *ni(d)* is used; see § 76 (ii).

(iv) After a preposition in adverbial clauses it is *na(d):*
"Am nad oedd gwyrthiau'r Arglwydd/Ar lannau Menai dlawd"
(W.J.G. ii, 9); Euthum adref *gan na* welais ef; *"Er nad* yw
'nghnawd ond gwellt"; Mi af ato *rhag na* all ddod yma.
Verbs are mutated after *ni* and *na,* so that with the loss of initial *g-* we
have *ni wn* 'I do not know' (*'wn i ddim)* and *er na anwyd ef yn ddall*
'though he was not born blind'.
The rule applies to *fel na(d), oblegid na(d), wrth na(d),* etc.

*It is shown in TC 361-3 that *ni, na* sometimes occur before vowels.

(v) In questions *na(d)* follows *paham, pa fodd,* etc.:

Paham (pam) na wnaethost ti dy waith? *Pa fodd nad* ydych yn gweld? *Paham na* chafodd ef fwyd?

Pa le is now followed by *na: Pa le na* cheir tlodi? *Pa le nad* oes angen? Formerly *pa le ni(d)* would be written:

"Piliwr adail, ple'r ydwyd?/Planed wyllt, *pa le nid* wyd?" (Maredudd ap Rhys FN 59) 'thou peeler of buildings, where art thou? Thou wild planet, where art thou not?'—to the wind).

(vi) For *O! na* in interjections see § 119 (ii).

(vii) *Na(d)* follows the conjunction *pe;* § 119 (ii). The infixed accusative pronoun *-s* can follow *pe na:*

"da fuasai i'r dyn hwnnw *pe nas* ganesid" (Mk. xiv. 21) 'good were it for that man if he had never been born'.

(viii) *Nid* is the form at the beginning of a negative mixed sentence, i.e. when any part, except the verb, is emphasised (§ 246):

Nid fy mrawd a roddodd hyn i mi; *Nid* anodd yw hyn; *Nid* yn y dref yr oedd hi; *Nid* cerdded a wnaeth, ond rhedeg (where the word emphasised is a verb-noun, not a verb); *Nid* cardod a roddir i chwi.

(The use of *nage (nace)* instead of *nid* in this construction is a late colloquial corruption heard in parts of S. Wales).

(ix) The conjunction *o* is joined to *ni(d)* to form the conjunction *oni(d)* 'if not'; § 236 (ii):

Oni ddaw yma ni chaf ei weld; *Onid oes* bwyd yma awn i ffwrdd. In speaking, and more and more in writing, *oni(d)* has been replaced by *os na(d): "Os nad* yw hi'n fawr, mae hi'n ddigon".

§ 222. **na(c):** *Na* before a consonant, and *nac* before a vowel. Following the natural spoken tradition and the written tradition as attested by poetry in the 'strict' metres, *nac* should be pronounced *nag.* However confusion with the conj. *nag* 'than' is avoided by preserving the old unphonetic spelling *nac.*

(i) *Na(c)* occurs before imperative verbs:

"*Na* ladd; *na* ladrata"; *Na* wna ddrwg am ddrwg; *Nac* oedwch wrth y drws; "*Na* thralloder eich calon".

(ii) Also in negative replies; (§ 227):

A wyt ti'n barod? *Nac* ydwyf; A weli di'r goeden? *Na* welaf. Mutations after the particles *ni, na, oni* are the same as those after the negative relative pronoun, *ni, na;* § 77.

INTERROGATIVE

§ 223. **a:** In direct and indirect questions the verb is introduced by *a: A* ydyw hi yma? *A* welaist ti ef? *A* ddaeth y post? *A* gafodd ef niwed? Gofynnodd imi *a* oeddwn wedi gweld ei frawd.

Interrogative *a* is followed by the soft mutation, like the rel. pron. *a;*
§ 77. (The use of *os* instead of *a* as an interrogative in speaking is
borrowed from the use of *if* in English in a conditional phrase as well
as with the meaning 'whether'. A sentence such as 'Ask *if (whether)* he
is going' should be 'Gofynnwch *a* ydyw ef yn mynd' in Welsh).

§ 224. ai: Any part of speech, except a verb, can follow *ai* in a direct
or indirect question:

Ai ceffyl sydd acw? 'Is it a horse that is yonder?' *Ai* gwyn yw ei
liw? 'Is its colour white?'; *Ai* cysgu y mae hi? (*cysgu* being a verb-
noun); Ni wyddai ef *ai* hwnnw oedd y trên iawn 'he did not know
whether that was the right train'.

In a double question we have *ai* . . . *ai:*

"*Ai* tydi yw yr hwn sydd yn dyfod, *ai* un arall yr ydym yn ei
ddisgwyl?" (Mt. xxii. 17).

The second *ai* can be followed by *nid:*

Ai gwir yw hyn *ai nid* gwir? 'Is this true or not true?'

In an indirect question we can have *a* . . . *ai na(d):*

Cei weld *a* wyt wedi llwyddo yn yr arholiad *ai nad* wyt 'you shall
see whether you have succeeded in the examination or not'.

The first alternative is often preceded by *pa un ai:*

Ni wyddem *pa un ai* byw *ai* marw oedd y dyn 'we did not know
whether the man was dead or alive'.

Instead of the second *ai* there is a tendency to say *neu* or *neu ynteu:*

Pa un ai yn y bore *neu/neu ynteu* yn y prynhawn y dewch yma? 'is it
in the morning or (else) in the afternoon you will come here?'

In indirect questions the alternatives may be introduced by *pa un
bynnag:*

Pa un bynnag ydyw hi, *ai* iach *ai* afiach, ni all aros yma 'whatever
she is, whether healthy or ill, she can not stay here'.

A statement becomes a question by the addition of *ai e?:*

Ti a wnaeth y drwg, *ai e?* 'it was you who did the mischief, was
it?'; Nid yma y mae hi, *ai e?* 'This is not where she is, is it?'

Ai e? can also be a question implying amazement or doubt:

'Fy ngwaith i yw hwn' meddai'r bachgen. 'Ai e?' meddai'r athro
('this is my work' said the boy. 'Is that so?' said the teacher').

For *naill ai* . . . *neu* see § 93.

§ 225. oni(d): *Oni(d)* introduces a question to which an affirmative
answer is expected. *Oni* with spirant mut. of *p, t, c,* and *onid* before a
vowel are used when a verb follows; but when any other part of
speech follows *onid* is always used; cf. *ni(d)* § 221 and § 246 (i):

Onid wyt ti'n frawd iddo?; *Oni chlywsoch* chwi'r gloch?; *Oni ddaeth* y
llythyr?; *Onid ti* yw ei frawd 'is it not you who is his brother?';
Onid melys yw mêl? 'is not honey sweet?'

The question may be indirect:

> Gofynnodd i mi *onid oeddwn* wedi gweld y rhybudd 'he asked me had I not seen the warning'; Dos i holi *onid hon* yw'r ffordd iawn 'go to ask whether this is not the right road'.

A statement becomes a question by the addition of *onid e?* (cf. *ai e?* above):

> Dy frawd yw Gruffudd, *onid e?* 'Gruffudd is your brother, is he not?'; Wedi blino y mae hi, *onid e?* 'she is tired, is she not?'

(In the dialects we have *yntê?*, *yntefe?*, *ontefe?* instead of *onid e?*)

REPLIES

§ 226. *Affirmative.* (i) When the question is introduced by *a* or *oni*, the verb is repeated in the reply, with any change of person that is needed:

> *A wyt* ti'n byw yma? *Ydwyf* 'do you live yere? Yes (I do)'; *A oeddech* chwi yno? *Oeddem* 'were you there? We were'; *Oni chlywent* hwy'r sŵn? *Clywent* 'could they not hear the noise? They could (hear)'; *Oni welir* y môr oddi yma? *Gwelir* 'is the sea not seen from here? It is (seen)'.

Instead of repeating the verb the auxiliary *gwnaf* is sometimes used:

> *A roddi* di rywbeth i mi? *Gwnaf* 'will you give me something? I will (do so)'; *A helpai* ef rywun tlawd? *Gwnâi* 'would he help someone poor? Yes (he would)'.

In replies no particle is put before the verb as a rule, but it can be put if the reply is repeated for emphasis or effect:

> *A wnei* di hyn? *Gwnaf, mi wnaf.*

In speaking the reply is frequently emphasised by repetition:

> *A ddaw ef? Daw, daw.*

When the verb of the question is in the past or perfect tense, instead of repeating the verb the reply is usually *Do:*

> *A welsoch* chwi hi? *Do* 'did you see her? Yes (we did)'; *Oni phrynodd* ef y bwyd? *Do* 'did he not buy the food? Yes'; *A ddaliwyd* yr aderyn? *Do* 'was the bird caught? Yes'.

If the question (with the verb in a past tense) is in the periphrastic form (§ 212 (ii)) the verb is usually repeated:

> *A ydych wedi gorffen?* *Ydym* 'have you finished? Yes (we have)'; *A wyt ti wedi darllen y llyfr?* *Ydwyf.*

In reply to this form of question *Do* is also used, more often in N. Wales:

> *A ydych wedi gweld y llun? Do.*

To the simple answer *Do* the full verbal answer can be added:

> *A brynaist ti ef? Do, fe'i prynais;*
> *A wyt ti wedi ei weld? Do, fe'i gwelais.*

(ii) When the question is introduced by *ai* or *onid* in a mixed sentence (§ 246), the affirmative reply is *Ie:*

Ai coch yw ei liw? *Ie* 'is its colour red? Yes (it is)';
Ai cysgu y mae'r baban? *Ie* 'is it asleep the baby is? Yes (it is)';
Ai yn y dref y buoch chwi? *Ie* 'is it in the town you have been? Yes';
Onid yn y car y daeth ef? *Ie* 'was it not in the car he came? Yes'.

NOTE. *Do* and *Ie* are sometimes used for emphasis with sentences which are not formal questions:

"Do, mi deflais dom a lludw,/Iesu, ar dy enw drud'' (Alun 194): 'Yea, I have cast filth and ashes, Jesus, on thy precious name'; *"Do,* bûm ganwaith yn dy garu,/Feinir wen a thithau'n gwadu'' (HB 122) 'Yes, I have a hundred times loved thee, fair maid, though thou didst deny it'; *"Ie,* pe rhodiwn ar hyd glyn cysgod angau . . .'' (Ps. xxiii. 4).

They are used also to confirm or agree with something that has been said, usually in conversation:

Dyma dywydd gwael!/*Ie, tywydd gwael iawn;*
Gresyn bod hynny wedi digwydd./*Ie, gresyn mawr;*
Fe weithiodd ef yn galed ar hyd ei oes./*Do, fe wnaeth.*

§ 227. *Negative.* (i) The negative reply to a question introduced by *a* has *na(c)* before the verb:

A wyt ti'n barod? *Nac (yd)wyf; A oeddynt* hwy yno? *Nac oeddynt; A garai* ef ei wlad? *Na charai; A ddowch* chwi? *Na ddown;* § 222.

The particle corresponding to *Do* in an affirmative question (i.e. after a question in a past tense) is *Naddo* in a negative reply:

A gawsoch chwi'r bwyd? *Naddo; A ddanfonwyd* y llythyr? *Naddo.*
A ydych wedi gwerthu'r cwbl? *Nac ydym* (or *Naddo*).

(ii) When a question is introduced by *ai* or *onid* before a mixed sentence, the negative reply is *Nage:*

Ai Owen biau'r cap hwn? *Nage; Ai* heddiw y daeth hi? *Nage.*
Ai cysgu yr oedd ef? *Nage; Onid* Mair a fu yno? *Nage.*

NOTE. Like *Do* and *Ie,* the negatives *Naddo* and *Nage* can begin a sentence for emphasis although it is not a reply to a question:

Naddo, ni welais neb tebyg iddo; *Nage,* nid peth i chwarae ag ef yw hwn; ''Ni chefais gymaint ffydd, *naddo* yn yr Israel'' (Luke vii. 9).

CONJUNCTIONS

§ 228. The conjunctions discussed below can join words or clauses or sentences.

(i) **a(c):** (a) *A* is used before consonants (including *h*) and is followed by the spirant mut.: *byr a hir; bara a chig; mawr a thrwm; carreg a phren; du a gwyn. Ac* is used before vowels and also before *mor, fel, felly, megis,* *mwyach, mai, meddaf;* before the particles *fe, mi,* and the two negatives *ni, na.* Before a consonantal *i,* the form mostly used is *ac: gwlad ac iaith; byw ac iach; eira ac iâ.*

(b) Sentences joined by *a(c)* are co-ordinate sentences: *Aeth ef at y drws ac agorodd ef* 'he went to the door and opened it'; *Gwelodd y plentyn ei fam a rhedodd ati* 'the child saw its mother and ran to her. (The use of the verb-noun instead of a personal verb in a series of co-ordinate clauses is discussed above, § 178 (v)).

In narrative in the biblical style the conj. *a(c)* is extensively used at the beginning of co-ordinate sentences in a series:

"*Ac* mi a welais angel yn disgyn . . . *Ac* efe a ddaliodd y ddraig . . . *Ac* mi a welais orseddfeinciau . . ." (Rev. xx. 1-4) cf. the use of *and* in the English Bible.

(c) As in the case of *nac* (§ 222) the natural and traditional sound of *ac* is *ag.* By keeping to the old spelling, *ac,* confusion between it and *ag* 'with, as' is avoided.

(d) *A(c)* is common at the beginning of absolute clauses, § 252:

Yr oedd Olwen yn llawen iawn, *a hithau wedi cael y fath newyddion da* 'Olwen was very happy, having received such good news'. Cerddasant ymlaen, *ac awel yn chwythu o'r môr* 'they walked on, with a breeze blowing from the sea'.

In this construction the preposition *â, ag* has frequently been used by writers instead of the conjunction *a(c):*

"*Ag* oerwynt hydre'n gyrru/Y gawod ddail yn gad ddu" (R.W.P.) In expressions such as *y ferch â'r gwallt melyn, y dyn â'r gaib, bachgen â phêl, rhywun ag arian* it is convenient to use the preposition *â, ag* to avoid ambiguity; see § 143 (i) (b).

(ii) **neu:** Nouns, verb-nouns and adjectives undergo soft mutation after *neu* 'or': *gŵr neu wraig; du neu goch; ennill neu golli; mynd neu beidio.* Formerly the same applied to verbs following immediately after *neu,* but nowadays verbs do not mutate: *Ewch allan neu byddwch ddistaw!*

Sentences joined by *neu* are co-ordinate: *Darllenai yn y tŷ neu âi am dro yn y prynhawn.*

The conj. *ynteu* is often added to *neu;* §§ 68 (vii); 224:

Ysgrifennaf atoch, *neu ynteu* ('or else') dof i'ch gweld.

(iii) **ond** (formerly **onid**): 'but'; followed by the radical. It can join two co-ordinate sentences or else it can introduce a new sentence, especially in a series in narrative, like *A(c).*

Agorwyd y drws, *ond* ni ddaeth neb i mewn. *Ond* ymhen ychydig amser clywodd sŵn traed, a gwelodd rywun yn rhedeg i ffwrdd.

Neb ond and *dim ond* occur frequently in negative sentences:

Nid oes *neb ond* ef yn y tŷ. *Ni* welodd hi *ddim ond* tlodi.

In such examples *neb* and *dim* are often omitted:

Ni ddaw yma *ond* adar gwyllt. *Ni* thrigai yn y pentref *ond* hen bobl.

Because of the tendency to give *dim* a negative meaning 'nothing', it came to be used as a negative at the beginning of a sentence in speaking:

Dim ond sŵn y gwynt oedd yno (= Nid oedd dim ond sŵn . . .).
This usage has spread to the literary language, e.g.,

"*Dim ond* lleuad borffor/Ar fin y mynydd llwm" (Hedd Wyn 157);
"*Dim ond* calon lân all ganu" (Gwyrosydd); "*dim ond* y trefniant cyntaf a oedd yn bosibl" (Morgan, TC 273).
(In ETM 765 *Dim ond calon lân* became '*Does ond calon lân*. The 'amendment' has not been generally accepted).

Ond often occurs after *pawb, pob un, y cwbl, i gyd, oll*, etc.:

Daeth *pawb* yn gynnar *ond* ('except') Tomos; Gwerthodd y ffermwr yr anifeiliaid *i gyd ond* un fuwch; Safodd pawb ar eu traed *ond* Ieuan; Yr oedd y defaid a brynodd ef yn wynion *oll, ond* un ddafad.

(iv) **Namyn:** 'but': This form occurs in early modern literature but is rarely used today except with numerals, e.g., *cant namyn un* 'a hundred but one'; "*y deugain erthygl namyn un*" 'the 39 articles'; The form *amyn* has been amended to *namyn* in recent editions of the Scriptures, e.g., in Mt. xviii, 12, 13; Luke xv. 4.

(v) **eithr:** 'except, but'; *Eithr* is used in the same way as *ond*, but its main function today is to join two co-ordinate sentences or to introduce a sentence in a narrative series:

"*Eithr* Pedr ac Ioan a atebasant . . ." (Acts iv. 19); "Clywsoch ddywedyd . . . *Eithr* yr ydwyf fi yn dywedyd . . ." (Mt. v. 21, 22).

(vi) **Naill ai . . . neu (ynteu);** see § 93.

§ 229. na(c): The negatives *na, nac* correspond to the affirmatives *a, ac* in usages noted in § 228 (a)—(c), except that this conj. *na(c)* does not occur before the particles *fe* and *mi* and the negative particles *ni, na*. Sometimes *na(c)* is added immediately before the first of the words joined:

Nid oedd *na glaswellt na choed nac unrhyw arwydd* o fywyd yno.

§ 230. (i) The conj. **â, ag** 'as' follows *cyn* + equative adj. and *mor* + positive adj.: § 50 (i).
Instead of a noun or adj., etc. a clause may follow *â, ag;*

(a) relative clause:

Yr oedd yr adeilad *mor llawn ag* y gallai fod 'the building was as full as it could be'.
Nid yw *cyn iached ag* y bu hi 'she is not as healthy as she has been'.
Llyncwch *gymaint* o'r gwlybwr *ag* a êl ar lwy de 'swallow as much of the liquid as will fill a teaspoon'.
Rhedwch *cyn gynted (mor gyflym) ag* y galloch 'run as quickly as you can'.

(b) verb-noun clause:

Fe fu ef *mor ffôl â* gwerthu ei dŷ 'he has been so foolish as to sell his house'. Byddwch *cystal â* gyrru'r llythyr yn ôl 'be good enough to send back the letter'. Buont *mor llwfr â* rhedeg ymaith 'they were so cowardly as to run away'.

A verb-noun clause may suggest 'sequence', e.g., if it is understood that the first example above *(Fe fu mor ffôl . . .)* means 'he was so foolish that he sold his house'.

(c) consequence clause (a construction now regarded as antiquated):

Y mae hyn *cyn symled ag* y gall plentyn ei ddeall 'this is so simple that a child can understand it'.

"Cystal yw meddylfryd pur *â*'i fod yn sancteiddio'r weithred gyffredinaf; a *chyn rheitied ag* na thâl ein gweithredoedd gorau ni ddim hebddo" (RBS 15); "This grace (purity of intention) is so excellent, that it sanctifies the most common action of our life: and yet so necessary, that without it the very best actions of our devotion are imperfect and vicious" (Taylor, *Holy Living* 13).

(In the second example above note that it is a *verb-noun, fod,* that follows *â,* in the first clause, but that in the second *ag* is followed by a *negative verb (na thâl)* as there is no negative verb-noun; see § 181.)

(d) adverbial clause with *pe* and *pan:*

Yr oedd ei llais *mor glir â phe* bai yn yr un ystafell â ni 'her voice was as clear as if she were in the same room as we were'. Y mae ef *mor hapus* yno *â phan* oedd yn byw yma 'he is as happy there as when he was living here'.

(ii) The conjunction *â, ag* also follows words with the prefixes *cyf-, cy-, cyd-* (§ 187), such as *cyfryw, cynifer, cyfwerth, cyfliw, cydradd:*

Daeth *cynifer ag* a oedd yno ymlaen ato; Mae'r darn hwn yn *gyfwerth ag* aur; Yr oedd ei gwisg yn *gyfliw â*'r lili; Mae'r ddau fachgen yn *gydradd â*'i gilydd; Tynnwyd y tŷ yn *gydwastad â*'r llawr.

(iii) Because several other expressions are synonymous with *cymaint* and *cyfryw* some writers have mistakenly made them be followed by *â, ag,* e.g., *popeth ag a welwyd; pawb ag a oedd yno; yr holl bethau â ddywedid.* This led to the misconception that *ac a* or *ag a* was the full form of the relative pronoun.

§ **231.** A comparative adjective is followed by **na(g)**; § 51 (1). As after *â, ag,* a clause may follow instead of a noun etc.:

Yr oedd y canu'n *wannach nag* y gallwn ei glywed yn iawn.

Mae *mwy* o bobl yn marw o ddamweiniau ar y ffyrdd *nag* a laddwyd mewn llawer brwydr.

For mutation and forms see § 229. *Na(g)* can be repeated if the comparison refers to more than two objects:

Yr oedd y mwynhad a gâi yn y gwaith yn *bwysicach* iddo *na*'r tâl *ac na*'r gwyliau. *"Gwell* yw ffafr dda *nag* arian, *ac nag* aur" (Prov. xxii. 1).

§ 232. The following conjunctions are used to join co-ordinate sentences: *canys, oherwydd, oblegid, (o) achos, o waith (waith):*

Gwyddwn nad oedd neb gartref, *canys* nid oedd golau yno. Aeth hi i'r siop newydd, *oherwydd* clywsai fod bargeinion yno. Ni chawsom fwyd, *(o) achos* yr oedd y siop wedi cau. "O! pam na ddeui ar fy ôl/Ryw ddydd ar ôl ei gilydd?/*Waith* 'r wy'n dy weld, y feinir fach,/Yn lanach, lanach beunydd" (Folk-song).

Oherwydd, oblegid and *o achos* are also prepositions; § 195. Note the difference between these examples:

(a) Ni phrynais ddim, *oherwydd nid* oedd gennyf arian 'I bought nothing, for I had no money'.

(b) Ni phrynais ddim *oherwydd nad* oedd gennyf arian 'I bought nothing because I had no money'.

In (a) *oherwydd* is a conj. joining two co-ordinate sentences. In (b) it is a preposition introducing a subordinate clause.

§ 233. Several prepositions are followed by *y* or *na* to serve as conjunctions introducing adverbial clauses (i.e., subordinate clauses), viz., *am, gan oblegid, oherwydd, o achos, er, rhag ofn, rhag, wrth, erbyn, fel, megis, er mwyn, hyd, cyn, wedi, gydag.* These clauses may denote (i) cause, (ii) sequence, (iii) purpose, (iv) time, (v) manner, (vi) concession.

(i) *Cause.*

Deuthum adref *am nad oedd gwaith i'w gael* '. . . because there was no work to be had'. Arhosais yn y cysgod *am y gwyddwn y dychwelai'r lleidr* '. . . because I knew the thief would return'. Ni allodd ysgrifennu ataf *oblegid na wyddai fy nghyfeiriad* '. . . because he did not know my address'. Ni phrynodd hi'r llyfr *oherwydd nad oedd ganddi ddigon o arian* '. . . because she did not have enough money'. Ni sychodd y dillad *(o) achos nad oedd dim gwynt* '. . . because there was no wind'.

(ii) *Sequence.*

Yr oedd hi wedi gweithio mor galed *fel y gallodd arbed arian* '. . . that she was able to save money'. Blinasai gymaint *fel na allai godi ar ei draed* '. . . that he could not get up on his feet'. Siaradodd mor dda *fel yr oedd pawb yn gwrando* '. . . that every one listened'. Mae sŵn y storm mor uchel *fel nad yw'r canu i'w glywed* '. . . that the singing is not heard'.

Fel is sometimes only implied before *y(r)* and *na(d):*

Yr oedd y cnau mor dda, *yr oedd pawb yn rhyfeddu* '. . . (that) every one was amazed'. Siaradai mor isel, *nad oedd neb yn clywed* '. . . (that) no one could hear'.

(iii) *Purpose.*

Dewch i ben y bryn, *fel y galloch weld yr olygfa* '. . . so that you may see the view'. "Na fernwch, *fel na'ch barner*" (Mt. vii. 1) '. . . that you may not be judged'. Tynnodd y ci ato *rhag y lleddid ef gan y cerbyd* '. . . lest it should be killed by the vehicle'. Bwytasant bryd da, *rhag na chaent ddim am amser hir* '. . . lest they would have nothing for a long time'. Gwrandewch arno, *megis y dysgoch rywbeth ganddo* '. . . that you may learn something from him'.

(iv) *Time.*

Rhaid i ni fod yn barod *erbyn y daw'r car* '. . . by the (time) the car comes'. Rhedwch adref *cyn y daw'r glaw* '. . . before the rain comes'. Gellwch aros yma *hyd y mynnoch* '. . . as long as you wish'. Fe welwch y darlun yn union *wedi yr eloch drwy'r drws* '. . . after you go through the door'. (A more common construction today is *wedi i chwi fynd drwy'r drws;* § 207 (iii) (c).)

(v) *Manner.*

Mi wnaf *fel y bydd fy mam yn dweud* '. . . as my mother will say'. Mae hyn yn wir heddiw, *megis y bu erioed* '. . . as it has always been'.

Megis and *fel* are sometimes followed by *ag:*

"ni a gawn ei weled ef *megis ag y mae*" (1 John iii. 2) '. . . as he is'. "Bydd digon o nefoedd dros byth/Ei weled E' *fel ag y mae*" (T.W. 48).

For *fel pe, megis pe, fel mai* see §§ 236 (iii) (e); 237 (iv).

(vi) *Concession.*

Gallwn fynd am dro, *er nad yw'r tywydd yn dda* '. . . though the weather is not good'. Gallodd gario'r baich *er nad yw hi'n gryf* '. . . though she is not strong'. "eithr mae e'n cael cennad . . . i ymweled â'r Ddinas . . . *er y gŵyr ef na wna hynny ond chwanegu ei gôsp*" (B.Cw. 44) '. . . though he knows that that will but add to his punishment'.

In an affirmative clause the usual construction today is *er i* + verb-noun: § 207 (iii) (c).

§ 234. There are also a few nouns and adjectives used with *y* or *na* to introduce adverbial clauses denoting time, place, cause, etc.: *pryd, pryd bynnag, lle, nes, hyd nes, cymaint ag, modd;* see § 88.

Bydd y cyfarfod am saith, *pryd y ceir anerchiad gan y Llywydd* '. . . when an address will be given by the President'. Cewch groeso *pryd bynnag y dewch* '. . . whenever you come'. Byddant yn

gweithio *(hyd) nes yr â'r haul i lawr* '. . . until the sun goes down'. Ni
ellir gweithio ar y tŷ *pryd na fydd y tywydd yn sych* '. . . when the
weather is not dry'. Af gydag ef *pa le bynnag yr êl* '. . . wherever he
my go'. Mae'r ci yn gorwedd *lle y mae cysgod* '. . . where there is
shade'. "Ac â i wlad *lle na raid cael/Byth lusern mwy na golau haul*"
(J.R. FG 160) '. . . where neither a lantern nor sunlight is needed
any more'.

As in the last example above *lle* is now followed by *na(d)*, but formerly
by *ni(d):*

"*. . . lle nid* oes na gwyfyn na rhwd yn llygru, a *lle ni* chloddia
lladron trwodd ac *ni* ladradânt" (Mt. vi. 20).

Lle often stands for *lle y* (§ 72):

"Crwydro am oes *lle y mynno ei hun,*/A marw *lle mynno Duw*"
(Eifion Wyn, *Caniadau* 27) 'Wandering throughout life where he
wills, and dying where God wills'.

The equative adj. *cymaint ag* becomes *yn gymaint ag* 'inasmuch as' as a
conjunction:

"*Yn gymaint ag nas gwnaethoch* i'r un o'r rhai lleiaf . . ." (Mt.
xxv. 45) 'Inasmuch as ye did it not to one of the least . . .'.

Instead of *(hyd) nes y* in an adverbial clause *(Rhedodd nes y blinodd* 'he
ran until he was tired') a verb-noun, with or without *i,* can be used:
Rhedodd nes blino or *Rhedodd nes iddo flino;* §§ 195; 207 (iii) (c).

§ 235. The following conjunctions denote time:

(i) **pan**: 'when'. In an affirmative clause it is followed immediately by
a verb (with soft mut.):

Pan fydd hi'n naw o'r gloch mi af allan. Neidiodd ar ei draed *pan
glywodd* y gloch yn canu. Ceisiodd ddianc *pan welwyd* ef.

If the infixed object is used (before the verb) it can be 'supported' by *y*
after *pan* (though this *y* is not the relative particle as in *pryd y):* but a
prefixed pronoun can take the place of *y* + infixed pronoun:

"*Pan y'm clywai clust* . . . a *phan y'm gwelai* . . ."(Job xxix. 11).
Ymserchodd ef yn y ferch *pan ei gwelodd.* "*Pan ei* gwelais, syth mi
sefais" (Folk-song).

Subordinate clauses following one introduced by *pan* can be joined by
y instead of repeating *pan:*

"Gwyn eich byd *pan y'ch* gwaradwyddant, ac *y'ch* erlidiant, ac *y*
dywedant bob drygair . . ." (Mt. v. 11). *Pan* eisteddai wrth y
ffenestr, *ac y* clywai'r adar yn canu, *ac y* gwyddai mai yn y coed yr
oeddynt, dyheai am fynd allan.

The verb after *pan* is commonly in the present subjunctive, especially
if the time referred to is indefinite:

Pan fo dyn yn mynd yn hen daw'r atgofion yn fyw iddo. "Bydd
glaswellt ar fy llwybrau i/*Pan ddelwyf* i Gymru'n ôl" (Folk-song).
"*Pan fyddo*'r don ar f'enaid gwan yn curo . . ." (Elfed CAN 796).
§ 118 (ii).

If it is necessary for the verb to be in the indicative mood, the form of the verb *bod* after *pan* is *yw* (not *y mae)*:

"a phaham y deuwch ataf fi yn awr, *pan yw* gyfyng arnoch?" (Judges xi. 7).

In a negative clause *pan* is followed by *na(d)*:

"*A phan na* allai hi ei guddio ef yn hwy . . ." (Ex. ii. 3). *Pan nad* oedd neb yn ei weld, rhedodd o'r ardd.

(ii) **er pan** 'since': See *pan* above; and § 203 (iv):

Mae'n amser hir *er pan* welais ef.

(iii) **tra** 'while': The radical of the verb follows it immediately:

"Ond cariad pur sydd fel y dur/Yn para *tra bo* dau" (Folk-song).

"Y ffôl, *tra tawo,* a gyfrifir yn ddoeth" (Prov. xvii. 28).

There have been inconsistences in the past (and some still remain) in the use of *tra*. It has sometimes been followed by the soft mutation, e.g., "gelwch arno *tra fyddo* yn agos" (Is. lv. 6); and in the same verse we find *tra y:* "Ceisiwch yr Arglwydd *tra y* galler ei gael".

As stated above, § 187 (ii), the adverb *tra* 'very' and the prefix *tra-* both take the spirant mut., and the practice of mutating in the same way after the conj. *tra* 'while' has been adopted by many writers. However, this departure from the oldest tradition is now not acceptable; see TC 379. As with *pan* there is a tendency to put the verb in the present subjunctive (§ 118 (ii)) after *tra*.

In a negative clause we have *tra na(d)*:

Aeth y lleidr i'r tŷ *tra nad* oedd neb gartref. Yno y gorweddai *tra na* ddaeth neb heibio.

(iv) **oni, hyd oni** 'until': since *oni* is a conjunction with two meanings, 'if not' and 'until', and also an interrogative particle, ambiguity is avoided by using *hyd oni* for 'until'. The mutations that follow are the same as after *ni;* § 77:

Arhosodd hi ar y bont *hyd onid* aeth y dorf heibio. Rhaid inni aros yma *hyd oni chawn* gyfle i fynd yng nghar rhywun. *Oni ddaw*'r meddyg gwell inni ofalu am y claf '. . . until the doctor comes'.

(v) **cyn** 'before': In § 233 *cyn* was included among the prepositions used with *y* as conjunctions. Formerly *cyn* could be so without an intervening *y* before the verb. It may be that there is an echo from this old construction in such expressions as *cyn bo hir* 'before long' or in the folk-song line *Cyn delwyf i Gymru'n ôl* 'before I (may) return to Wales'.

§ 236. Os, o, oni and **pe** are conjunctions introducing conditional clauses:

(i) *os, o, od* 'if': (a) The form commonly used in prose today is *os,* which has supplanted *o* (before a consonant) and *od* (before a vowel), except in some poetry and some rather pedantic prose. The verb follows immediately after *os,* except when some other part of the clause is emphasised:

> *Os credwch* chwi hynny, fe gredwch unrhyw beth. Fe'ch gwelaf yno, *os af* i'r cyfarfod.

All three forms occur in biblical Welsh, almost indiscriminately:

> *"Os gofynnwch* ddim yn fy enw i, mi a'i gwnaf. *O cherwch* fi, cedwch fy ngorchymynion" (John xiv. 14, 15). *"Os yw* neb . . . *od oes* neb" (2 Tim. ii. 5).

Like *oni* the conj. *o* takes the spirant mut.:

> *O phalla hyn* 'if this fails'; *O chredwch; O theli* 'if thou payest'.

(b) When any part of the clause other than the verb is emphasised, it comes immediately after *os:*

> *Os hyn* yw dy ddymuniad, af ymaith 'if this is your wish, I shall go away'. *"Os mab Duw* wyt ti, arch i'r cerrig hyn fod yn fara" (Mt. iv. 3). *Os dy dad* a ddywedodd wrthyt am fynd, mae popeth yn iawn. *Os cysgu* y mae'r plant, peidiwch â'u deffro.

There are many examples of placing some part other than the verb after *os* when no emphasis is intended, thus producing a clause on the pattern of an Abnormal Sentence (§ 247). This construction, though common in the Bible and later writing, is avoided by standard writers:

> *"Ac os myfi* a af . . . mi a ddeuaf drachefn" (John xiv. 3). (In meaning this is *Os af fi . . .* 'If I go', without any emphasis on *myfi).* *"Os chwychwi* . . . a fedrwch roddi rhoddion da . . ." (Mt. vii. 11).

There is a tendency in some dialects to insert *mai* or *taw* between *os* and the word(s) emphasised, e.g., *Os mai (taw) fi sydd yn mynd* instead of *Os fi fydd yn mynd.* This can not be regarded as correct in writing.

(ii) (a) The conj. *o* and the negative *ni(d)* are combined to form *oni(d)* 'if not, unless':

> Rhaid i mi fynd, *oni ddaw neb* i agor y drws '. . . unless someone comes . . .' *Onid arhoswch* yma i gysgodi, fe fyddwch yn gwlychu 'If you do not stay here to shelter . . .' Byddai'n ddrwg iawn arni, *oni bai* bod cymdogion yn gofalu amdani' She would be in a bad way, if neighbours did not look after her'.

The verb following *oni(d)* is in the indicative except that in the case of *bod* it can be in the imperfect subjunctive or the pluperfect:

> *Oni byddai'r tywydd yn ddrwg iawn,* gwelid ef yn y pentref bob dydd 'Unless the weather were very bad . . .'. *Oni buasai amdano ef, byddai pawb wedi eu lladd* 'Had it not been for him, all would have been killed'.

(b) The negative form corresponding to *os* before the word or words emphasised is *onid:*

> *Onid hwn yw dy lyfr di,* ni wn pa le y mae ef 'If this is not your book . . .'. *Onid yn erbyn y goeden* y gadewaist y rhaw?' Was it not against the tree you left the spade?'

An abnormal construction with *os . . . ni + verb,* and with no emphasis on what follows *os* sometimes occurs in biblical Welsh; cf. (i) (b) above:

"*Ac os Crist ni chyfodwyd, . . . os y meirw ni chyfodir . . .*" (1 Cor. xv. 14).

(c) In speaking *oni(d)* 'if not, unless' has been generally supplanted by *os na(d),* and this change has spread to the written language:

Mi ddof i'ch gweld yfory *os na* fydd fy nhad yn waelach. Ef oedd un o'r beirdd mwyaf, *os nad* y mwyaf oll, yn y cyfnod hwnnw. "*Os nad* yw hi'n fawr, mae hi'n ddigon . . ."

(iii) (a) After *pe(d)* the verb is in the imperfect subjunctive or the pluperfect (§§ 119 (i); 117 (ii)):

"Fy nghalon a'i carai, *pe gwyddwn* y cawn" (Folk-song). "*Pe buasit* ti yma, ni buasai farw fy mrawd" (John xi. 21). *Ped addefai*'r gwir, ni chosbid ef 'If he were to admit the truth, he would not be punished'.

The form *pes* contains the infixed pronoun, 3 sing. and plur., -*s* as object; § 72. Its use is now antiquated.

In addition to *pe bawn, pe bait,* etc., and *pe buaswn, buasit,* etc., the following forms (contracted from medieval expressions) are commonly used:

Imperfect		Pluperfect	
petáwn	petâem	petaswn	petasem
petáit	petâech	petasit	petasech
petái	petâent	petasai	petasent

(b) In a negative clause we have *pe na:*

Byddai'n dda gennyf *pe na ddywedaswn* ddim wrtho 'I would be glad if I had not said anything to him'. "Da fuasai i'r dyn hwnnw *pe nas* ganesid" Mk. xiv. 21).

(c) Other parts of speech can be inserted between *pe* and the verb for emphasis:

Pe deillion fyddech, hawdd fyddai maddau ichwi 'If you were blind . . .' *Pe gwir* fyddai hyn, byddai'n gywilydd i bawb.

(d) Sometimes *am y* + verb in the pres. subj. is equivalent to *os* + verb in the indicative:

"yna pawb a'i stori . . . os gwir, os celwydd, nis gwaeth, *am y bo* hi'n ddigrif" (B.CW. 23) '. . . provided it be funny'. Fe gânt fwyd, *am y bônt* hwy'n talu amdano '. . . provided they pay for it'. § 118 (ii).

In the spoken language other means of expressing 'if only, provided that' have become prevalent, e.g.,

Dim ond iti ddweud y gwir, fe gei fynd adre 'If you only tell the truth ⸏ . .'. *Ond ichi dalu* am y rhaglen, cewch fynd i'r cyngerdd 'Provided you pay for the programme . . .'.

(e) *Fel* and *megis* can be followed by *pe:*

Yr oedd hi'n chwerthin *fel petai* hi ar hollti '. . . as if she were about to burst'. Yr oedd y plant yn y wlad honno yn dringo coed *megis petaent* yn gathod neu deigrod '. . . as if they were cats or tigers'.

§ 237. (i) **Mai** 'that (it is)' precedes a noun-clause when a part of it, other than the verb, is emphasised:

Gwn yn iawn *mai yng Nghymru* y mae Gwent. "Gwybyddwch *mai yr Arglwydd* sydd Dduw" (Ps. c. 3).

(ii) As well as *mai* the conj. *taw* is heard in some S. Wales dialects, and used by some writers:

"Diau *taw*'r gair hwn sydd yn yr enw *Porth y Rhyd*" (DIG 3) 'It is doubtless that this is the word which is in . . .'.

"barnai eraill *taw* gwell iddynt fyned yn eu blaen" (YS 119) 'others believed that it was better for them to go on'.

(iii) The negative conj. corresponding to *mai* is *nad:*

"canfyddwn, mi gredaf, *nad* hollol gywir y farn hon" (R.T.J. 9) '. . . that this opinion is not completely correct'.

"a chofia, *nad digon* i ddyn fyned i ffordd dda . . ." (LlTA 253) 'and remember that it is not enough for a man to go . . .'.

In speaking, *nad* in this construction has largely been supplanted by *mai (taw) nid*, which has appeared in writing from the 18th century onwards. Such usage, however, is not regarded as acceptable in literary Welsh. A far worse corruption is the substitution of *nage (nace)* for *nad* and *nid* in some S. Wales dialects.

(iv) *Fel* can be followed by *mai:*

Yr oedd y twll yn y berth mor fach *fel mai* prin y gallodd fynd trwyddo '. . . that he could hardly go through it'. Mae'r mwyar wedi cympo o'r fasged, *fel mai* ychydig sydd ar ôl '. . . so that only a few are left'.

Comparison, rather than sequence, is implied by *mai fel* in:

"*fel mai* byw yr Arglwydd, pe gadawsech hwynt yn fyw, ni laddwn chwi" (Judges viii. 19) 'as the Lord liveth, if ye had saved them alive, I would not slay you'.

§ 238. **Po** is considered to be a conjunction before a superlative adjective in proportionate equality (§ 52 (iii)), although it was originally a verb, viz. *bo*, 3 sing. pres. subj. of *bod:*

Gorau *po gyntaf* y dychweli 'the sooner you return, the better'.

Po dywyllaf yr âi, cyflymaf y cerddai hi 'the darker it became, the faster she walked'.

INTERJECTIONS

§ 239. (i) Simple interjections: *a, ha, o, ho, och, ach, ych, ha-ha, o-ho, wfft, gwae, ust, twt, pw, wel,* etc. In the dialects several others are heard, e.g. *ew, whiw, dir, heisht, hei.*

(ii) Interjectional expressions: (a) greetings and wishes, e.g., *Bore da!; Prynhawn da!; Da boch ch(w)i!; Dydd da ich(w)i!; Nos dawch* (= Nos da iwch/ichwi); *Yn iach (iti)!* 'Farewell'; *Diolch (iti); Iechyd da!; O! na . . . Gwyn-fyd na* 'would that' (+ verb); *Croeso!; O'r gorau/* 'very well'.

(b) blessings and curses, e.g., *Bendith arno!* 'bless him'; *Melltith arnoch!* 'curse you'; *Rhad arnynt!* 'bless them (ironical)'; *Yn boeth y bo!* 'may he burn'; *Rhag cywilydd!* 'for shame'. *Yr achlod!* 'shame'.

(c) oaths (mild), e.g. *Myn* (obscure *y*) + noun, *Myn f'enaid i!; Myn cythraul!; Myn gafr!; Ar f'enaid!; Er mwyn dim!; Yn enw popeth!; Yn enw dyn!,* colloq. *Neno dyn!* (for *Yn enw Duw); Nefoedd fawr!; Bobol fawr!; Bobol annwyl!; Hawyr bach!*

(d) entreaties, e.g., *Da chwithau (chwi)! Atolwg!* 'pray'.

(e) interjection + pronoun or noun: *Gwae fi; Gwae ninnau; Och Gymru!; Ach fi!,* colloq. *Ach y fi, Ach a fi, Ych y fi!*

(f) interjection + preposition: *Wfft iddo!; Ffei ohonynt!*

(g) expressions of compassion or despair: *Duw a'i helpo!; A'n helpo ni!; Duw a'n catwo ni (bawb)!,* colloq. *Dyn cato ni! Cato'n bawb (pawb).*

(h) expressions of amazement or surprise: *Wele!; Felly'n wir!; O'n wir!; Dyna drueni!; Gresyn mawr!; O! druan bach!; Druan ohono!; Dyna hi!; 'Does bosib!; Wel* (for *wele) dyna beth mawr!*

(iii) An interjection may be the predicate in a noun predicate sentence:

> "*Gwae fi* fy myw mewn oes mor ddreng" (Hedd Wyn 47) 'Woe is me that I live in an age so sorrowful'. *Croeso* iddo ddweud hynny 'he is welcome to say so'.

(iv) An interjection is often followed by a noun in the vocative case: *Ha fab; Ust blant; Och wraig; Hylô fachgen;* "Ffarwél, ffarwél, dwyllodrus fyd" (T.W. 49); "Ac yn iach ganu'n uchel" (L.G.C., BU 49); "O Dduw, 'rwy'n anobeithio" (T.W. 17); "Och Feuno, uchaf onnen" (T.A. 365). The name of a person in the vocative case is not generally mutated now in speaking, nor always in writing, especially when it comes first in the sentence: "Dafydd, tyrd adref!'"; "Duw mawr y rhyfeddodau maith" (CAN 728); "Crist, gwared ni!" A loose compound is formed when an adj. precedes the vocative, and the second element therefore mutates: *Annwyl gyfaill.* The vocative word may be a pronoun, and a following noun in apposition is mutated: *Ti, frawd; Chwithau, wrandawyr.* (For a full discussion of mutation after interjections see TC 416—424).

SYNTAX

(THE SENTENCE)

§ 240. A sentence may be a statement, a question, a command, a wish, or an exclamation:

Statement: Gwelodd y plentyn geffyl. 'The child saw a horse'.

Question: A welodd ef y ceffyl? (The reply is usually a statement: Do (fe welodd y ceffyl); Ni wn i.)

Command: Edrychwch ar eich llyfrau! 'Look at your books!'

Wish: O! na ddeuai'r rhyfel i ben! 'Would that the war would end!'

Exclamation: Hardded y nos! 'How beautiful is the night!'

Every sentence has two elements, the *predicate* and the *subject.* The subject is not always named; it may be understood from the context or from the situation of which the listener is aware, or it may be denoted by the form of the verb in the predicate. When the predicate is a *verb* (usually with other words relevant to the meaning) we have a *Verb-predicate Sentence.* When the predicate is a *noun* (in the fullest sense of the word, i.e., a noun, pronoun, verb-noun, adjective or adverb) we have a *Noun-predicate Sentence.*

§ 241. The Noun-predicate Sentence.

(i) The predicate is shown in italics in the following examples of noun-predicate sentences (mostly proverbial sayings):

Hir pob aros.
Popeth newydd *dedwydd da.*
Drych i bawb ei gymydog.
Nes penelin *nag arddwrn.*
Hawdd tynnu gwaed o ben crach.
Pechodau athrawon *athrawon pechodau.*
Digrif gan bob aderyn ei lais.
Gweddw crefft heb ei dawn.
Gorau cof, cof llyfr.
"*Gwyn eu byd* y tangnefeddwyr".
Da gennyf eich gweld.
Drwg gennym glywed hynny.
Nid aur popeth melyn.
Nid hawdd dringo mynydd.

A sentence such as 'Llawer gwir, gwell ei gelu' can be regarded as a noun-predicate sentence with *llawer gwir* as subject and *gwell ei gelu* as predicate. Also *gwell ei gelu* alone can be so regarded, with *gwell* as predicate and *ei gelu* as subject. ('Many a truth is better hidden').

(ii) One of the forms of *bod* can be inserted in a noun-predicate sentence to denote the time to which the predicate refers. This verbal form is called the *copula,* as its main function is to join the subject and the predicate.

(a) The copula can be between the predicate and the subject:

Hir *yw* pob aros.
Nid aur *yw* popeth melyn.
Da gennyf *oedd* ei weld/Da *oedd* gennyf ei weld.
Dymunol *fyddai* cael mynd am dro.
Drwg iawn *fu*'r tywydd.
Eu twyllo hwy *fydd* dweud hynny.
Saer *fuasai* fy nhad.

(b) The copula can begin the sentence, and in such a case the predicate, if it is a noun or verb-noun or adjective, is preceded by *yn,* the predicative *yn* mentioned in § 141:

Y mae pob aros *yn* hir.
Nid yw popeth melyn *yn* aur.
Yr oedd fy nhad *yn* delynor.
Bydd hyn *yn* dorri tir newydd.
Yr oedd yn dda gennyf glywed hynny/*Yr oedd* clywed hynny *yn* dda gennyf.
Buasai Dafydd *yn* frenin da.

In sentences of the type given in the above examples the predicate is sometimes called the *complement,* as in § 142 (i), and this is often a convenient term.

This construction was formerly used without the predicative *yn,* and still is in some traditional expressions:

"Byddwch lawen a hyfryd" (Mt. v. 12).
"Canys bûm newynog" (Mt. xxv. 35) (The subject is here indicated by the form of the copula, *bûm (i)*).
Byddwch wych!

(The complement-predicate is mutated in the above, as after *yn*).

(c) When the predicate is adverbial it can not be preceded by *yn:*

Y mae pawb *felly.*
Yr oedd ei gnawd *fel eira.*
Byddai fy nwylo *mor ddu â'r glo.*

NOTE: The verb *bod,* of course, has its own verbal function with the meaning 'to exist', e.g.,

Y mae bydoedd eraill. *Nid oes* gobaith iddo. *Bu* haf sych y llynedd. A *oes* heddwch? Fe *fydd* etholiad.

The distinction between the two functions of *bod* is not always clearly defined. In the periphrastic construction, e.g., in *Mae'r plentyn yn cysgu* the predicative *yn* suggests that this is a noun-predicate sentence, with *mae* as copula. However, the fact that the sentence is but another way of saying *Cwsg y plentyn*, a verb-predicate sentence, one must regard this as being the same. It is when predicative *yn* is followed by a noun or adjective (and not a verb-noun) that we have a noun-predicate sentence; § 213 (iii). *Mae* may be regarded as an auxiliary in *Mae . . . yn cysgu*, in an expression equivalent to a verb.

§ 242. The Verb-predicate Sentence.

In a verb-predicate sentence a verb is the predicate or an essential part of it.

(i) When the subject is a noun, a demonstrative pronoun (§ 89), or one of the pronominalia in §§ 92-98, the verb is always in the *third person singular*, even when the subject is plural (§ 113):

Daeth y dyn. Daeth y dynion. Daeth rhywun. Daeth rhywrai. Rhedodd hwnnw. Aeth y rhai hynny.

(ii) The personal ending of the verb may denote the subject:

Gwelaf. Cei. Daw. Rhedwn. Rhoddwch. Dywedant. Cefais. Rhoesoch. Credasom.

These personal forms are commonly followed by auxiliary personal pronouns; §§ 69(c); 74:

Gwelais i. Buoch chwi. Aethant hwy. Clyw ef. Credaf fi. Gweli di.

They can also be preceded by independent pronouns; § 67:

Mi ddywedaf (fi). Chwi wyddoch. Fe gaiff. Fe gânt. (See § 68 (iv)).

These personal pronouns are not the subjects of verbs; they are extensions of verbal endings.

(iii) The subject of an impersonal form of a verb is neither expressed nor implied:

Cychwynnir yn brydlon 'One will start promptly, i.e., a prompt start will be made'.

The doer of the action can be indicated by means of a noun preceded by the preposition *gan*, or by an inflected form of *gan* without a noun (§ 121):

Cenir y gân *gan Iwan* 'the song will be sung by Iwan'. Rhoddwyd y llyfrau i'r plant *gan y cadeirydd*, a chafwyd anerchiad *ganddo* 'The books were given to the children by the chairman, and an address was given by him'.

The object is not mutated when it follows immediately after an impersonal form; § 123 (iii).

When a verb-noun is used instead of an inflected form of the verb (§ 178 (v), (vi)) the sentence is considered to be a verb-predicate sentence:

Aeth y dyn ymlaen ac *agor y drws.*

§ 243. A Co-ordinate sentence is one which contains two or more simple sentences joined by co-ordinating conjunctions; § 228:

Aeth hi i'r tŷ *ac* eisteddodd wrth y tân.

Edrychais drwy'r ffenestr *ond* ni welais neb.

Cei fynd i'r cyngerdd *neu (ynteu)* gelli aros gartref.

§ 244. In a **Complex Sentence** there is a Main Sentence and a Subordinate Sentence (or Subordinate Sentences). A Subordinate Sentence is conveniently called a (subordinate) Clause:

Main Sentence	*Clause*
Aeth allan i weithio	pan alwodd ei feistr arno.
Mi af i lan y môr	os bydd y tywydd yn braf.
Ni wyddai hi	pwy oedd yno.
Mi af i weld y dyn	a werthodd y peth hwn i ti.

§ 245. A Relative Clause is either adjectival or adverbial in function. As a rule it refers to an antecedent, viz., a noun, pronoun, or other equivalent expression, in the main sentence. The antecedent is sometimes implied instead of being expressed.

When the relative pronoun is in the nominative or accusative case the clause is called a Proper Relative Clause. When the relative is in one of the oblique cases, or when it is governed by a preposition, it seems appropriate to call the clause an Oblique Relative Clause. The various types of relative clauses, with examples, are discussed above in §§ 76-87. Following is a summary:

(i) Proper Relative Clause: (a) where the relative is the subject:

Hwn yw'r ci *a achubodd y plentyn.*

Rhaid torri'r coed *na ddygant ffrwyth.*

Ni wn i am *a ddigwyddodd* (with the antecedent not expressed) 'I do not know of what happened'.

(b) where the relative is the object:

Ai hon yw'r het *a brynasoch?*

Gwrthodais y rhai *na(s) hoffwn.*

Mi gredaf *a welaf* (with the antecedent not expressed).

(ii) Oblique Relative Clause: (a) where the relative is in the genitive:

Aethom i'r tŷ *yr oedd ei ddrws yn agored* '. . . the door of which was open'.

Gall y rhai *y gwelais i eu gwaith* fynd adref '. . . those whose work I have seen . . .'.

Fe welwch bethau *na fyddwch yn hoffi eu gweld* '. . . that you will not like to see (lit. . . . not like the seeing of them)'.

(b) where the relative is governed by a preposition:

Hon yw'r gadair *yr eisteddai ef arni* '. . . on which he would sit'.

Aeth y plant *nad oedd cotiau glaw ganddynt* yn ôl i'r ysgol '. . . with whom there were no raincoats . . .'   —

(c) where the relative is in an adverbial case:

Dyna'r unig dro *y gwelais ef* 'That is the only occasion (when) I saw him'.

Ni wn beth yw'r rheswm *yr aeth i ffwrdd* '. . . the reason why he went away'.

Yr oedd y gyllell mewn lle *nad oeddwn wedi edrych* '. . . where I had not looked'.

Nid yw hi cystal ag *y bu* (after *ag* here the antecedent is not expressed; see §§ 230 (i) (a); 242 (iii).

§ 246. The Mixed Sentence.

The normal order of the simple sentence in Welsh is *verb + subject + object + extension of predicate:*

Rhedodd y ferch i ganol yr heol 'The girl ran to the middle of the road'.

Prynodd y ffermwr geffyl (ddoe).

Cynhelir eisteddfod yn yr haf. (The impersonal forms of verbs have no expressed subject; § 121).

The verb can be preceded by prefixed and infixed pronouns, preverbal particles, and adverbs: *Fe redodd; Mi welais; Ni ddaeth; A roddodd?; Oni phrynodd; Fe'm gwelsoch; Yna safodd; Ac felly cododd; Bob bore darllenai'r papur.*

If it is desired to emphasise any part of a simple sentence other than the verb, that part is placed first and then followed by a relative clause. By so doing the simple sentence becomes a *Mixed Sentence:*

Simple Sentence	Mixed Sentence	Part emphasised
Rhedodd y plentyn adref.	*Y plentyn* a redodd adref.	Subject
Prynodd y dyn geffyl.	*Ceffyl* a brynodd y dyn.	Object
Rhoddais lythyr iddo.	*Llythyr* a roddais i iddo.	Object
Mi glywais y gloch.	*Fi/Myfi* a glywodd y gloch.	Subject
Fe'th welwyd ganddo.	*Ti* a welwyd ganddo.	Object
Canai'r aderyn ar y pren.	*Ar y pren* y canai'r aderyn	Adverb
Ni fydd ef yn y capel.	*Nid yn y capel* y bydd ef.	Adverb
Byddwn yn bwyta yma.	*Bwyta* y byddwn ni yma.	Predicate

For the use of *a, y(r); ni(d), na(d)* as relatives see §§ 80-82; also the relatival form *sydd,* § 83; *piau,* § 84; and *a'r, a,* § 85.

NOTE. When the *complement* is placed before the copula in a noun-predicate sentence, whether it is emphasised or not, no relative clause follows, and the sentence is still simple. Initial *b-* of copula forms is mutated to *f-* after the complement, § 154:

"*Yr Arglwydd* yw fy mugail". *Gwyn* (yd)oedd lliw'r aderyn. *Cadeirydd f*yddwch chi i'r pwyllgor. *Beth f*ydd y bachgen? *Onid ti* yw ei fab?

On the omission of *a* before forms of *bod* in a relative clause see § 153.

§ 247. The Abnormal Sentence.

There is another kind of sentence in which the subject or the object (or the object of a verb-noun) comes first but bears no emphasis. This is called an *Abnormal Sentence*. It is a construction very commonly found in literature as late as the beginning of the present century, when grammarians began to condemn it. In the Welsh translation of the scriptures the simple sentence has to a considerable extent been supplanted by the abnormal sentence. In form the examples following are similar to mixed sentences, but in meaning they are not, because there is no emphasis on the subject or object at the beginning. The verb in the quasi relative clause agrees in number and person with the subject, whereas the verb in the true relative clause is always 3 sing. after *a*:

"A'i ddisgyblion a ddaethant ato, ac a'i deffroasant" (Mt. viii. 25).
"Canys efe a draddodir i'r Cenhedloedd, ac a watwerir, ac a amherchir, ac a boerir arno" (Luke xviii. 32).
"a'm pechod sydd yn wastad ger fy mron" (Ps. li. 3).

The above examples could be re-written as co-ordinate sentences without altering the meaning:

Daeth ei ddisgyblion ato a deffroasant ef.
Canys traddodir ef . . . a gwatwerir ef, ac amherchir ef, a phoerir arno.

Or as simple sentences:

Y mae fy mhechod yn wastad ger fy mron.

On the use of pronouns and particles before verbs see § 68 (iv).

(N.B. *Mi gefais anrheg* 'I received a gift'—Simple Sentence.
Myfi a gefais anrheg 'I received a gift'—Abnormal Sentence.
Myfi (fi) a gafodd anrheg 'It was I who received a gift'—Mixed Sentence.

§ 248. The Noun-clause.

A clause can take the place of a noun as the subject of a sentence, or it may be the object of a verb-noun or verb, or be in apposition to a noun or pronoun. Such a clause is called a *Noun-clause*. (This should not be confused with a Noun-predicate Sentence, §§ 240-41).

§ 249. *The Noun-clause with a verb-predicate:*

(i) The noun-clause is introduced by the affirmative particle *y(r)* or the negative particle *na(d)* placed before its verb:

Gwn *y daw ef* 'I know that he will come'. Gwyddwn *y deuai ef* 'I knew that he would come'. Ni chredaf *y gwyddant hwy* 'I do not believe that they know'. Yr oedd ef yn dweud *yr âi* 'He was saying that he would go'. Gwn *na ddaw hi* 'I know that she will not come'. Gwelaf *na fu neb yma* 'I see that no one has been here'.

In the above examples the noun-clause is the *object* of the verb or of a verb-noun in the main sentence. In the following it is the subject of the main sentence:

Ai gwir yw *y gwneir arbrofion?* 'Is it true that experiments will be done?' Mae'n dda gennyf *y bwriedwch ddyfod* 'I am glad that you intend to come'. Digon gwir *y byddwn yn galw i'w gweld* 'That we shall be calling to see her is true enough'. Mae'n amlwg *na wnaethoch ddim* 'It is obvious that you did nothing'. Mae'n bosibl *na fydd ef gartref* 'It is possible that he will not be at home'. Dichon *y gwelwch ni* 'It may be that you will see us'.

On the use of the imperfect tense in noun-clauses see §§ 115 (iii) (v) (vi); 117 Note. On the use of the present subjunctive after commands, see § 118 (iii).

In the following examples the noun-clause is in apposition to a pronoun or noun:

Yr wyf yn sicr o *hyn, y bydd ef yma yfory* 'I am sure of this, that he will be here tomorrow'. Mi wyddwn i *hynny, nad oedd hi'n dweud y gwir* 'I knew that, that she was not telling the truth'. Amlwg iawn oedd y *ffaith, na welsai'r mab ei frawd erioed* 'The fact that the son had never seen his brother was very obvious'.

Sentences such as the following also contain a noun-clause:

Yr wyf yn siŵr *y daw llythyr* 'I am sure that a letter will come'.

Yr wyf yn siŵr can be paraphrased as *Credaf/Gwn yn siŵr*. Otherwise one may consider that words such as *o hyn* or *o un peth* are understood after *yn siŵr*, and that the noun-clause is in apposition to the pronoun or noun understood.

Formerly one could have a negative noun-clause equivalent to a verb-noun used negatively:

"Canys ni allwn *na ddywedom*" (Acts iv. 20) [= *beidio â dywedyd*]; see §§ 118 (iv); 181 Note.

(ii) When any part of a noun-clause, other than the verb, is to be emphasised it is preceded by *mai, taw* or *nad;* § 237:

Rhaid iti ddeall *mai gwell iti ufuddhau* 'You must understand that it is better for you to obey', Gwyddom *nad gwiw inni gwyno* 'We know that it will not do for us to complain'.

(iii) An equative adjective at the beginning of a noun-clause emphasises some special quality:

Mynnai ddangos i bawb *gystal ysgolhaig ydoedd* 'He wanted to show everybody what a good scholar he was'. Ni chredech *mor fwyn ydoedd hi* 'You would not believe how gentle she was'. Gwelwyd y dydd hwnnw *ddewred y gallant ymladd* 'It was seen on that day how bravely they could fight'. (See § 50 (iii)).

(iv) Every indirect question is a noun-clause:

Gofynnwch iddi *a oedd ganddi arian.* Dechreuodd holi *ai fi a wnaeth y drwg.* Ceisiwch wybod *pwy a fu yno.* Gofynnais wedyn *a oedd ei dad yn gwybod.* Cei weld a *fu ef yno.* 'You shall know whether he has been there'.

§ 250. *The Noun-clause with a verb-noun predicate.*

When the 'action' in the noun-clause is affirmative and in a tense other than the future or the imperfect (including the future from the standpoint of the past, § 115 (vi)), a verb-noun is used instead of a verb in the noun-clause. But a future meaning can be conveyed also in one construction with a verb-noun; see (iii) below.

(i) The subject of the verb-noun in the noun-clause can be governed by a preposition, either *i* or *o,* or else the subject can follow an 'intransitive' verb-noun without a preposition; see § 179 (iii):

Mae'n dda gennyf *iti ddweud y gwir* '. . . that you told the truth'. Gwn *iddo fynd yno ddoe.* Clywodd y ferch *ddarfod i'w thad ennill y gadair* '. . . that her father had won the chair'. Wedi'r ymdrech bu *iddynt orffwys ar y traeth.* 'A hon yw'r ddamnedigaeth, *ddyfod goleuni i'r byd a charu o ddynion y tywyllwch''* (John iii. 19).

In the above examples the action of the verb-noun is in the past.

(ii) If the action in the noun-clause is in the present or the imperfect tense, the verb-noun *bod* is used, or else *bod* + *yn* + another verb-noun, and the subject of the noun-clause is expressed by a noun or pronoun:

Credaf *fod bara yn y gell* '. . . that there is food in the larder'. Diau *fod digon o fwyd gennym* '. . . that we have plenty of food'. Ni wyddant hwy *fy mod yn dlawd* '. . . that I am poor'. Gwyddent hwy *ei bod hi'n gyfoethog* '. . . that she was/is rich'. Dywedais wrtho *fy mod yn byw yma* '. . . that I am/was living here'. Clywswn *fod Olwen yn cadw siop* '. . . that O. was keeping a shop'. Dyna oedd y drwg, *fod tyllau yn y berth* '. . . that there were holes in the hedge'. Ni allwn i wybod *fod rhywun yn gwrando* '. . . that someone was listening'. Cafodd ef neges *fod ei dad yn wael* '. . . that his father was ill'.

[In the present century *bod* has been written perhaps more frequently than *fod* at the beginning of a noun-clause, except after a personal verb, or when the radical or some other mutation was required (e.g., after *ein, eu, fy,* etc.), or after a parenthesis. However, *bod* and other verb-nouns have traditionally been mutated, so that *fod* must be considered to be correct, as shown in TC 236-7].

(iii) If the action in the noun-clause is in the past perfect or pluperfect tense, the formula is *bod* + *wedi/heb* + another verb-noun:

Clywais *ei fod wedi ysgrifennu llyfr* '. . . that he has/had written a book'.

Gwelodd *fod y newyddion wedi cyrraedd o'i flaen* '. . . that the news had reached there before him'.

Mae'n wir *fod y lleidr wedi ei ddal* '. . . that the thief has been caught'.

Gwelais *ei fod heb orffen y gwaith* '. . . that he had not finished the work'.

Dywed hi *fod y tŷ heb ei godi* '. . . that the house has not been built'.

[In the last two examples with *heb* the noun-predicate clause is a variant of a negative verb-predicate clause: . . . *nad oedd ef wedi gorffen y gwaith* and . . . *nad oedd y tŷ wedi ei godi*].

(iv) To express an action in the future in a noun-clause the following formula: *bod* + preposition *(ar, ar fedr, ar fin)* + verb-noun:

Dywedodd *ei bod ar fin cychwyn* '. . . that she was about to start'.

Mi wn *fod y trên ar gyrraedd* '. . . that the train is about to arrive'.

Mae hyn yn arwydd *eu bod ar fedr hwylio* '. . . that they are on the point of sailing'; § 200 (i).

(v) The preposition *ar* may be used to introduce a noun-clause which is the object of verbs of entreaty or command *(erfyn, deisyf, gweddïo, gorchymyn, erchi,* etc.), or which follows an expression equivalent to an entreaty, etc. Thus the two prepositions, *ar* and *i,* sometimes occur together:

"gweddïwch bob amser, *ar gael eich cyfrif yn deilwng"* (Luke xxi. 36) '. . . that ye may be accounted worthy'.

"Dyma fy ngorchymyn i; *Ar i chwi garu eich gilydd"* (John xv. 12).

"Eithr ysgrifennu ohonom ni atynt, *ar ymgadw ohonynt* oddi wrth halogrwydd delwau" (Acts xv. 20) '. . . that they abstain from . . .'.

In another construction the noun-clause is not introduced by *ar* after a verb of entreaty, etc.:

"yr wyf yn atolwg i chwi . . . *roddi ohonoch eich cyrff yn aberth byw"* (Rom. xii. 1) '. . . that ye present your bodies . . .'.

"Ac yr wyf yn atolwg i chwi . . . *ddywedyd o bawb ohonoch chwi yr un peth"* '. . . that ye all say the same thing'. See § 179 (ii).

Many verbs take *ar* before a following noun object (§ 200 (v)) in a simple sentence, e.g., *Yr wyf yn deisyf ar y bobl; Galwodd ar ei fam;*

Erfyniaf arnoch. Such sentences can be followed by noun-clauses introduced by a repetition of *ar:*

"gweddïa *ar* yr Arglwydd, *ar yrru ohono ef y seirff oddi wrthym*" (Num. xxi. 7).

(vi) When *dweud* means 'tell, command' the substance of the command is conveyed by a noun-clause introduced by *am;* § 199 (x); i.e. an indirect command:

Dywedwch wrthynt *am roi bwyd i'r anifeiliaid* '. . . to give food to the animals'. Dywedodd y fam wrth y plentyn *am fod yn ddistaw* '. . . to be quiet'.

(vii) If the indirect command or entreaty is negative it is now expressed by the use of *peidio â* before the verb-noun:

Yr wyf yn gofyn iti *beidio â dweud hynny;* § 181 (i).

An older construction is the use of *na* + verb in the subjunctive; § 118 (iii):

"yr wyf yn atolwg i ti *na'm poenech*" (Luke viii. 28) 'I beseech thee, torment me not'. Cf. § 181 (i) and Note.

§ 251. The function of an **Adverbial Clause** is the same as that of an adverb, viz., to modify an adjective or the action of a verb.

All the conjunctions (including prepositions + *y/na*) listed in §§ 142 (iii); 233—236, serve to introduce adverbial clauses. So also do *fel mai,* § 237 (iv) and *po,* § 238.

Some clauses following equative adjectives are adverbial clauses; see §§ 230 (i) (c); 50 (iv).

§ 252. The **Absolute Phrase** is one that is added to a sentence but is independent of the syntax of that sentence. It is not a subordinate clause, although it may be equivalent to an adverbial clause, inasmuch as it is an extension of what is said in the main sentence. It may precede the main sentence, or it may follow it, or it may be a parenthesis. It is always introduced by the preposition *a(c),* and in form is one of three patterns:

(a) subject + predicative *yn* + noun or adjective.

(b) subject + adverbial phrase.

(c) subject + preposition ('pre-verb-noun' *yn, ar, ar fin, ar fedr, wedi, heb)* + verb-noun.

(a) "Mair Magdalen a ddaeth y bore, *a hi eto yn dywyll*" (John xx. 1) 'when it was yet dark'.
Fe wnaeth y mab hynny lawer tro, *a'i rieni eto'n fyw.*
"*A minne'n llawer rhwymedicach,* weithieu mi gyd-bynciwn â'r côr ascellog" (B.Cw. 83) 'Being much more obliged myself, I would sometimes join the winged choir in song'.

"Beth gymmwysach, eb ynte, *a hi'n Ben-lladrones ei hun?*" (B.Cw. 21) 'What is more fitting, said he, she being a head robber-woman herself?'

(b) *"A'i gwisg ddeilios dlos hyd lawr*/Mi a ganfum wig enfawr" (R.W.P. 51) 'Its beautiful dress of tiny leaves being strewn on the ground, I perceived a great wood'.

Adnabu'r plentyn ei fam, *a hithau ymhell oddi wrtho* '. . . she being far away from him'.

A hwy yn yr eglwys, ysbeiliwyd eu tŷ 'They being in the church, their house was plundered'.

(c) *"Ac a hwy yn gwrando ar y pethau hyn,* efe a chwanegodd . . . ddameg" (Luke xix. 1).

Taerodd na fu erioed yn y lle, *a minnau'n gwybod gwell* 'He insisted that he had never been in the place, while I knew better'.

Mynnodd fynd i'r gwaith, *a'r meddyg wedi dweud wrtho am orffwys* 'He insisted on going to work, though the doctor had told him to rest'.

Clywodd y cloc yn taro tri, *ac yntau heb gysgu o gwbl* '. . . he not having slept at all'.

Lladdwyd ei gŵr yn y ddamwain, *ac ef ar ymadael â'r chwarel* 'Her husband was killed in the accident, when he was about to leave the quarry'.

A'r llong ar fedr hwylio, gwelwyd rhywun yn rhedeg ati 'The ship being on the point of sailing, someone was seen running to it'.

"A mi yn ewyllysio iacháu Israel, datguddiwyd anwiredd Ephraim". (Hos. vii. 1) 'When I would have healed Israel, the iniquity of Ephraim was discovered'.

APPENDIX A

CONSONANTAL CHANGES
THE INITIAL MUTATIONS

(i)

Radical Consonant	Soft Mutation	Nasal Mutation	Spirant Mutation
p	b	mh	ph
t	d	nh	th
c	g	ngh	ch
b	f	m	
d	dd	n	
g	—	ng	
ll	l		
rh	r		
m	f		

(ii) The Soft Mutation or Lenition. References to instances of mutation:

Noun and adj. after the article	§§ 8; 26(iii); 30 (ii).
Adj. and noun after fem. noun:	§§ 42; 43.
Adj. after *mor, cyn*, etc.:	§§ 48; 50
Equative adj.:	§ 50 (iii).
Noun and adj. after *yn:*	§§ 51 (iv); 213 (iii-v) and Note.
Superlative adj. after *po:*	§ 52 (iii).
Superlative adj. as adverb:	§ 52 (v).
Second element of a compound:	§ 42; 53, i; 96; 186 and Note.
Noun after superlative adj.	§ 53 (iii).
Adj. after proper noun:	§ 54.
Noun in apposition:	§ 55.
Numeral after plural noun:	§ 58.
Noun after numerals:	§ 62.
Noun after ordinals:	§§ 59; 63.
Verb after independent pronouns and particles:	§§ 68 (iv); 152 (iii).
Noun after prefixed pronoun (*dy, ei*):	§ 71.
Noun after infixed pronoun (*'i, 'w*):	§ 73.
Noun after relative pronoun:	§ 77.
Noun after *wele, dyna, dyma*:	§ 83.
Mutation of *piau*:	§ 84.
Noun, etc. after *pa*:	§ 88.
Noun after *naill*:	§ 93.
Noun after *rhyw, amryw, cyfryw*:	§§ 96-97.
Adverbial and adjectival pronominalia:	§§ 98 (vi); 100 (v); 101 (v); 102 (iii); 103 (i); 104 (iii); 106; 107 (iii); 110 (iv).
Subject and object:	§§ 123; 242 (iii).
Debygaf, gredaf, etc.:	§ 114 (ii).

Noun predicate after *sydd*, etc.:	§§ 143 (iii); 241 (iib).
Bod (b- forms) after noun predicate:	§§ 154; 246 (ii).
Verb-noun subject (doer):	§§ 179; 207 (iii).
Byw and *marw* after forms of *bod*:	§ 184.
After prefixes:	§ 187 (i).
After inflected prepositions:	§ 189 (i).
After the uninflected prep. *hyd*:	§ 195.
Adverbial nouns:	§ 216.
Adverbial adjectives after adjectives:	§ 217.
Verbs after the particles *mi, ti, ef, a,* etc.:	§§ 219; 220.
Verbs after the particles *ni, na*:	§§ 221; 222 Note; 227.
Verbs after the interrogatives *a, oni*:	§§ 223; 225.
Noun, etc. after the conjunctions *neu, ynteu*:	§ 228 (ii).
Verbs after the conj. *pan, oni* 'until':	§ 235 (i-iv).
Verbs after the conj. *oni* 'if not':	§ 236 (iia).
Noun after interjection:	§ 239 (iv).
Noun in the vocative case:	§ 239 (iv, v).
Ni before *rhaid, gwiw, gwaeth*:	§ 221 (i).
Bod, fod beginning a noun-clause:	§ 250 (ii).

(iii) The NASAL MUTATION.

After the numerals *pum, saith, naw, deg,* etc.:	§ 62.
Blynedd and *blwydd* after *un* in compounds:	§ 62.
After the prefixed pron. *fy*:	§ 71
After the prep. yn 'in':	§ 213 Note.

Examples:

(a) *fy*: plas—fy *mh*las; tir—fy *nh*ir; cefn—fy *ngh*efn; bara—fy *m*ara; drws—fy *n*rws; gên—fy *ng*ên.

In speaking initial *f-* is dropped: *'y nhŷ*; *'y ng*wlad; and even *'y* is very often dropped, but the mutation remains: *'nh*ad i; *'ngh*effyl i; *'mh*en i. This loss sometimes occurs in writing, e.g.,

"Mae *'m*linion, hirion oriau/A'm nos hir yn ymnesáu" (RGD 63) 'My weary, long hours and my long night are approaching'.

(b) *yn*: Pen-y-bont—ym *Mh*en-y-bont; Talgarth—yn *Nh*algarth; Caerdydd—yng *Ngh*aerdydd; Brynaman—ym *M*rynaman; Dowlais—yn *N*owlais; Gwynedd—yng *Ng*wynedd; pen uchaf y stryd—ym *mh*en uchaf y stryd; drws y tŷ—yn *n*rws y tŷ; gwaelod yr ardd—yng *ng*waelod yr ardd; Tan-y-bryn—yn *Nh*an-y-bryn; cartrefi Cymru—yng *Ngh*artrefi Cymru; basged Mari—ym *m*asged Mari.

Yn also becomes *ym* before a radical *m*: ym Merthyr; ym Môn; ym meysydd y wlad.

[In some dialects there is a tendency to keep the radical after *yn*, and even to substitute the soft for the nasal mutation. Careful speakers shun such irregularities.]

The modern practice is to retain the initial radical of a book-title after *yn*: yn *Gwaith Tudur Aled;* yn *Cofiant Ieuan Gwynedd.* But in referring to particular numbers of periodicals, newspapers, etc., the mutation is shown after *yn*: yng *Ngheninen* Mawrth; yng *Nghymro*'r wythnos hon; yng *Ngoleuad* yr wythnos nesaf; yn *Nysgedydd* y mis hwn. An alternative method is to write *rhifyn . . . o* before the title: yn *rhifyn* y gaeaf *o'r Traethodydd;* yn *rhifyn* 5 Awst *o'r Cronicl.*

(iv) The SPIRANT MUTATION.

After the numerals *tri* and *chwe:*	§ 62.
After the fem. sing. prefixed pron. *ei:*	§ 71.
After the genitive fem. sing. infixed pron., and after the fem. *'w:*	§ 73.
After *ni, na*	
relative pronoun:	§ 77.
pre-verbal particle:	§ 221; 222.
conj. following comparative adj.:	§ 51 (i); 231.
Co-ordinate conj.:	§ 229.
After the prep. *â (gyda, tua, efo,* etc.):	§ 195.
After the conj. *a:*	§ 228.
After the conj. *â* 'as':	§§ 50 (i); 230 (i).
After the interrogative particle *oni:*	§ 225.
After the conj. *oni* 'if not':	§§ 222 Note; 236 (ii).
After the conj. *oni* 'until':	§ 235 (iv).
After the adverb *tra* 'very':	§§ 187 (ii); 217 (iii).

(v) MEDIAL and FINAL MUTATIONS.

Soft in second element of proper compounds:	§ 186 (i) and Note.
Soft after prefixes:	§ 187 (i).
Nasal after prefixes:	§ 187 (iii).
Spirant after prefixes:	§ 187 (ii).
Nasal in some words before plur. ending:	§ 12 Note II.
Pum (pump), can (cant) before nouns:	§ 57 (b).
Pumed 'fifth', *canfed* 'hundredth':	§ 56.
Deng (deg), deuddeng, etc.:	§ 62.
Ym, yng (yn):	(iii) above; § 186 Note.
Prynhawn (pryd + nawn):	§ 186 Note.
Chwephwys, triphwys, etc.:	§ 186 Note.

(vi) PROVECTION (MEDIAL).

b + b = p; d + d = t; g + g = c; b + h = p; d + h = t; g + h = c. f + h = ff; dd + h = th (these last two changes are rare).
    Provection occurs as above by adding a termination to a word or by joining two words:

adding *-ed (-hed), -ach, -af (-haf)* in comparison of adjectives:	§ 44.
in proper compounds *(pt, tb, tg, cb, tch, cff):*	§ 186 and Note.
adding *-ha, -ha-u* to form verb-nouns:	§§ 175 (xv); 172.
a few verbal forms in the subjunctive:	§ 131 (i).
some abstract noun endings (*-der, -did, -dra, -had* becoming *-ter, -tid, -tra, -cad/-tad*):	§ 31 (i).
exceptions after prefixes *all-, dis-:*	§ 187 (i).
merchetos, merchetach, pryfetach:	§ 19 (i).

(vii) Aspiration.

When the aspirate *h* belongs to a medial or final syllable, it is lost if the syllable becomes unaccented: bren*h*inoedd (pl.), brenin (s.); cyn*h*aliaf, cynnal; bren*h*iniaeth, breniniaethau; ang*h*enus, angen; di*h*areb, diar*h*ebion, etc.: §§ 12 Note; 170 (v).

After prefixes the aspirate is retained in unaccented syllables: ym*h*oliadau, ar*h*oliadau, ym*h*elaethu, ang*h*aredig, ann*h*erfynol, etc.: § 187 (i, iii).

It is also retained in an unaccented syllable in the following words: *enghraifft, anrheg, anrhaith, penrhyn, olrhain.*

A vowel is preceded by *h* after the following pronouns: prefixed *ei* (fem.); infixed *'i* (fem.) and *'w* (fem.); infixed accusative *'i* (masc. and fem.); prefixed *ein, eu;* infixed *'m*: §§ 71; 73.

The aspirate is inserted after *ar* before *ugain (un ar hugain,* etc.), and the adjective *holl* and the adverb *hollol* are aspirated, but not the adverb *oll:* §§ 56; 103.

APPENDIX B

VOWEL AND DIPHTHONG CHANGES

(i) Affection

(a) A vowel in the final syllable of a word tends to cause an anticipated change in a vowel in a preceding syllable, by assimilating its sound to that of its own. This occurs, e.g., when -*i* is added to a syllable containing -*a*-, such as *gardd* and *gerddi*. The name given to this change is 'affection'.

The affection remains in many words which have lost old terminations which contained the vowels that caused the change, viz. *a* and *i*. The change spread to many other words by analogy, i.e., words which did not have terminations containing sounds capable of causing the change.

(b) The kind of affection formerly caused by *a* is seen in the feminine forms of adjectives:

Original sound	Affection	Examples (§§ 39; 40)
y	e	byr, ber; gwyn, gwen; brych, brech;
w	o	llwm, llom; tlws, tlos; crwn, cron.

(c) The kind of affection formerly caused by *i* is seen in plural forms of nouns and adjectives, and in 3 pres. sing. indicative of verbs:

Original sound	Affection	Examples (§§ 11; 33 (i); 125)
a	ai	sant, saint; brân, brain
a	ei	bardd, beirdd; marw, meirw; galw, geilw
a	y	alarch, elyrch (eleirch); gwasgar, gwesgyr
ae	ai	draen, drain; cyrraedd, cyrraidd
ae	ey, ei	gwaell, gweyll/gweill
e	y	bachgen, bechgyn; ateb, etyb
o	y	corff, cyrff; deffro, deffry

Original sound	Affection	Examples (§§ 11; 33 (i); 125)
w	y	asgwrn, esgyrn; (arddwrn, erddyrn)
oe	wy	oen, ŵyn; croen, crwyn
aw	au	taw, tau
aw	y	gwrandaw-af, gwrendy; gadaw-af, gedy

(d) Where the affection noted above occurs in multisyllabic words, *a* of the penult becomes *e*, i.e., *a . . . e* become *e . . . y*, and *a . . . a* become *e . . . ai* or *ei* or *y*: e.g., castell, cestyll; llawes, llewys; dafad, defaid; alarch, eleirch/elyrch; aradr, erydr; llannerch, llennyrch; ateb, etyb.

The change is from *a . . . a . . . e* to *e . . . e . . . y* in maharen, meheryn; from *a . . . o* to *e . . . y* in anfon, enfyn; annog, ennyg; datod, detyd; and from *o . . . o* to *e . . . y* in gosod, gesyd; ymosod, ymesyd.

(e) A sound in the ending of a word can affect the penult:

Original sound	Sound in ending	Affection	Examples (§§ 13; 124; 170 (iii))
a	i	e	gwlad, gwledig; can-af, ceni; par-af, peri; gardd, gerddi.
a	i	ei	gwas, gweision; truan, trueiniaid; par-af, peiriant
a	y	e	nant, nentydd; plant, plentyn
e	i	ei	pencerdd, penceirddiaid; gorwedd, gorweiddiog: niwed, niweidiol
ae	i	ei	gwaedd, gweiddi; maen, meini; saer, seiri
ae	y	ey	maes, meysydd; caer, ceyrydd
ae	u	eu	*(exceptional forms,* aeth, euthum; daeth, deuthum; gwnaeth, gwneuthum)
aw	i *or* y	ew	gwrandaw-af, gwrandewi, gwrandewych; taw-af, tewi, tewych; cawr, cewri.

(f) *a* remains unaffected in the penult in many words before *i*, or *ia:* nouns ending in *-iad, -iaid:* cariad, caniad, llafariad, lladdiad 'slaughter' *(ctr.* lleiddiad 'killer'); casgliad, anwaria(i)d, hynafa(i)d, Piwritaniaid, Protestaniaid, Americaniaid, *(ctr.* cyfneseifiaid 'kinsmen');

a few nouns with plur. ending *-ion:* manion, eithafion, carthion, amcanion;

-asid (but also *-esid*) in impersonal forms of pluperfect verbs; § 124;

-it, -asit (from *-ut, -asut*) in 2 sing. imperf. and pluperf. of verbs: canit, canasit, etc., § 128;

in compounds: *(a . . . i/y)* caswir, rhandir, cyfandir, canrif, gwanddyn, talgryf, candryll, talgrib; in prefixes before *i, ia, y:* athrist, afiach, amgylch, canlyn, datrys, etc., § 187; (exception; where the *y* of the ending is itself affected from *o*, it affects *a* in the penult; datro-, detry; datglo-, detgly; § 125 (i(a)).

If the final syllable is not a termination, but part of the word, there is no affection: anian, arian, arial, anial.

(g) In the 2 plur. pres. indic. of verbs *a* is affected to *e* although there is now no apparent reason for the affection, the sound *(i/y)* which caused the affection having been lost: *car-, cerwch; cân, cenwch.* In speaking these forms are commonly pronounced *canwch, carwch,* and seem to be increasingly adopted in writing, e.g., in the 1975 translation of the New Testament into Welsh.

(h) 'Reversion'. The affection is sometimes found in the suffixless form of a word, while the original vowel remains unchanged when a termination is added; **§** 13: *gwraig, gwragedd; rhiain, rhianedd; cainc, cangau; lleidr, lladron; cenau, cenawon; edau, edafedd; Sais, Saesneg, Saeson; adain, adanedd* (now supplanted by *adenydd,* from which a singular *aden* came into use, the artificial plural *edyn* being spurious). This change from the affected to the original sound is called 'reversion'.

(ii) Vowel Mutation

(a) Certain vowels and diphthongs in final syllables and monosyllables undergo change merely through change of position when a termination or another word is added. This change is called Vowel Mutation, of which examples are given below:

In the ultima & monosyllables	*Mutation*	*Examples*
ai	ei	gwair, gweiriau; gwaith, gweithio; llai, lleiaf; rhaid, rheidrwydd; craig, creigle
au	eu	traul, treulio; dau, deuddeg; amau, amheuaeth; aur, euro, euraidd; cynnau, cyneuodd
aw	o	ffawd, ffodus; tlawd, tlodion; brawd, brodyr; llaw, llofnod, lloffa; ansawdd, ansoddair; awr, oriau, orig, oriog.
w	(obscure) y	cwm, cymoedd; cwestiwn, cwestiynau; ffrwd, ffrydiau; twf, tyfu, tyfiant; trwm, trymach; cwmwl, cymylau
(clear) y	(obscure) y	llyn, llynnoedd; gwyn, gwynnach; dilyn, dilynaf; terfyn, terfynu; mynydd, mynyddoedd; byw, bywyd, bywydau (see **§** 3)
uw	u	buwch, buchod, buches; uwch, uchel, uchaf; cuwch, cuchio; lluwch, lluchio (*also* lluwchio)

(b) There are may exceptions to the rules of vowel mutation:

(i) Although there is no exception to the rule that *ai* becomes *ei,* the sound *ei* does occur before *l* or *r* and another consonant in final syllables and monosyllables; (i) (c) above: *beirdd, heirdd, beilch, ceirch, meirch, geifr, lleidr, eleirch, teifl, gweheirdd, dieithr;* and in *deil* 'holds', *ceir* (noun 'cars'), *lleill, eich.* Also in the contraction of *e-i* to *ei* in impersonal forms of verbs: *ceir* 'one has', *ceid, gwneir, gwneid, eir* 'one goes', *eid, caniateir, parheir,* etc.; *Cymreig, bwyteig. (Cair, gwnair* are sometimes so written artificially to rhyme with *gair, gwair,* etc.)

(ii) There is no exception to mutating *au* to *eu*, but *eu* may occur in accented final and monosyllables as a contraction of *e-u* or *eu-u:* *cyfleu, cyfleus, dileu, dyheu, amheus* (amheu-us), *gweu* (gwe-u), *cyd-weu,* (but also *gwau),* *creu, heu* (but more usually *hau).*

Where *-ha-u* has given *-hau* (*-au*) in verb-noun endings, it is to the stem *-ha-*(or affected *-he-*) that endings are added in the verb conjugations: *parhau, parhaodd; mwynhau, mwynheais; gwastatáu, gwastatewch; bywiocáu, bywioceir;* see §§ 134; 136.

(iii) There is no mutation of *aw* to *o* in *mawrion, llawnion, athrawon, awdur, cawswn, hawsaf, iawnder, cyfiawnder, gwawdio, hawlio, canllawiau, tawaf, llawen, awen, addawaf,* etc.

We have *ow* instead of *aw* in *ardderchowgrwydd, lluosowgrwydd, godidowgrwydd,* but it is *o* in *enwogrwydd, gwresogrwydd.*

Although *aw* remains unmutated before a vowel in *addawol, gwrandawaf, trawaf,* it becomes *o* in a final syllable: *addo, gwrando, taro.* This change of *aw* to *o* in final syllables occurs regularly: *dwylo* (dwy-law), *anodd* (an-hawdd), *ffyddlon* (ffydd-lawn), *cariadlon,* etc.

(iv) In many words there is no mutation of penultimate *w;* when followed by *w,* e.g., *cwmwl, cwrcwd, cwmwd, bwgwth* (also *bygwth), mwdwl, cwpwrdd, cwcwll* (but both mutate when termination follows: *cymylau, myrthylion, cyrcydu);* also *gwrol, gŵraidd, gŵra* (from *gŵr); bwthyn* (pl. *bythynnod), cwsmer, cwmni, cwstwm* and other borrowings; *gwgu, bwriad, gwthiaf, twrio, twmpath, swnio, swnllyd, wrthyf,* etc.; and the prefix *gwrth-: gwrthwynebu, gwrthblaid, gwrthglawdd, gwrth-ddweud, gwrthod,* etc.

(v) Clear *y* does not become obscure before another vowel in the penult: *gwestyau, gwestywr, ysbytywr* (two obscure *y*'s followed by clear), *dyall* (usually written *deall), ysbytyau* (also *ysbytai), lletya, lletywr, gwelyau, distrywio, amrywiaeth, benywaidd, gwrywaidd.* The *y* is obscure in the prefix *rhy-* in *rhywyr* 'high time', but clear in *rhy hwyr* 'too late'; and obscure too in *-yw-* in *bywyd, cywydd, llywydd, tywydd, tywod.*

In an antepenultimate syllable *y* is obscure: *cyfarfod, hysbysu, cynhaeaf, mynyddoedd, ystrydoedd, ymweled,* etc. In loose compounds, however, the prefixes *cyd-* and *cyn-* have clear *y,* and are accented: *cyd-weld, cydymdeimlo, cyn-faer, cyn-gadeirydd* (§ 187 (i)). Most other loose compounds have clear *y* in the first element: *llyfr-rwymwr, brysneges, gwyn-galchu, rhydd-ddeiliad, Rhyddfrydwr, sych-dduwiol, synfyfyrio,* etc. If the first element of a loose compound is polysyllabic the sound of *y* depends on its position in it (as a separate word): *llygadrythu* (*y* being obscure in the penult of each element), *cynffonlonni, prysur-gerddded;* in *cyflym-redeg* the first *y* is obscure and the second clear; § 3.

In the diphthong *ey* the *y* is an integral part, and can not mutate. When *wy* is a rising diphthong the vocalic element in it, *y,* can mutate: *gwyn, gwynnaf,* §§ 4; 5 (ii).

In a few monosyllables *y* is obscure; § 1 (b).

In *sylw* and *gwyry* (*gwyryf*) the *y* of the penult is clear because both words were formerly monosyllabic; but in *sylwi, sylwodd* it is obscure.

(vi) There is no mutation of *uw* in *duwiol, duwies, duwdod,* etc.

INDEX

References to paragraphs

I. TERMS

absolute phrase, 68, 178, 212, 228, 252.

accentuation, 6.

adjectives: formation of pl., 33-8; no pl., 34; pl. as noun, 35; concord, 36-7; gender, 39-43; mut. of fem. adj., 42-3; comparison, 43-6; syntax of comparison, 50-3; adj. preceding noun, 53, noun following adj., 53-4, adj. after proper noun, 54; verbal adjs., 183.

adverbial phrases, 215-7; adverbs, 214-7.

affection of vowels, 125, 170; Appendix B (i).

alternatives, 92-3.

antecedent, 78, 86-7, 98, 225.

apposition, noun in, 55.

article (def.), 7-9; mut. after, 8; with veb-noun, 177.

aspiration, Appendix A (vii).

case: adverbial, 79, 82; governed by prep. 81, 88; vocative, 239; nomin., 76, 78; acc., 68-9, 72, 76, 123, 180, 195; genitive, 43, 60, 69, 92, 99, 145, 148, 150.

clauses: adverbial, 118, 147-50, 178, 207, 211, 221, 230, 233-7, 251; conditional, 115, 117, 119, 146, 150; noun-clauses, 118, 199, 207, 221, 237; noun clause with verb predicate, 249; relative clause, 68, 76-87, 118, 143-150, 221; proper and oblique relative, 76, 79-86, 218, 221, 245.

complement (predicate), 88, 142, 143, 149, 154, 241.

compounds, 5, 42, 185-7; proper and improper, 186-7; strict and loose, 42, 96, 186

conjunctions, 228-238.

consonantal mutations: soft, spirant, nasal, medial and provection; Appendix A (i)—(vii).

copula, 50, 142, 241.

diphthongs, falling and rising, 4-5.

interjections, 239.

interpolation, 123.

nouns: 10-31; concrete and abstract, 10; formation of pl., and sing., 11-24; dual no., 25; gender, 26-31; gender of derivatives and compounda, 31; epicenes, 27; classification by gender, 30-1; noun in

apposition, 54; double plurals and diminutive endings, 19.

numerals, 56-65; adjectival, 57; ordinals, 59; substantive numerals, 60; mutations after, 62-3.

object, 68, 76, 123, 242-50.

passive voice, 121, 182.

predicate, 88, 141, 239, 240, 249-50.

prefixes, 187, 217, 230.

prepositions: 188-219; conjugated, 190-4; uninflected, 195-6; constructions etc.: adverbial forms, 196-213, 215.

pre-verbal particles, 68 (indep. pronouns), 113-4, 152, 218-227; affirmative, 218-220; interrogative, 141, 223-5; negative, 221-2; relative particle, 80, 88, 218, 246.

pronominalia, 92-112, 141, 213.

pronouns; personal, 67-74; independent; simple, reduplicated, conjunctive, 66-8, 123, 196; dependent; prefixed, infixed, affixed, 69-74, 246; possessive, 75; demonstrative, 9, 89-91, 98, 212.

relative pronoun, 72, 76-85, 87, 153, 210, 245-7; verbal relatival forms *(sydd, piau)* 83-4.

replies, 141, 226-7.

reversion, Appendix B(i) (h).

sentence, the, 204-7; noun-predicate sentence, 207, 241; verb-predicate sentence, 242; co-ordinate sentence, 243; complex sentence, 244; mixed sentence, 148, 246; abnormal sentence, 143, 178, 218, 247; periphrastic sentence, 114, 117, 141, 181-2, 212-3; main and sub-ordinate sentence, 244.

subject, 76, 84, 113, 123, 240, 242-50.

sub-predicate, 178, 205, 209.

verbs: tenses and moods, 114-169; impersonal forms, 121; regular verb, 124-132; contracted forms, 133-9; irregular verbs, 140-168; *Bod,* 140-154; 3 pers. s. indic. and constructions, 141-152.

verb-nouns, 122, 170-182; as nouns and verbs, 177-8; object of, 180; verb-noun and negative, 181; verb-noun and passive choice, 182; 207.

vowel and dipthong changes, Appendix B.

vowels, length of, 2.

II. WORDS

(important or exemplary)

a, ac *(conj.)*, 228.
a *(relative pron.)*, 72, 76, 89, 153, 245-7.
a *(particle)*, 68, 219; interrogative, 223.
â, ag *(prep.)*, 143, 195, 198, 228.
â, ag *(conj.)*, 50, 230.
ai, *(interrogative particle)*, 224; ai ê, 224
aberth, ebyrth, 11.
adwaen (adwen), adnabod, 155, 160.
af, mynd, 2, 162.
amrant, amrannau, amrantau, 12.
amryw, 97.
ar, 169, 191, 200.
a'r a, 85.
arall, 93.
ardderchowgrwydd, 31.
aroglau, arogleuon, 13.
asen, ais, asennau, 15.
at, 191, 201.

bach, 42, 46.
bellach, 51.
beudy, beudyau, beudai (beudái), 18.
biau, bioedd, 84.
blwng, blong, 39.
blwydd, blwyddiaid, 35.
blwyddyn, blynyddoedd, blynedd, 18.
bod, 83, 140-154, 250.
braf, 42.
braint, breintiau, breiniol, 12.
brych, brech, 39.
bustach, bustych, 11.
bynnag, 86, 99, 214.
byw, 34, 184.

caf, cael, 137, 182.
canfyddaf, canfod, 155.
câr, ceraint, 2, 13.
carw, hydd, ewig, 29.
caseg, cesig, 11.
castell, cestyll, 11.
celain, celanedd, 13.
cenau, cenawon, cenawes, 13.
cennad, cenhadon 'missionaries', cenhadau, 12, Note I.
cleddyfod, 31.
codaf, cyfodaf, 139.
collen, cyll, 15.
conyn, cawn, 15.
credadun, credinwyr, 18.
crwydryn, crwydraid, 16.
crych, crech, 39.

cwbl, 104.
cwta, cota, 39.
cydnabyddaf, 155, 161.
cyf-, cy-, cyd-, 230.
cyfarfyddaf, 155.
cyfnesaf, cyfneseifiaid, 35.
cyngor, cynghorau, cynghorion, 21.
cymaint, 46, 50, 53, 87, 203.
cymar, cymheiriaid, 13.

chwegr, chwegrwn, 29.

damwain *(verb)*, 169.
dan, tan, 191, 209, 233.
darfod, 156, 169.
dau, dwy, deu-, dwy-, 8, 25.
daw, gwaudd, 29.
derwin, 34.
deuaf, dof, 162, 198.
dichon, 163.
digon, 107.
digwydd, 169.
dim, 101, 141, 228.
do, 226-7.
dros, (see *tros*).
dydd, diau, 18.
dylwn, 164.
dyma, dyna, 87, 214, 239.

ebe, eb, ebr, 165.
er, 50, 52, 192, 195, 203, 235.
erbyn, 204.
ers, 195, 203.
euraid, 34.
ewyllys da, 42.

gadawaf, gadaf, 138.
gan, 50, 99, 123, 177-8, 193, 205.
gefell, gefeilliaid, 13.
gilydd, 112.
gorfod, 155-6.
gormod, gormodd, 108.
gras, -usau, 18.
gwaethaf, 46, 52, 208.
gwaudd, 29.
gwaun, gweunydd, 13.
gweddu, 169.
gwesty, -au, gwestai, 18.
gwir, 186.
gwn, gwybod, 155, 159.
gwnaf, 162.

gwŷn ('passion, pain'), 5.
gwŷs ('summons'), 5; gwŷs, gwyddys *(verb)*, 5, 159.
gynt *(adverb)*, 51; cynt *(comp. adj.)*, 46.

haearn, heyrn, 18.
hanfod, 158.
heb, 181-2, 192, 206.
hesbwrn, hesbin, 29.
hun, -an, -ain, 95.
hwn, hon, 9, 89.
hwde, hwre, 168.
hyd oni, 235.
hynod o, 217.

i *(prep.)*, 179, 184, 207, 250.
ie, 226.

llawer, 51, 101, 141, 214.
llysewyn, llysau, llysiau, 15.

maen, main, meini, 11, 13.
mai *(conj.)*, 236, 237, 249.
maint, 99.
marw, meirw, -on, 33, 184.
math, 26.
meddaf ('I say'), 166.
methu, 169.
mewn, 195, 213.
miaren, mieri, 17.
moes *(verb)*, 168.
mor, 48, 50, 230, 240.
mwy, -ach, 46, 48, 214.
mwynhaf, 133.

na, nac *(conj.)*, 229; *(pre-verbal particle)*, 120, 141, 222, 227; naddo, 227.
na, nad *(rel. pronoun or particle)* 2, 76, 80-2, 86, 245; *(pre-verbal particle)* 119, 221-2, 249.
na, nag *(conj.)*, 86, 231.
neb, 86, 111, 150, 213, 228.
nemor, nepell, 111.
nes, 2; *(prep.)*, 195, 234; *(adverb)*, 118; *(comp. adj.)*, 46.
ni, nid *(rel. pronoun or particle)*, 76-80, 83, 144, 221; *(pre-verbal particle)* 141-5, 221; nid *(before complement)* 87, 142, 234, 241; *(in negative mixed sentence)* 221, 246.
nos da, 42.

o *(prep.)*, mo, 72, 179, 191, 208, 217, 250.
oll, holl, 103.
ond, 87, 228.
oni, onid *(conj. 'until')*, 118, 235; *(conj. 'if not')*, 119, 221, 236; *(interrog. particle)*, 141, 225.
os, o, od, *(conj.)*, 146, 150, 236.

pa, 88, 94, 213.
pan, 118, 235.
pawb, pob, 102, 213.
pe, 115, 117, 119, 236.
peidio, 120, 181.
pennog, penwaig, 11, 18.
peth, 2, 86, 100; (pa) beth bynnag, 214.
piau, pioedd, 84, 161.
po, 52, 238.
pobl, y bobl, y bobloedd, 8.
pryd y, 82, 234.
pwdr, pydron, 38.
pwy, 86, 88, 213.

rhaeadr, 11, 18.
rhag, 50, 192, 210.
rhagor, 47, 109, 214.
rhai, 86, 90-1, 98, 208.
rhaid, 47, 143, 221.
rheidus, 35.
rhiain, rhianedd, 13.
rhyw, 96, 101, 106, 141; rhywbeth, rhywbryd, rhywfaint, rhywun, unrhyw, 4, 51, 146, 216.

sawl, 86, 105.
serch *(prep.)*, 203.
swrth, sorth, 39.
sydd, 83, 140, 143, 151.
synnu, 169.

tan, dan, 191, 205 (v, Note); 209, 233.
taw, (see under *mai*).
tra *(adverb)*, 118, 187, 217; *(conj.)* 235.
trof, 133.
tros, dros, 192, 202.
trwsgl, trosgl, 39.
twn, ton, 39.
tycio, 169.

un, 56, 62, 86, 94-7, 213.
unrhyw, 97, 213.

wedi, 117, 178, 195, 212.
wele, 83, 239.
wrth, 193, 207, 211.

y, yr 'r *(article)*, 7-9, 25-6, 30, 90-3.
y, yr *(adverbial particle)*, 118, 218, 249; *(relatival particle)*, 80-82, 118, 218, 246.
ych, ychen, 13.
ychydig, 51, 106, 214.
ymdrin, ymdrîn, 6.
ymdroi, 6.
ymddwyn, ymddŵyn, 6.
ymladd, ymlâdd, 6.

yn *(prep.)*, 2, 192, 213; *(predicative)*, 114, 141, 143, 213; *(with verb-noun)*, 114, 178, 182, 213.

yrhawg, 6.
ysgrech, 6.